The Way Through the Trees

The Way Through the Trees

An Introduction to Faith Development

Sarah Brush

scm press

© Sarah Brush 2025

Published in 2025 by SCM Press

Editorial office
3rd Floor, Invicta House,
110 Golden Lane,
London EC1Y 0TG, UK
www.scmpress.co.uk

SCM Press is an imprint of Hymns Ancient & Modern Ltd
(a registered charity)

Hymns Ancient & Modern® is a registered trademark of
Hymns Ancient & Modern Ltd
13A Hellesdon Park Road, Norwich,
Norfolk NR6 5DR, UK

All rights reserved. No part of this publication may be reproduced,
stored in a retrieval system, or transmitted,
in any form or by any means, electronic, mechanical,
photocopying or otherwise, without the prior permission of
the publisher, SCM Press.

The Author has asserted her right under the Copyright, Designs and
Patents Act 1988 to be identified as the Author of this Work

British Library Cataloguing in Publication data

A catalogue record for this book is available
from the British Library

ISBN: 978-0-334-06664-4

EU GPSR Authorised Representative
LOGOS EUROPE, 9 rue Nicolas Poussin, 17000, LA ROCHELLE, France
E-mail: Contact@logoseurope.eu

No part of this book may be used or reproduced in any manner for the
purpose of training artificial intelligence technologies or systems.

Typeset by Regent Typesetting

Contents

Acknowledgements	ix
Introduction	1
The Structure of the Book	2
What is Faith?	5
How Do We Develop?	9
How Does Faith Develop?	13
The Field of Faith Development	14
How Does Knowing About Faith Development Help Us?	20
1 Faith Development in the Christian Tradition	25
Teresa of Avila	34
John of the Cross	36
2 Progressive Stages	46
James Fowler	46
Sharon Parks	62
Fritz Oser and Paul Gmünder	64
M. Scott Peck	70
Alan Jamieson	76
3 Progressive/Regressive Stages	89
Willow Creek	90
John Westerhoff	97
Nicola Slee	104
Janet Hagberg and Robert Guelich	109
Richard Rohr	115

4 Cycles   126
    Dick Hall   130
    Richard Blackaby   132
    John Westerhoff   134
    Brian McLaren   135

5 Styles   144
    Heinz Streib   146
    Rebecca Nye   155
    David Csinos   161
    James Hopewell   168
    Maria Harris   174

6 The Way Through the Trees   188
    The Landscape   188
    The Model   204

7 Exploring the Way Through the Trees: Application of the
   Model in the Parish   210

Bibliography   224
Index of Bible References   233
Index of Names and Subjects   237

List of Tables and Figure

Tables

Faith development models categorized	4
Gardner's Intelligence mapped against Fowler's seven lenses for assessing faith stage	145

Figure

The cyclical movement of communities	173

Acknowledgements

To my parents Pam and Bill Hamilton, who helped nurture the seed of all that this is.

To the parish of All Saints', High Wycombe, who helped me grow in faith and ministry.

To all the young people I have worked with throughout the years who have taught me so much about life, God and myself, and especially to the young people of the project 'Every Good Work' in Wakefield with a logo inspired by my model.

To Nicola Slee for her supervision of the thesis from which this grew and her wisdom in asserting that I couldn't present an overarching and all-encompassing model of Faith Development in a 12,000-word dissertation, it needed a whole book. For her encouragement since then when she was chair of the British and Irish Association for Practical Theology and even more so when I took on that role.

To all those who responded to a survey about faith and art whose responses gave me the encouragement to think that I had something worth exploring.

To the congregations of the Halas team, especially those who responded so warmly to this model at our retreat in Glastonbury, for supporting me in my first years of ordained ministry and to my wonderful clergy colleagues there – Katryn Leclezio, Rob Hall, Dominic Melville, Mike Rutter and Hazel Charlton – for three happy years in parish ministry.

To Alison Baxter, Suzanne Johnson and Gemma Birt, who made sure there were more images of trees in my life, and to Robert Latham for conversations about apple trees.

To David Shervington and Rachel Edge for their professional and supportive work as my editors, for pushing me beyond a small project to something more challenging and ultimately more fulfilling.

To Ronni Lamont for such enthusiasm for the model that she placed it alongside Westerhoff and Fowler and made me think I could really do this.

To Mary Hawes for persistently nagging me to get this published so that she could buy it.

To Margaret Whipp for her enthusiasm, encouragement and friendship.

To my spiritual directors; Sue for her conversations and wisdom about the mystics, and Emily for working with me in a different season.

To Sir David Hockney for his clear love of trees and his thought-provokingly beautiful exhibition, *The Bigger Picture*.

To Ian Macdonald for his friendship and humour over many years and for conversations about young people, faith and life.

To members of both the International Association of the Study of Youth Ministry and the British and Irish Association for Practical Theology who asked good questions when I presented this model to them at their conferences and helped me see things from some new perspectives.

To those who came to the Growing Faith Research conference and whose responses encouraged a significant change in the model.

To the ordinands of the Queen's Foundation for Ecumenical Theological Education alongside whom I studied and those who helped me explore this model with them soon after it was first developed. To seven generations of ordinands at Ripon College Cuddesdon for their response and insights to the model.

To my academic colleagues at Ripon College Cuddesdon: Alison Walker, Buki Fatona, Cathy Ross, Ellie McLaughlin, +Humphrey Southern, Hywel Clifford, Jacky Sewell, James Grenfell, Jane Baun, Jen Brown, Joanna Collicutt, Mark Chapman, Michael Brierley, Michael Dormandy, Michael Lakey, Oliver Keenan, Rebecca Dean, Richard Wyld, Roger Latham, Susie Snyder, Tim Naish, Tobais Tanton, Tom Clammer and Victoria Turner, for their support, especially those who enabled me to take time for study leave to complete this book and for their warmth and friendship. I also want to thank other colleagues at Cuddesdon, including Abi, Aiden, Aline, Cally, Clint, Eveline, Fiona, Gary, Hayley, Jane, Joji, Julianna, Julie, Karen, Malcolm, Michael, Molly, Nicole, Nigel, Ravi, Sam, Sarah, Sarah-Jane, Shei, Sonia, Sophie and Travis, for keeping me fed, watered and sane.

To those who saw me through the winter: Ally, Eleanor, Fi, Helen, Mike and Michael, Ian, Louise, Lily and Connie, Hannah, Elisabeth and Fred, Lynda, Ron and Anne, Hannah, Richard, and The Moog.

Introduction

Although we may not sense the maturing of our faith day to day, I am convinced there is some sense of development in faith throughout our lives through the various experiences we have, through our continued engagement with ideas and imagination, through our interaction with others and, especially for those who practise a faith, through interaction with the divine. Arguably, this development of our faith may not be discernible to most of us except in contrasting early faith and matured faith. Many of us can look back on our younger selves and remember a simpler understanding of our faith. (We may go on in later life to see how we overcomplicated our faith in middle age!) Yet this expectation of growth is not universal. Indeed, some see faith as a certain, sure and unshakeable thing which, in order to be faith, does not and should not change. Kenneth Stokes described how, of those questioned in a US study of church members, 32% said they believed a person's faith should not change throughout life.[1] This stems from a focus on faith as a one-off conversion from no faith to faith and thus surety. The tradition, however, through monastic theologies, teaches us the value of seeing conversion of life as an ongoing practice. There has been much focus in recent decades on church growth in terms of numbers converted. I think a focus on the growth of faith of individuals and communities in terms of ongoing conversion of life would be much more fruitful.

Our focus is on theories of Faith Development, by which I mean models that have endeavoured to map how people experience their faith and how it changes throughout their lives. Over the centuries, many have sought to describe this experience of growing faith and offer models to help others understand their own faith or the faith of those for whom they have pastoral care. In more recent years, this has been in the field of Faith Development, which draws on a variety of disciplines outside of theology to explore the psychological, sociological and spiritual aspects of the development of the individual with regards to faith.

This book will also describe some secular sources that explore the lived experience of human beings and how that develops, grows and changes, as such models cover much of the terrain that features in Faith

Development. However, charting the development of people's faith and growth is not an invention of the last few decades. In previous centuries, spiritual writers sought to explain how humans grow in faith and how to help others chart their discipleship. These earlier writers used a different mode of engaging with Faith Development, drawing on the richness of metaphor, something that theologians have been recently rediscovering in the discipline of theopoetics.[2]

> Theopoetics contends that whether theology is inscribed in the genre of poetry, in the form of story, or in a thicker, more theoretical style of prose, it remains a poiesis: an inventive, intuitive, and imaginative act of composition performed by authors.[3]

Gloria Hernández focuses her attention on theopoetics through the works of medieval mystic John of the Cross (whose work we explore later) alongside a similar mystical work in Sanskrit.[4] Gabriel Moran commented on this mixed ecology of development models and the misconception about differences between modern and more ancient ideas: 'The arrogant presumption that the world moves from religion to metaphysics to science has to be rescinded. While the mathematical-empirical sciences have made valuable contributions to human life, they cannot discern the purpose of life.'[5] Though these modes of engaging with Faith Development differ, they each have much to offer us as we consider our own faith journeys and the mission of the church in supporting others in their Faith Development.

The Structure of the Book

In this Introduction we will explore the concept of faith, how it might grow and the way scripture talks about it, before going on to explore the field of Faith Development and how it might be useful to the church and its ministers.

In Chapter 1, I give a brief overview of the richness of the Christian tradition with reference to Faith Development through various spiritual writers who have described stages or deepenings of faith. I am dealing with these separately, first as a grounding for the concept of how our faith grows, and second exploring how their origins are rooted in personal reflection and experience (rather than based on engagement with modern research). This makes them distinct from most of the late twentieth- and early twenty-first century models for Faith Development.

Joann Wolski Conn also turned to voices from the Christian tradition before introducing the then new model proposed by James Fowler.[6] Wolski Conn included the wisdom of Catherine of Siena, Teresa of Avila and John of the Cross, and other contributors to the volume explored Ignatius of Loyola and Thérèse of Lisieux. In this book our section on the tradition is necessarily briefer; it also includes some of those described by Wolski Conn as well as the works of John Climacus, Bonaventura, Meister Eckhart, Hugh of St Victor, Walter Hilton, the anonymous *The Cloud of Unknowing*, the rather more controversial Marguerite Porete, as well as Origen and Bunyan. There are doubtless other models from across the centuries which could have been included here if space had allowed.

As there are so many contributors to the modern field of Faith Development, I have endeavoured in this book to explore them as families of models.[7] Others have offered similar explorations, basing their grouping of theories on the underpinning models of research that serve as the foundation for identifying a commonality between specific stages from different models. James Estep and Jonathan Kim's recent review of Faith Development theories[8] categorizes various models according to what they call soft/hard developmental theories,[9] functional models of development and cultural-age models of development, and suggests that four of the models we will explore in this book share common stages that can be identified as Subjective Assimilation, Instrumental Reciprocity, Social Conventionality, Individual Systematization and Dialogical Consolidation.[10] Nicola Slee suggests that Faith Development models can be seen as belonging to various types, namely lifespan theories, structural stage theories or dialectical/socio-psychological theories.[11] I have chosen to group the models according to the mode of movement that each model describes (see Table 1), and will be introducing these models in these groupings. I have included the models from the Christian tradition in the table for ease of comparison.

The first group I call 'progressive' as these chart people's experience of spirituality in terms of forward-moving maturation. This group includes the work of James Fowler and his contemporaries Sharon Parks, M. Scott Peck, and Fritz Oser and Paul Gmünder, and a more recent work from Jamieson. These all emphasize a mono-directional path forwards, though some models that are progressive also accept the concept of regression to a previous stage, so we will explore these as a subset that I term 'progressive/regressive' models. These models include the work of Nicola Slee and the principal model of John Westerhoff, as well as the rather different research from Willow Creek churches. Also

3

Table 1: Faith development models categorized

	Progressive		Cyclical	Style
	Single trajectory	Progression/regression		
Social science based	Peck, *The Road Less Travelled* (1978) Fowler, *Stages of Faith* (1981) Parks, *The Critical Years* (1986) Oser & Gmünder, *Religious Judgement* (1991)	Hagberg and Guelich, *The Critical Journey* (1989) Westerhoff, *Will our Children Have Faith* (2000) Slee, *Women's Faith Development* (2004) Willow Creek, *Reveal: Where are You?* (2007) Rohr, *The Art of Letting Go* (2010) [Streib (2020)]	Westerhoff, *Living the Faith Community* (1985) McLaren, *Naked Spirituality* (2011)	Streib *Religious Styles* (2001) Csinos, 'Four Ways of Knowing God' (2010) Hopewell, *Congregation: Stories and Structures* (1988) Nye, 'Psychological Perspectives on Children's Spirituality' (1998)
Metaphor based	Underhill, *The Mystic Way* (1913) Jamieson, *Chrysalis* (2007) From the Christian Tradition: John Climacus, *The Ladder of Divine Ascent* (7th century) Hugh of St Victor, *The Soul's Three Ways of Seeing* (d.1141) Bonaventure, *The Soul's Journey Into God* (d.1274) Meister Eckhart, *The Book of Benedictus* (d. 1328) Marguerite Porete, *The Mirror of Simple Souls* (d. 1310) Walter Hilton, *The Ladder of Perfection* (d. 1396) *The Cloud of Unknowing* (14th century) John of the Cross, *The Dark Night of the Soul* (1578/79) John Bunyan, *The Pilgrim's Progress* (1678 and 1684)	From the Christian Tradition: Teresa of Avila, *Interior Castle* (1577)	Blackaby, *The Seasons of God* (2012) Hall, *For Everything a Season* (1986)	
			Harris, *Dance of the Spirit* (1989)	
Story		Brush, *The Way Through the Trees* (2014)		

within this group are two other works: that of Richard Rohr and of less well-known theorists Janet Hagberg and Robert Guelich. The second group I term 'cyclical' as they explore the way a person experiences faith as a series of modes or seasons that follow one after the other in a repeating cycle. Though there are some other models that refer to faith cycles, some do not actually function as cycles (despite their name), so this group is relatively small, comprising the creative works of Richard Blackaby and Dick Hall (with some mention of related work by Ross Thompson), a later model by Westerhoff, and the original model proposed by Brian McLaren. The final group are those models that focus more on a person's particular 'style' of faith. These do not chart a progression from one stage to another but instead describe a person's faith as a development of self into a fuller expression of their particular spiritual personality. This may involve movement between various styles or modes of spirituality but not in any specific cycle or hierarchy. This is true of Rebecca Nye and Heinz Streib, the latter one of the chief proponents of this position in current academic theology for some time (though we will note some change in his model over time). The strongest example of a style model is the work of David Csinos on the faith lives of children. I also include, in this section, James Hopewell's exploration of congregations in four modes, and the metaphoric work of Maria Harris. Finally, I will bring together all this wisdom and introduce the concepts that underpin my own model and then present the model itself. Being based not on stages, cycles or styles, it encompasses both stages and cycles into what I call a story model.

What is Faith?

When he set out to chart how faith developed, Fowler endeavoured to establish a model that would be open to those of all faiths, not simply those who were Christian. His definition of faith was, "a person's or group's way of responding to transcendent value and power as perceived and grasped through forms of cumulative tradition".[12] For Fowler, faith could develop in and out of religious belief; the faith system of an individual could be of one credal confession at one stage and later of another. Fowler's endeavour to provide a universal definition of Faith Development that encompasses all faiths and none was a worthy object. However, it led some, such as Estep and Kim, to suggest that his model of Faith Development might not have anything at all to say about faith as Christians would understand it. They suggest instead that what modern Faith Development models measure is not faith as such but "relates more closely to the biblical concept of wisdom".[13] Though in his later works Fowler explores other aspects, his initial definition focuses somewhat on a cognitive worldview. Of course, Anselm's concept of *fidens quaerens intellectum* (faith seeking understanding) would suggest that a quest for wisdom is not so far from the Christian journey of faith. Bonnie Miller-McLemore is rather more generous about Fowler's definition, saying that he deliberately makes a distinction

> between institutional religion and ultimate concern or between doctrinal belief and loyalty to centering values [because] he purposively focuses on universal values and cognitive structures of faith instead of substantive dogmas and faith differences in order to reach a more diverse religious audience and the wider public of nonprofit organizations, public schools, and prisons.[14]

Others have sought to extend this understanding of a faith that develops to include specifically emotional aspects of spirituality. Ronni Lamont pointed to the work of Rabbi Sandy Eisenberg Sasso who frames faith as something that is the result of '"experience" followed by "contextualising the story", culminating in our "theology"'.[15] Jeff Astley summarizes this differently, referring to faith as something that brings together 'thinking, valuing, feeling, making sense'.[16] It should already be apparent that the field of Faith Development lacks consensus so, wherever possible, I include the definition of faith for each of the modern theorists. For Christians, a primary source on the nature of faith alongside our reason and experiences is the tradition of the church, and first among that tradition is scripture.

Scripture talks about faith in various ways. In the Hebrew scriptures, the words אֱמֶת (*e.met*), 'truth, faith(ful)', and אָמַן (*a.man*), 'be faithful', are used in different ways. אֱמֶת (*e.met*) is used to mean faithfulness,[17] though also translated as true[18] or even to describe security[19] or purity.[20] אָמַן (*a.man*) is generally used in the context of covenantal relationships, both those kept and those broken,[21] though also as a sense of belief.[22] It is also used variously to describe someone committing to an act of caring[23] or as something that is reliable.[24] In the New Testament, πίστις (*pistis*), 'faith', is something that gives confidence in a certain outcome,[25] or describes adherence to a certain belief or set of beliefs.[26] Yet it is also described as being something that has no meaning without an outworking[27] and is also more powerful than adherence to the law.[28]

In one parable, Jesus speaks of faith not as something that has to be large or impressive to be effective.[29] In response to the disciples asking him, 'Increase our faith!' (Luke 17.5), Jesus compares both faith and the kingdom to a mustard seed, implying strongly that faith for Jesus is not just about beliefs or indeed individuals. Other scriptural texts speak not simply about faith but about levels of faith and of faith growing. Jesus describes the people as being 'of little faith' when the disciples are caught in a storm on the lake (Matt. 8.26), when commenting on the material desires of his listeners (Matt. 6.30 and Luke 12.28), when Peter tries but fails to walk on water to meet Jesus (Matt. 14.31), and when the disciples have forgotten to bring food with them (Matt. 16.8). Jesus describes the centurion and the Syrophoenician woman who each come to him asking for a miraculous cure as having 'such great faith' (Matt. 8.10, 15.28 and Luke 7.9). Jesus also speaks of faith, though, as something that takes work. The parable of the wise and foolish builders tells us that we cannot have a firm foundation to our lives without spending time to ensure we build our faith on something solid as we would build our house on rock (Matt. 7.24–27).

The relationship between Jesus and Peter, though mapping rather too short a time of Peter's life to be described as a model of Faith Development, shows that faith is something that changes over time and can be encouraged. Peter makes confident statements about Jesus (Matt. 16.16; Mark 8.29; Luke 9.20), shows great enthusiasm (Matt. 17.4; 26.35; Mark 9.5; 14.29; Luke 9.33; 22.33; John 13.9.), questions him in order to learn (Matt. 15.15; Luke 12.41), gets it wrong (Matt. 16.22; 26.40; Mark 8.32–33; 14.37; John 13.6; 18.10–11), rejects Jesus (Matt. 26.69–75; Mark 14.54–72; Luke 22.55–61; John 18.17–27) and on repenting returns with renewed strength (Luke 24.12; John 21.7–17; Acts 2.14; 3.6; 4.13; 9.34), as predicted by Jesus when he said to Peter, 'I have prayed for you that your own faith may not fail; and you, when once you have turned back, strengthen your brothers' (Luke 22.32).

In Acts, it is clear that faith takes some effort. Paul is said to have 'strengthened the souls of the disciples' and encouraged them to 'continue in the faith', saying, 'It is through many persecutions that we must enter the kingdom of God' (Acts 14.22). In scripture it is clear that faith can become stronger (Acts 16.5; Rom. 4.20) and also be something that opens up (Acts 14.27). Elsewhere there is a greater ambiguity and intangibility of the meaning of faith. Jesus suggests that it is not automatic or a guarantee, asking, 'when the Son of Man comes, will he find faith on earth?' (Luke 18.8). Faith, according to Paul, is a gift (1 Cor. 12.9) and something that is not the same in everyone, but that is God-given, and not equally so, but in varying measure (Rom. 12.3). Paul speaks of faith as something that can be encouraged mutually (Rom. 1.12) and as something at which a person can excel as they could at a skill like knowledge or oratory (2 Cor. 8.7). He asserts that, however powerful, faith is useless without love (1 Cor. 13.2). Hebrews suggests that there are different levels of maturity in faith: 'for everyone who lives on milk, being still an infant, is unskilled in the word of righteousness. But solid food is for the mature, for those whose faculties have been trained by practice to distinguish good from evil' (Heb. 5.13–14). Paul suggests something similar to the Corinthians when he uses such a metaphor of food to describe the teaching he could offer them (1 Cor. 3.1–3). In this same letter Paul describes his own growing faith:

> When I was a child, I spoke like a child, I thought like a child, *I reasoned like a child*; when I became an adult, *I put an end to childish ways*. For now we see in a mirror, dimly, but *then we will see face to face*. Now I know only in part; *then I will know fully*, even as I have been fully known. (1 Cor. 13.11–12)[30]

Paul continues this theme of maturing faith in his other extant letter to the Corinthians, saying, 'our hope is that, *as your faith increases*, our sphere of action among you may be greatly enlarged' (2 Cor. 10.15). Indeed, Paul is possibly the biblical author who writes most about faith as something that grows. He not only describes the maturity in faith of the Corinthians (1 Cor. 2.6), he also does so twice in his letter to the Colossians (Col. 1.28 and 4.12) and again in his letter to the Philippians (Phil. 3.15). The idea of renewal of faith is present in scripture in the concept of a second birth. Jesus describes the need for disciples to both be 'born from above' (John 3.3) and also to become like children, saying, 'Truly I tell you, unless you change and become like children, you will never enter the kingdom of heaven. Whoever becomes humble like this child is the greatest in the kingdom of heaven' (Matt. 18.3–4). This concept supports some of the faith transitions that we will explore in the models described in the following chapters.

Considering these passages and my reading of Faith Development thinkers, what we are talking about when we talk about a faith that develops is an understanding of the place of self in connection to other people, the world (or universe) and God (which some might call something different, such as a higher power or the universe). This is an evolving system of meaning-making that might include specific credal and doctrinal elements alongside the sense of meaning in terms of oneself and of interpersonal relationships; a sense of connection with

God and the other, practices of connection to God and the other, and outworkings of those relationships in terms of actions, character and dispositions. If this definition were to be narrowed to simply a Christian context, the dominical commandments offer a perfect framework for faith. Jesus speaks of our calling to love God with all aspects of our being; he tells us to love God 'with all your heart, and with all your soul, and with all your mind, and with all your strength', and also presents us with the need for our calling to involve not simply God but also those around us and ourselves, as we love our 'neighbour as [y]ourself' (Luke 10.27). So, focusing exclusively through the Christian lens of faith, it would be possible to be more specific, as follows: Christian faith that develops is an understanding of the place of the self in connection to our neighbour, creation and God the Father, Jesus Christ and the Holy Spirit as one Holy Trinity. It is an evolving system of meaning-making including an ongoing exploration of the scriptures, the creeds and the teachings of the church through the tradition and in its current expression. It involves meaning-making in terms of oneself as a member of the Body of Christ, through corporate worship and personal practices of contemplation and devotion, as well as enacted works of discipleship through service to others, the church and creation as an individual and as part of the church. It involves the individual in reflective practice of their beliefs in terms of their own character and lifestyle.

How Do We Develop?

In addition to the models of specifically Faith Development that we will explore in this book, there are general models of human development that account for the maturing process in various facets of experience. Some focus strictly on the distinctions between people at various ages, often linked to biological and specifically cognitive changes. Others account for the development of concepts of the self, moral development or the development of interaction with others. Many of the Faith Development models that we will explore in this book refer to some of these development models as foundations either individually or corporately. This being the case, it is sensible in this brief section to set out some of the more common models that are referenced in Faith Development.

Swiss theologian Jean Piaget composed a model for cognitive development in children establishing that children think in a way that is not merely incomplete in comparison to the thinking style of adults but qualitatively distinct.[31] He charted the cognitive development of children and the implications of their biological maturation for their developing interaction with the world. Piaget's model has four stages. He asserted that these transcended cultural differences and were sequential without any change in order. The child in infancy (0–2) is deemed to be in the *sensorimotor stage* when the main focus of the child is physical. They learn to move their bodies and engage with the world through sight, touch, sound, taste and smell. In this stage children begin to learn that they are a person distinct from others and they begin to learn that objects have permanence even if they are not seen. Earliest childhood (2–7) is described as the *preoperational stage* when children begin to use symbols and to sort things into categories. Their thinking is centred on their own view and is intuitive rather than logical. Late childhood (7–11) is the *concrete operational stage* when a child, due to particular development within the brain, can begin to use logic in relation to their world and the things that happen in it, and work out things in their head without having to be doing something physically in relation to the problem they are solving. In adolescence (12 upwards) children enter the *formal operational stage* with the beginnings of abstract thought. Teens can think hypothetically as well as systematically, opening up the ability to understand issues such as politics and ethics. These stages were based in part on observation but also on biological changes.

Building on Piaget's work, Lawrence Kohlberg, an American psychologist with German heritage, suggested a scale of moral development based on the responses of his research participants to hypothetical situations.[32] In his model there are six stages, grouped in three pairs of levels. He terms Level 1 *Pre-Conventional Morality* and associates it with childhood up to the age of about nine. The two stages in this level are, first, an obedience and punishment orientation, in which an individual seeks to avoid punishment, though, if punishment is not evident, will consider any activity acceptable and Stage 2 is about individualism and exchange in which the child exhibits a willingness to do something if an obvious reward is evident, and gains awareness that there are different viewpoints about what is right and wrong. Level 2 is attributed to those aged approximately nine up to early adolescence. Kohlberg describes it as a time of *Conventional Morality* and comprises Stages 3 and 4. Stage 3 has an emphasis on interpersonal accord and conformity. This is the stage of abiding by social norms to be a 'good person' in the eyes of others. Stage 4 is about maintaining the social order whereby the adolescent becomes aware of the wider societal rules and laws. Level 3 is a stage that can come in adolescence or early adulthood but that Kohlberg also identifies as not coming for all adults.

It is the *Postconventional* level, comprising Stages 5 and 6, which configures morality through the social contract and the concept of individual rights. Stage 5 is a nuanced stage where an understanding develops that a law for the greater good may not be in the best interests of a minority. Stage six comprises those who have come to their own formulation of moral guidelines or universal principles, which may mean going against the rest of society. Kohlberg considered that very few people reach this final stage, something we will observe in other models such as Fowler's.

Erik Erikson grew up in Germany in complex family circumstances with Jewish/Danish origins, which prompted his later focus on identity. Writing in the 1950s–60s, he suggested that there were eight stages of psychosocial development (the interrelation of social interaction with others and an individual's thought and behaviour).[33] His eight stages, being linked to certain age ranges, come in a particular order. At each stage there are two competing factors that the individual must balance in what he calls a psychosocial crisis. In infancy (0–1½) the crisis relates to *Trust vs Mistrust* of the adults caring for them. Successful psychosocial development to Stage 2 depends on predictable and reliable care, without which a child develops mistrust and confusion. In very early childhood (1½–3) the crisis is *Autonomy vs Shame* as the child develops personal control and begins to exercise independence. Healthy development at this stage is supported by encouragement. Children who are excessively controlled or criticized can become overly dependent and lack self-esteem.

In early childhood (3–5) the child is presented with the conflict of *Initiative vs Guilt*. As they become more independent of adults and spend time with other children, healthy development involves imaginative play. Children are beginning to assert themselves and too much criticism of such use of initiative can lead to an unhealthy development of guilt. At primary school age (5–12), the psychosocial conflict is *Industry vs Inferiority*. The child's peer group gains greater significance and this involves a sense of needing to prove themselves. Encouragement in these endeavours to prove their competence will lead to healthy development, while failure in a skill perceived as key in their immediate society can lead to a sense of inferiority. In adolescence (12–18) the conflict is *Identity vs Role Confusion*.

Teenagers search for their own identity as they transition from childhood to adulthood identifying what roles they will assume as an individuated adult. This involves becoming at home in one's own skin at a time when physical changes can be rapid. A healthily developing young person becomes used to their new body and has a sense of how they fit into the world without undue pressure to conform to others. Without this, an adolescent can experience an identity crisis, experiment with a variety of identities or indeed end up in a negative identity and attendant distress. In early adulthood (18–40) the balance must be found in *Intimacy vs Isolation*. Having established their individual identity and role in the community in adolescence, young adults face the need to establish healthy, loving relationships with others. Individuals explore intimacy and establish longer-term commitments outside of existing family. Individuals unable to establish intimacy or fearful of commitment can end up feeling isolated and suffering from depression.

From mid-life onwards (40–65) the crisis comes in *Generativity vs Stagnation*. Individuals feel the need either to nurture or to create things that will outlive them. This can be in the form of children or creative or professional production. Healthy development induces a sense of accomplishment and self-worth derived from feeling useful. Conversely, without a constructive way to contribute to society, individuals become stagnant, feeling unproductive and disconnected from community. Finally, over the age of 65 productivity slows and the crisis is rooted in *Ego Integrity vs Despair*. Individuals look back over their life for a sense of having accomplished what they thought their life would be and maintain a sense of the person who they had hoped they would become. Erikson describes this as 'the acceptance of one's one and only life cycle as something that had to be'.[34] Without this ego integrity, an individual will look back on their life with dissatisfaction, which can lead to hopelessness or depression.

Some models have sought to account for the diversity of individuals in a way that does not specify progressive change and have instead chosen to talk about a continuum. American psychologist Carl Rogers maps a person's psychological health into seven stages (from rigidity to fluidity in psychological functioning) but suggests it could equally be broken into three, fifteen or fifty stages.[35] His 'river' tracks the confluence of several streams of personality, frozen at first and becoming more flowing, as they converge to a holistic state of psychological stability. Rogers describes each aspect of the person's development separately through seven stages, differentiating someone's relationship to feelings, degree of incongruence, manner of experience, communication of self and construing of experience. For the final two streams (relationship to problems and manner of relating to others) he does not track progress across the seven stages but instead talks in more general terms of progression.

INTRODUCTION

How Does Faith Develop?

Working with my own definition of faith as given above, faith, therefore, develops in relation to all those aspects described. Our understanding of how faith develops can be explored in terms of our evolving sense of our relationship with God, with our neighbour, encompassing all creation, human and otherwise, and in relation to our evolving sense of self. We can also chart how our faith grows in terms of how we grow and change in our familiarity, comprehension and interpretation of the teachings of the church in scripture and the wider tradition. Faith also develops through our exploration of practices of devotion and contemplation, through our various experiences as a member of the Body of Christ; through our learning more about our own calling and our self-awareness; and in the operation of our faith in terms of virtues and character. Our faith develops in relation to both positive and negative experience in all these things. As St Paul writes, 'endurance produces character, and character produces hope, and hope does not disappoint us' (Rom. 5.3b–4). Indeed, the late great Professor John Hull observed wisely about the nature of learning (and the lack of learning):

> The desire to be right, the need to be right are very important in the lives of most adults. This is no less true of religious adults ... The need to be right carries with it the fear of being wrong. In the lives of many Christian adults these factors prevent learning. To be ready to learn is to be ready to admit that there is much one does not know, that one may not be entirely right.[36]

Though we may not be comfortable with it, developing our faith sometimes involves exploring some of our most dearly held beliefs and practices, which may be affirmed by that exploration or may be challenged. Yet without such exploration, our faith cannot change and develop. When Jesus talks to Nicodemus, he talks about a pivotal moment in someone's faith life as being born from above/again/of the spirit.[37] This has often been linked to the conversion experience of those adopting Christianity as adults. Yet here Jesus is talking to someone he acknowledges as a mature person of faith. Jesus is here speaking of that need to take a step into something new. This is echoed in a few of the models that reference something like what one writer calls the dark night of the soul and what I term a hiatus in spiritual growth. We will see evidence of the importance of this kind of development of faith in some of our modern models and most especially in some of the models from the tradition.

As we explore each model of Faith Development, we will see many ways in which faith has been considered to develop; for many in the church these have been sources of encouragement and inspiration.

The Field of Faith Development

Modern Faith Development is a discipline that spreads across a number of fields. There is a distinction to be made between the origin of models that fall in roughly three camps. First, there are Empirical Models; those that are strongly founded on empirical research (often by teams including psychologists or sociologists, perhaps alongside theologians or those with interest in more than one field). Empirical Models are based on the exploration of the faith lives of individuals who have been interviewed and their responses analysed in order to say something about more general trends in the Faith Development of the wider population. Then there are Collated Models based on the exploration of several Empirical Models, bringing together different sets of empirical data, or at least the analysis of them, to present something new that combines the wisdom of others either recognizing common findings or juxtaposing the differences between models and coming to a new model. The third category, Discipleship Models, are written for a universal rather than academic readership and might have little or no engagement with academic models (or at least demonstrate no such engagement due to minimal, or a total lack of, referencing to sources).

This diversity presents anyone exploring the variety of models with the difficulty of trying to compare things that do not have enough in common to properly be weighed by the same measure. As I present the various models in this book, I have endeavoured to give you a sense of which categories each of these models falls into. That said, there are occasionally models that straddle particularly the second and third categories and I hope I make that clear also. Slee suggests that the study of Faith Development requires

> the rigorous dialogue between different accounts of faith in order to tease out the strengths and weaknesses of each, and to see where fresh enquiry is needed. But dialogue depends upon the integrity and mutual respect of each partner, rather than replacement of one, inevitably limited, understanding by another.[38]

She reiterates this with a call for an 'ongoing conversation' between models that I hope this book can offer.

In addition to those authors who propose new models of Faith Development, there is a considerable field of writing which sets out instead to survey the existing field or in some way comment on the models already proposed. For example, Parker's review article includes a thorough literature review of the study of Fowler's theory and a comprehensive list of empirical studies using various models of faith.[39] Other works engaging with Fowler's theory, including Astley and Francis[40] or Dykstra and Parks,[41] provide models for applying Fowler's theory to practical research. Kelcourse edited a collection of essays in relation to Faith Development not presenting any particular models but inviting contributors to each look specifically at faith at various stages such as infancy, middle age, etc.[42] Watts, Nye and Savage cover Faith Development as one aspect of their exploration of *Psychology for Christian Ministry*, suggesting some discernment is necessary when bringing Faith Development to bear on lived ministry. Rather than something for the whole people of God, they suggest Faith Development models are best reserved as a heuristic tool for ministers to consider when helping other people. The inherent hierarchy in Faith Development models, they suggest, makes them less useful for the wider church membership as we should be

> cautious about the tool's ability to predict the future course of a person's faith journey. People are more likely to respond to the power of these stages to make sense of changes retrospectively, recognising a similar sequence to their faith history ... at best it suggests what growth could be like, but not what it should be ... The sharp demarcation of separate stages does not always fit with people's experience of development in adulthood; there is often a stronger sense of continuity and gradual unfolding.[43]

Stokes' and Astley's books both sought to introduce the concepts of Faith Development to a wider audience through an accessible text.[44] Nonetheless it remains a field that has not had considerable impact on the models of ministry and mission of the church.

What this brief introduction to the field has not yet made clear is that there are a number of critiques of the field. There is a considerable preponderance of white, western writers and thinkers in the field, just as there is in the field of human development that we explored earlier. Fowler, Westerhoff, Peck, Hawkins, Guelich, Rohr, McLaren, Hopewell, Csinos, Blackaby and Buchanan are all white, male North

American thinkers. Streib, Oser, Gmünder and Hall are all white, male European thinkers and Jamieson is a white New Zealander. Harris, Hagberg, Parkinson and Parks are all white, female North American writers, and Slee and Nye are white female European writers. I am conscious that I also fall into this latter category and have endeavoured to address my own potential biases in my contribution to the field.

Some journal articles and dissertations have focused on the faith lives of particular communities but almost all the major writers on Faith Development are white, male westerners. This imbalance in modern, theological study can partly be balanced by the voices from the Christian tradition who offer a different perspective, though, of course, the voices from the tradition also include a predominance of white and male voices. These major voices receive critique from female academics and from some academics of global majority heritage (GMH) in smaller studies[45] and a substantial project on the faith lives of women and girls.[46] This predominance of the white, male voice means that established models of Faith Development fail to account fully for the faith lives of genders other than male or those of GMH. It is obvious, from a survey of those writing on Faith Development, that issues of diversity in the field have not been fully reflected in those who have proposed models, and equally we will see that those interviewed about their faith have not fully reflected the diversity of human lived experience.

Another critique of Faith Development models has been that identifying the development of faith towards a 'proper' and 'mature' faith negates the faith experience of children or those whose faith does not develop beyond the preliminary stages of a model due to particular life experiences or to mental capacity. Miller-McLemore critiques Faith Development models for their lack of attention to the validity of the experience of the child. Even though she acknowledges that the likes of Fowler and Westerhoff did consider children as part of their research, she notes that Fowler focused on adults rather than children, saying of his research that 'his primary subject is not the child but the individuating adult who is looking back over life to judge where one stands and where one is going'.[47] Fowler's focus on 'becoming adult', Miller-McLemore argues, undermines the validity of any statements about the faith lives of children. Of Westerhoff, she acknowledges that his work makes clear that 'children deserve respect as equal participants in religious life and as part of God's promise and not as a means to some other, adult end'.[48] Nonetheless, he too, she considers, fails to pay due attention to the faith lives of children because, 'even in books with "children" in the title, Westerhoff talks more about adult crises in religious education than about children and family'.⁴⁹ The very title of Westerhoff's principal text, *Will Our Children Have Faith?* speaks from a position of adult or parental anxiety, as Mark Yaconelli observed:

> Adults want youths to conform to adult standards. They want youth to act responsibly. They want them to sit down and listen. They want youth to hurry up and get their identity fixed and grounded. Adults want youth to have a roadmap for a secure and reasonable future and they get rattled when they notice that most youth aren't carrying one.⁵⁰

Some people have constructed Faith Development models that are intended to cover whole lifespans, including childhood. Of these, some nonetheless treat the Faith Development of children and young people as something inherently lesser that needs to be grown out of or mature into what it is really meant to be. This can lead to a lack of valuing earlier stages as apt for the right time. It also highlights a concern for the way that those of different stages might be regarded by others, especially how those of 'higher' stages might view those of 'lower' stages. Although adult models may not account well for younger people, there are researchers who have endeavoured to establish models of Faith Development specifically for children or young people, and a number of quantitative studies from the field of child psychology and sociology. Sungwon Kim recently set out a bold ambition 'to develop a faith scale for young children that is theologically sound, faithful to the development theories, and scientifically proven'.⁵¹

Kim used a questionnaire focused initially on three facets of faith, namely, '"knowing" ("who God is" and "what God has done"), loving ("You can have a relationship with God"), and living ("You can be all God wants you to be") and ("You can do all God wants you to do")'.⁵² He ultimately revised this to suggest a scale with implied progression of children from factor one through to incorporate also factor two and factor three. Kim seems to suggest that Faith Development in childhood moves from confessional faith life to missional life, and then to distinctive life. The resulting model is based on the principle that 'young children's faith is defined as a system of life that manifests itself in the attitudes and actions of knowing, believing in, and loving, God'.⁵³ In contrast to other models that see a maturing of faith as somewhat stepping away from childhood understandings of faith, Kim suggests that a childhood foundation is something to be built upon in the future:

> Given that early childhood is a time when basic images and affective maps of life are formed, children form a basic attitude toward others, the world, and God through interaction with significant others, and they likewise form a basic system of spirituality. Children's faith can then grow into a holistic spirituality when they learn theological concepts and biblical values that are consistent with the emotional map they have already embodied.[54]

However, if we apply Miller-Mclemore's critique of Westerhoff to it, Kim's work may not be considered a true reflection of childhood faith as it is based on parental observation. Kim references work by Song exploring children's faith in several facets: image of God, faith and resurrection in Jesus, heaven, prayer and forgiveness, as well as the spirituality scales of Howden and of Stoyles et al.[55] The latter of these can be used with children of varying faith traditions and is based on a combination of Hay and Nye's 'three sensitivities' (see p. 158 below), Champagne's 'concept of 'relational consciousness' and Bradford's assertion 'that children seek out and recognise relationships between self and others'.[56] They explored spiritual sensitivity in combination with measures for a child's sense of both self-esteem and hopefulness, concluding that children scoring higher on the spiritual sensitivity scale were also likely to score high in both hope and self-esteem.

I hope in this book, and in my own model, to honour the faith lives of children, young people and others as sometimes distinct from the faith lives of adults (though having common elements), which have no need for hurrying up towards anything and certainly not as something lesser. To this end, I include Faith Development models that focus specifically on children to reinforce one of the distinctions of the field: there is no one concept of a fully matured person. Faith Development, as a field, negates the idea that once someone has reached a certain point in their faith, such as by becoming an adult, they are 'mature' and 'complete'. Miller-McLemore credits Erikson with this concept as it was his work that resulted in 'extending Freud's stage theory from childhood to adulthood. No longer did people assume adulthood was a static state.'[57] Such completion is, of course, not possible in this lifetime, as St Paul attests: 'Now we see as in a mirror, dimly, but then we will see face to face. Now I know only in part; then I will know fully, even as I have been fully known' (1 Cor. 13.12).

Finally, it is evident from the reception of certain models that some parts of the church seem more reluctant to engage with Faith Development than others. Estep and Kim acknowledge their struggles with a model that is founded on a principle that the pinnacle of maturity in faith lies in liberalism.[58] Nonetheless they also acknowledge that Fowler, along with Oser and Gmünder, have identified clear evidence of certain patterns in the religious lives of those whom they studied. The work of Willow Creek in exploring the faith experience of their members somewhat bucks this trend though their research methods depart from those of other Faith Development models. Indeed, much of the disquiet with Faith Development seems to be rooted in a reticence about the academic roots of the field itself and in two particular aspects of the field. First, the field of Practical Theology is still young, and some Christians are not yet sure of a discipline that is rooted in practice or, as some might misconstrue it, draws on 'mere experience' rather than on scripture. Second, Practical Theology takes seriously various sources of theology, scripture and experience included. It also draws on other fields of academic study, such as sociology and psychology, alongside more traditional theological sources. Some Christians are uncomfortable with this interdisciplinary approach. Yet the reticence about Faith Development is more than a rejection of Practical Theology.

As most Faith Development models engage with issues of doubt, struggling with the faith, in the tradition of Jacob (Gen. 32.22–30), or some form of critical engagement with issues of faith, there are those who might naturally resist these models, preferring a secure adherence to the *via positiva* and an unquestioning reliance on trust in God in matters that might challenge the teachings of the church. The third reason for some to reject models of Faith Development is that most models, though not all, tend towards viewing a more liberal and inclusive theological viewpoint (even encompassing an openness to the revelation of other faiths) as the development beyond a more conservative theological viewpoint.

Aligned to the study of Faith Development is the significant field of work in religiosity. As Marsha Cutting and Michelle Walsh identified over a decade ago, there were then nearly 200 different scales for measuring religiosity in the fields of psychology and sociology.[59] They note that despite this great number, there was a lack of consensus on what exactly is being measured. They also suggest that the scales represent a bias towards a particular kind of religiosity, namely an 'American Protestant orientation', though studies do not always specify the demographic spread of participants in the description of the formation of the scale. They list Fowler's scale as one of the few with a more nuanced approach. Cutting and Walsh identify the roots of many of these religiosity scales in quantitative methods (focusing on counting various factors) while only a few had been based in qualitative methods (focusing on the nature of data). From their description, it's clear that many of these scales used in sociology do not have much in common with what models of Faith Development talk about. For this reason, I have not chosen to include any within this book. However, there are other secular development models that are worth including to give context to the Faith Development models we explore.

How Does Knowing About Faith Development Help Us?

Having explored the field and the ways in which this field has been criticized we might wonder why it is a field of interest at all. I believe it is an important field to support individuals in discipleship and ministers in pastoral care and mission as it enables us to understand fully why people join churches, why they act as they do as members of churches and why some feel the need to leave and join another church, or in some cases leave church completely or indeed change religions. Indeed, there has been increasing research into the faith experience of those who previously but no longer attend church and some of this has been usefully linked to Faith Development.[60]

As individuals, we are each on a journey of discovery in our faith. These models offer us not maps so much as travelling tales from those who have been there or know the area. Rather than wandering aimlessly, a journey of faith should be one that is reflected upon and taken with an awareness that we are on that journey. For those in ministry, this is something that is encouraged during the discernment process, yet for many of the people in our congregations it is not something that they have ever considered, and 'there is virtue in encouraging people to talk (or write) about their faith in a way that listens out for the ways that changes in it are connected to other aspects of their lives'.[61] I hope this book and my model will help people get a sense of where they might currently be in their faith journey, as well as understand where they have come from and perhaps give some reassurance about any experiences that may have been difficult to explain or understand.

A model of Faith Development might also help someone understand how their faith could develop in the future. For those of us charged with the care of the spiritual lives of individuals and communities, these models offer a way of supporting those for whom we have care. As those who lead church communities, understanding Faith Development models should enable ministers to be aware of the variety of religious experience that might be present in a community at any one time. This should help with planning discipleship and worship that can support individuals appropriately at their current stage or through a period of transition from one stage to the next. These models can also make leaders more aware of why we might feel more affinity with some members of our communities than with others. There are some stages that share much less in common with others, even to the point of hostility to differing outlooks. Some models we explore in this book map faith in general (rather than specifically Christian faith) so might also help us work with those of all faiths and none in our local communities.

Notes

1 Stokes, Kenneth, 1989, *Faith is a Verb: Dynamics of Adult Faith Development*, Mystic: Twenty-third Publications, p. 3.

2 Theopoetics was first so named by Stanley Hopper. For a good introduction to theopoetics, see Keefe-Perry, L. C., 2014, *Way to Water: A Theopoetics Primer*, Eugene: Wipf and Stock.

3 Holland, Scott, 2014, 'The Return of Theopoetics', *CrossCurrents*, Vol. 64, No. 4, December, pp. 496–508.

4 Hernández, Gloria Maité, 2021, *Savoring God: Comparative Theopoetics*, Oxford, Oxford University Press.

5 Harris, Maria, and Moran, Gabriel, 1998, *Reshaping Religious Education: Conversations on Contemporary Practice*, Louisville: Westminster John Knox Press, p. 64.

6 Wolski Conn, Joann, ed., 1986, *Women's Spirituality: Resources for Christian Development*, New York: Paulist Press.

7 Cutting and Walsh catalogued almost 200 religiosity scales in the fields of psychology and sociology. Cutting, Marsha and Walsh, Michelle, 2008, 'Religiosity Scales: What are We Measuring in Whom?' *Archive for the Psychology of Religion*, Vol. 30, pp. 137–53.

8 Estep, James Riley, and Kim, Jonathan H., eds, 2010, *Christian Formation: Integrating Theology and Human Development*, Nashville: B. and H. Academic.

9 Power, C., 1991, 'Hard versus Soft Stages of Faith and Religious Development', in Fowler, J., Nipkow, K., and Schweitzer, F., eds, *Stages of Faith and Religious Development: Implications for Church, Education, and Society*, New York: Crossroad Publishing, pp. 116–29.

10 Estep and Kim, *Christian Formation*, pp. 185–8.

11 Slee, Nicola, 2004, *Women's Faith Development: Patterns and Processes*, London: Routledge, p. 17.

12 Fowler, James W., 1995, *Stages of Faith: The Psychology of Human Development and the Quest for Meaning*, San Francisco: Harper, originally published 1981, p. 9.

13 Estep and Kim, *Christian Formation*, pp. 163 and 189.

14 Miller-McLemore, Bonnie, 2006, 'Wither the Children? Childhood in Religious Education', *Journal of Religion* 86, pp. 635–57, p. 641, fn. 21.

15 Lamont, Ronni, 2020, *Faith in Children*, Oxford: Lion Hudson, p. 91.

16 Astley, J., ed., 1991, *How Faith Grows: Faith Development and Christian Education*, London: National Society and Church House Publishing, p. 1.

17 Gen. 24.27, 49; Josh. 24.14; Judg. 9.19; 1 Kings 3.6.

18 Deut. 13.14; 17.4; Ps. 15.21; 19.9; 25.5; Eccles. 12.10.

19 Isa. 39.8; Jer. 33.6; 2 Kings 20.19.

20 Jer. 2.21.

21 Ex. 21.8; Lev. 5.15; Num. 5.6, 12, 27; Deut. 32.51; Josh. 7.1; 22.16, 20–22, 31; Judg. 9.15–16, 19; 1 Chron. 2.7; 5.25; 9.1; 10.13; Ezra 10.2, 10; Job 39.12; Ps. 106.24; 146.6.

22 Gen. 15.6; Ex. 4.1–9; 2 Kings 17.14; 2 Chron. 20.20; Job 15.22; Ps. 78.22; Isa. 28.16; Lam. 4.12; Jonah 3.5; Hab. 1.5.

23 Ruth 4.16; 2 Kings 10.1, 5; Esth. 2.7.

24 Gen. 42.20; 1 Kings 11.38; Isa. 8.12; Hos. 5.9.

25 Matt. 6.30; 8.10; 9.2, 29; 14.31; 15.28; 21.21; Mark 2.5; 4.40; 5.34; 10.52; 11.22; Luke 5.20; 7.9, 50; 8.48; 9.25; 12.28; 17.5, 6, 19; Acts 3.16; 14.9.

26 Acts 13.8.

27 James 2.18.

28 Rom. 9.32.

29 Matt 17.20 and Luke 17.6; Matt. 13.31–32; Mark 4.30–32; Luke 13.18–19.

30 See also Col. 1.28; 4.12; 1 Cor. 2.6; Phil. 3.15; 2 Tim. 3.7.

31 Piaget, Jean, 1950, *The Psychology of Intelligence*, London: Routledge and Kegan Paul Ltd.

32 Kohlberg, L., 1969, 'Stage and Sequence: The Cognitive-Developmental Approach to Socialization.' in Goslin, David A., ed., *Handbook of Socialization Theory and Research*, Chicago: Rand McNally, pp. 347–480; Kohlberg, L., and Levine, C., 1984, *Moral Stages: A Current Formulation and a Response to Critics*, Abingdon: S. Karger; Colby, A., and Kohlberg, L. eds, 1987, *The Measurement of Moral Judgment*, New York: Cambridge University Press.

33 Erikson, E. H., 1950, *Childhood and Society*, 1st edn, New York: Norton; Erikson, E. H., 1968, *Identity: Youth and Crisis*, New York: W. W. Norton.

34 Erikson, *Childhood*, p. 268.

35 Rogers, Carl, 1959, 'A Tentative Scale for the Measurement of Process in Psychotherapy', in Rubinstein, E., and Parloff, M., eds, *Research in Psychotherapy: Proceedings of a Conference, Washington, D.C. April 9–12, 1958*, Washington: American Psychological Association, pp. 96–107.

36 Hull, John, 1985, *What Prevents Christian Adults from Learning*, London: SCM Press, p. 91.

37 John 3.3.

38 Slee, *Women's*, p. 168.

39 Parker, Stephen, 2010 'Research in Fowler's Faith Development Theory: A Review Article', *Review of Religious Research*, Vol. 51, No. 3, pp. 233–52.

40 Astley, Jeff, and Francis, Leslie J., eds, 1992, *Christian Perspectives on Faith Development: A Reader*, Grand Rapids: Eerdmans, Leominster: Gracewing.

41 Dykstra, Craig, and Parks, Sharon, 1986, *Faith Development and Fowler*, Birmingham: Religious Education Press.

42 Kelcourse, Felicity B., 2005, *Human Development and Faith: Life-Cycle Stages of Body, Mind, and Soul*, St Louis: Chalice Press.
43 Watts, Fraser, Nye, Rebecca, and Savage, Sara, 2002, *Psychology for Ministry*, London: Routledge, pp. 112–13.
44 Stokes, *Faith is a Verb*; Astley, *How Faith Grows*.
45 For example, see Kim, Sungwon, 2021, 'Development and Validation of a Faith Scale for Young Children', *Religions*, Vol. 12, No. 197, pp. 1–14; King, P. E. et al., 2021, 'The Measure of Diverse Adolescent Spirituality (MDAS) and Refined Findings from Mexican and Salvadoran Youth', in Ai, A. L., Wink, P., Paloutzian, R. F., Harris, K. A., eds, *Assessing Spirituality in a Diverse World*, Cham: Springer, pp. 383–410; Nynäs, Peter et al., 2021, 'The Faith Q-Sort: In-Depth Assessment of Diverse Spirituality and Religiosity in 12 Countries' in Ai, A. L. et al., *Assessing Spirituality*, pp. 553–73; Ng, Greer Anne Wenh-In, 1996, 'Toward Wholesome Nurture: Challenges in the Religious Education of Asian North American Female Christians', *Religious Education*, Vol. 91, No. 2, Spring, pp. 238–54; Seager, James, 2022, 'Reimagining discipleship pathways for pluralist societies: Faith development theory and the theology of Christian formation in conversation', *Journal of Pentecostal and Charismatic Christianity*, Vol. 43, No. 2, pp. 1–18.
46 Slee, Nicola, Porter, Fran and Phillips, Anne, eds, 2013, *The Faith Lives of Women and Girls: Qualitative Research Perspectives*, London: Routledge; Slee, Nicola, Porter, Fran, and Phillips, Anne, eds, 2018, *Researching Female Faith*, London: Routledge.
47 Miller-McLemore, 'Wither', p. 639.
48 Miller-McLemore, 'Wither', p. 643.
49 Miller-McLemore, 'Wither', p. 644.
50 Yaconelli, Mark, 2006, *Contemplative Youth Ministry*, London: SPCK, p. 13.
51 Kim, 'Development', p. 3.
52 Kim, 'Development', p. 9.
53 Kim, 'Development', p. 8.
54 Kim, 'Development', p. 9.
55 Howden, Judy W., 1992, *Development and Psychometric Characteristics of the Spirituality Assessment Scale*, Texas Woman's University unpublished dissertation; Stoyles, Gerard John, Stanford, Bonnie, Caputi, Peter, Keating, Alysha-Leigh and Hyde, Brendan, 2012, 'A measure of spiritual sensitivity for children', *International Journal of Children's Spirituality*, Vol. 17, No. 3, pp. 203–15.
56 Stoyles et al., 'A Measure', pp. 204–5.
57 Miller-McLemore, 'Wither', p. 640.
58 Estep and Kim, *Christian Formation*, p. 165.
59 Cutting and Walsh, 'Religiosity Scales', pp. 137–53.
60 Aisthorpe, Steve, 2016, *The Invisible Church: Learning from the Experiences of Churchless Christians*, St Andrews: St Andrew Press. See also Jamieson, Alan, 2002, *A Churchless Faith: Faith Journeys Beyond the Churches*, London: SPCK; Mclaren, Brian, 2022, *Do I Stay Christian? A Guide for the Doubters, the Disappointed and the Disillusioned*, London: Hodder and Stoughton.
61 Watts et al., *Psychology*, p. 113.

I

Faith Development in the Christian Tradition

In the Introduction we considered the scriptural understandings of faith and how it develops. Following this, throughout church history theologians have expressed the idea of faith as something that matures and grows over time. Mostly this has been in manuals and handbooks on spirituality. In encouraging others to grow in holiness, some writers have presented works that fore-echo Faith Development models. These were not composed as a measure of how faith develops but rather as a guide for those wishing to mature in their faith, so they do not stand scrutiny in terms of having empirical foundations. They were based instead on individual religious experiences of a deepening relationship with God; a form of medieval auto-ethnographic theology. They evidence a desire in the historic church for disciples to progress from an initial faith to one of a deeper nature. They used images and ideas to tell the story of Faith Development. Some images are unique, while others echo across the centuries. Some use a basic image as nothing much more than a structure for their ideas, while others engage more earnestly in a metaphorical exploration of the experience of faith, prayer and relationship with God.

The use of analogies, images and stories to help people understand how to deepen or grow their faith can be powerful. Yet we can be so accustomed to metaphorical language that we do not notice the metaphor. The most common example today is also a motif that features in the tradition. I even used it in our Introduction. It is so natural to talk about one's 'journey of faith' that we barely notice it being a metaphor. We do not literally go on a journey, rather we use journey as an idea through which we can understand the changing nature of what we experience in our relationship with faith. We might talk about a 'difficult path' or how we are 'stepping out in faith'. It is no surprise that this image has such power for us. Jesus calls himself 'the way, and the truth, and the life' (John 14.6) and the earliest Christians described themselves as followers of 'the Way' (Acts 9.2). It is a recurring image in scripture from the journeys of Abram and Sarai on their way to becoming Abraham and Sarah (Gen. 12), Moses and the Israelites in the wilderness (Ex. 16—40), right through to Jesus' own parables such as the Good Samaritan (Luke 10.29–37) and the Lost Son (Luke 15.11–32). Arguably, the most powerful encounter with the risen Christ is the journey of Cleopas and his companion on the road to Emmaus (Luke 24.13–25). Journeying is the most popular motif in the historical models of Faith Development. Journey, then, is perhaps the most familiar of metaphors for our faith lives, though other metaphors have been used throughout the history of the church and we will explore some briefly before devoting more time to more significant models.

Hugh of St Victor lived as part of a twelfth-century monastic community in Saxony and wrote widely on theology, particularly mysticism. In his exploration of mystical experience, he uses a metaphor of fire to talk about a deepening meditation. He compares the first stage of seeking right counsel amid temptation as a time when smoke and flame are mixed, until a deeper place is reached when 'the heart's attention is given purely to the contemplation of the truth'.[1] This is the time of a flame without smoke until a state of *completion* is reached: 'the whole heart being turned into the fire of love, God is known truly to be all in all.'[2]

In the first chapter of the anonymous Middle English text *The Cloud of Unknowing*, the author suggests that there are four stages of faith that progress like a form of intimacy of relationship, namely, in the original text, 'Comoun, Special, Singuler, and Parfite',[3] or, as often translated, ordinary, special, singular and perfect.[4] The author suggests that only three of these stages can be begun and completed in this life. The fourth may be begun in this life but will then endure for ever in the eternal life. The author specifies that these stages go in one particular order. The *ordinary* stage they describe as 'the Christian life in a day-to-day mundane existence along with your friends'.[5] The next stage, *special*, is initiated not by the individual but by God who 'drew you closer to himself ... He called you to be his friend and, in the company of his friends, you learned to live the interior life more perfectly than was possible in the common way.'[6]

The third stage, again initiated by God, is a stepping stone or a turning towards the fourth stage, *singular*: 'you live now at the deep solitary core of your being, learning to direct your loving desire toward the highest and final manner of living.'[7]

To summarize the nature of these three stages the author suggests that there is a kind of outward-only expression of faith (ordinary), a learning to live in the interior stage (special), and a solitary mode of living at the core of your being (singular) which will ultimately lead to directing a loving desire towards God (perfect). Other medieval theologians used the idea of relationship with stronger descriptions of intimacy.

Meister Eckhart and his contemporary Marguerite Porete both describe the growing intimacy with God. Porete was a French Béguine who was burned at the stake in Paris in 1310 and about whom we know little outside the documents of her trial.[8] She wrote *The Mirror of Simple Souls* in Old French sometime in the 1290s.[9] Her trial and execution were possibly motivated not simply by the deeply intimate tone of her writing, shocking as it was to some, but primarily by ecclesiastical politics involving the Inquisition striving for legitimacy and trying to win over the Franciscans by targeting their rivals the Béguines.[10]

Porete describes 'seven stages of ascent', which could be termed stages towards annihilation of the self.[11] The first stage is to *love God and neighbour* (and, more controversially, to 'lose' the ability to sin). The second stage involves *self-mortification in search for perfection*. The third stage involves *abandonment of works of charity in favour of works of spiritual perfection*. The fourth stage is a kind of false zenith of *ecstasy of love*. The fifth stage is a *handing over of will to God*, and the sixth a *loss of self* entirely. Her seventh stage, she says, is indescribable as it could only be known when *the soul is with God*.[12]

Meister Eckhart, born *c.*1260, was a Dominican prior who became Master of Theology in 1302 and Prior Provincial for the Dominicans in Saxony in 1303. He also served as magister at the University of Paris more than once.[13] He became embroiled in a fevered period of accusations of heresy within the Dominicans of Cologne in the later 1320s, being accused by others who had themselves been accused.[14] Before there was a full resolution to the trial, Eckhart died in 1328.[15] Eckhart wrote in both Latin and German. In Latin he wrote commentaries on Ecclesiasticus, Genesis, Exodus, Wisdom and the Lord's Prayer, and there are also extant sermons. He wrote various theological texts on topics of doctrine called *Quaestiones* and a work called *Opus Tripartitum*, which discusses the nature of the work of a theologian as 'reading of the texts, disputation and preaching'.[16] It's among his German works that we find his stages of Faith Development, namely in a text called *The Nobleman*. Eckhart, acknowledging the influence of Augustine, suggests that there are various stages in the development of the 'inner man' in which 'God's seed and God's image are impressed and sown, and how the seed and the image of divine nature and divine being, God's Son, appears'.[17] Eckhart combines two metaphors. The first few stages he relates to the growth of a baby from infancy. He doesn't explicate the first of these stages but presents just a metaphor:

> The first stage of the inner man and the new man, St. Augustine says, is that a man lives by the example of good and saintly people, though he still holds on to chairs and supports himself by walls, and subsists on milk.[18]

After this first stage he gives a little more explanation of his metaphor describing an individual turning towards God:

> The second stage is when he not merely regards the outward examples and good people, but runs and hastens to the teaching and counsel of God and divine wisdom, turns his back on mankind and his face toward God, crawling forth from his mother's lap to smile up at his heavenly Father.[19]

There is a similar treatment of the third stage, whereby, he says, a person

> withdraws more and more from his mother and, being further and further from her lap, escapes from care and casts off fear so that, even if he might with impunity do evil and injustice to all, he would have no wish to do so, for he is so bound to God with love in eagerness, until God establishes and leads him in joy, sweetness, and bliss, wherein he cares nothing for whatever is repugnant and alien to God.[20]

The child-centred metaphor is less identifiable in Eckhart's fourth stage when he says an individual 'grows more and more, and becomes rooted in love and in God, so that he is ready to welcome any trial, temptation, adversity, and suffering willingly, gladly, eagerly, and joyfully'.[21] After these initial four stages, Eckhart abandons the metaphor almost entirely and describes the fifth stage as 'when he lives altogether at peace with himself, resting calmly in the richness and abundance of the supreme ineffable wisdom'.[22] Like others in the tradition, Eckhart's final stage of development is otherworldly. He even implies theosis as a part of it:

> The sixth stage is when a man is de-formed and transformed by God's eternity, and has attained total forgetfulness of transitory, temporal life and is drawn and translated into a divine image, having become the child of God.[23]

Colledge suggests this model has two essential stages: 'The two great stages under which Eckhart discusses the inner appropriation of God are the "Birth of the Son in the Soul", and the "Breaking Through to the Divine Ground".'[24] This is enabled through a process of what Eckhart calls 'detachment'. Eckhart presents other models which are somewhat simpler. In one he suggests four steps in two slightly different forms. Firstly, he suggests:

> This virtue has four degrees. The first breaks through and makes a way for a man away from all transient things. The second takes them away from a man altogether. The third not only takes them away, but causes them to be altogether forgotten as if they had never been – and this is part of the process. The fourth degree is right in God and is God Himself ... How, then, does He become yours? By your becoming entirely His. If God is to be as much mine as His own, I must be as much His as my own.[25]

In a different sermon, Eckhart uses the image of steps in a ladder,[26] though this is an image expanded more fully by other writers in the tradition.

A ladder features in Jacob's vision (Gen. 28.10–19) as a place where heaven and earth meet, representing a direct route from one to another. This was a popular image in Hellenistic philosophy, including the works of Plato and the lesser-known Plotinus. Ladder imagery therefore comes into Christian literature via both the Hebrew scriptures and the writings of classical philosophy (which influenced other areas of theology). There are proponents of the ladder model for faith throughout the history of the church from the earliest writers, including Gregory of Nazianzus (*Oration* 43.71)[27] and John Chrysostom (*Homilies on John* 83.5),[28] to Reformation theologian John Calvin. In his work on ascent, Calvin makes the distinction that this is not about an individual's journey but the journey of the church as the Body of Christ, in imitation of Christ's own ascent.[29] Augustine of Hippo's ladder describes the stages of the soul as first *the giving of life*, second *the gift of the senses*. These, Augustine says, are common to all living things, but from the third level, *memory*, upwards, they belong only to humanity. Memory encompasses the inheritance of knowledge in countless fields of human endeavour. The fourth level is *moral virtue*, which leads a person to do what is right and purge themselves of all wickedness. Such purification leads to the fifth level, which is the *tranquillity of knowing purity*. The sixth and seventh levels are to *approach God* and *unity with God*.[30] John

Climacus (*c.*579–649), a monk at the monastery at Sinai, presents a series of 30 'steps' on a ladder towards sanctity, from early stages relating to moral practice (e.g. renunciation of life, detachment, obedience) through to more contemplative final stages (e.g. stillness, discernment, dispassion).[31] Later medieval models also offer explorations of ladders of faith.

Bonaventure served the church in the thirteenth century as a professor of theology, bishop and cardinal. He wrote a biography of St Francis, approved by the Franciscan Order in 1266 and widely distributed.[32] He was a prolific writer whose thinking on doctrine, the Bible and spirituality strongly influenced the Franciscan movement for centuries.[33] His spiritual writings include *De triplici via* (*On the Threefold Way*), which offers a simple model of three ways or stages of spiritual engagement: the purgative, the illuminative and the unitive.[34] His *Itinerarium mentis in Deum* (*The Mind's Journey into God*) describes six stages, each represented by one of the six wings of a seraph whom Bonaventura saw in a vision:

> Therefore, according to the six stages of ascension into God, there are six stages of the soul's powers by which we mount from the depths to the heights, from the external to the internal, from the temporal to the eternal – to wit, sense, imagination, reason, intellect, intelligence, and the apex of the mind, the illumination of conscience ('Synteresis'). (1.6)[35]

Bonaventure describes these stages shifting through certain forces: 'These stages are implanted in us by nature, deformed by sin, reformed by grace, to be purged by justice, exercised by knowledge, perfected by wisdom' (1.6). He describes these stages as steps on Jacob's ladder (1.9). The path combines three sources of enlightenment: the use of senses, the contemplation of the eschaton, and rational enquiry. Through these three modes, individuals progress through the six stages from the first stage where *an individual perceives God's traces in the universe*. The second stage is *an embodied engagement of the five senses as sources of divine encounter*, or the reflection of God in his image stamped upon our natural powers. The third stage is where an individual turns from these bodily experiences to *inner contemplation*. The fourth stage is described as *the reflection of God in his image reformed by the gifts of grace*. This means that the individual must cease to rely on intellectual capacity and open themselves to God's grace to progress further. Bonaventure's fifth stage is *the reflection of the divine unity in its primary name, which is being*. This is a philosophical reflection on the nature of being and non-being that leads to a full awareness of God's being as the ultimate example of being without non-being. It is, in essence, contemplation of God as the ultimate. The final sixth step on Bonaventure's ladder is *the consideration of God as ultimate goodness*, or the reflection of the most blessed Trinity as all-powerful and good.

Though he is better known for his *Dark Night*, John of the Cross also talks about a ladder, comparing it to that seen in Jacob's dream and as a means for God to come down and for humans to ascend with ups and downs:

> We can call this secret contemplation a ladder for many reasons. In the first place, because, just as men mount by means of ladders and climb up to possessions and treasures and things that are in strong places, even so also, by means of this secret contemplation, without knowing how, the soul ascends and climbs up to a knowledge and possession of the good things and treasures of Heaven.[36]

His ladder has ten steps or degrees. The first step of *love* causes the individual to languish and lose satisfaction in material things.[37] The second step is about *seeking God unceasingly*. The third step 'causes the soul to work and gives it fervour so that it fails not'[38] and is therefore termed *humble service to God*, which the individual can never consider sufficient for service to God. The fourth step is typified by 'habitual suffering because of the Beloved, yet without weariness'.[39] From this *willing suffering*, the individual moves to the fifth step, which is *a longing and impatient desire for God*. This desire is satisfied in the sixth step where the soul '*runs swiftly to God and touches Him again and again*'.[40] The seventh step is one of *vehement boldness*, and the eighth step is where *the soul seizes God*. These two steps are recounted with much reference to the Song of Solomon. The ninth step involves *the soul burning with sweetness and being perfect*. The final step embodies theosis as *union with God*, which 'causes the soul to become wholly assimilated to God'.[41]

In his *Ladder of Perfection*, Walter Hilton, a fourteenth-century British Augustinian canon and mystic, talks about the degrees of contemplation and their various stages.[42] He gives three basic 'degrees' of contemplation, breaking them down into substages. The first is '*knowledge of God and of spiritual matters*'.[43] The second is '*loving God*' and splits into two stages, the latter distinguished by greater depth of prayer life, which he also calls 'love on fire with devotion'.[44] The final degree of contemplation 'consists of both knowledge and love' when '*God and the soul are no longer two but one*'. He also calls this stage of theosis 'love on fire with contemplation'.[45]

In addition to ladder images there are also models describing steps on journeys. Origen Adamantius was a third-century ascetic who devoted his life to study and stood alongside those who were delivered to martyrdom. Although his own writing on martyrdom hailed it as something wonderful and was almost a plea of 'feed me to the lions', he did not suffer martyrdom directly. He was tortured under the persecution of Decian, later dying from wounds.[46] Origen begins his model of spiritual development by indicating that

> Christians exhibit varying degrees of spiritual maturity, which reflect the degree of their decline and the state of their spiritual progress. As such, 'not everyone is nourished by one and the same Word,' since their receptivity to the Word depends on their spiritual capacity ... As children are nourished by milk, so spiritual infants are nourished by 'the more obvious and simpler teachings, as may usually be found in moral instructions.' At the opposite end of the spiritual spectrum, mature Christians, like the physically strong, need nourishment in the 'meat' of scripture: the mystical teachings.[47]

Origen charts the journey of the people of Israel as a commentary on the journey of the ascent of the soul: 'Therefore, the ascent from Egypt to the promised land is something by which, as I have said, we are taught in mysterious descriptions the ascent of the soul to heaven and the mystery of the resurrection of the dead.'[48] The first stage, according to Origen, is being ensnared by the devil just as the Israelites were enslaved in Egypt. Origen then enumerates 42 stages of ascent, named after different cities on the Exodus (Elim, Raphaca etc.), each of which he says Christ has inhabited, 'the person who ascends, ascends with Him who descended from there to us, so that he may arrive at the place from which He descended not by necessity but because he deemed it right'.[49] Origen conveys a sense of personal growth, not simply a deepening spirituality: 'by passing through each of the different stages that is those "many stages" that are said to be with the Father (John 14.2) it will be increasingly enlightened as it passes from one to another'.[50]

Origen suggests that the many stages he describes are all necessary and must be in the order he describes: 'The order of setting out and the distinction of the stages are quite necessary and must be observed by those who follow God and set their minds on progress in the virtues.'[51] The soul moves from *corruption* to *wandering*, then to *struggle* and on to *moderate self-control*, then *contemplation of hope*, before *encountering dangers and temptations*. Overcoming these temptations leads to a *place of refreshment* before an encounter with the *wilderness of sin*, followed by *a place of health*. At this point, Origen himself seems to realize that 42 stages is too many to cover in detail. So he begins instead to write much more briefly about each, establishing the principle of twin movement between spiritual challenge and resultant reward before further challenge. He brings the model to a conclusion with arrival at Gelmon Deblathaim (scorn of figs), as a symbolism of the complete abnegation of earthly things, then on to Nabau (passage), as the place of separation, saying, 'For when the soul has made its journey through all these virtues and has climbed to the height of perfection, it then "passes" from the world and "separates" from it.'[52] The last stage of Origen's model is Moab by the Jordan, as the soul arrives at the river of God as 'neighbours of the flowing Wisdom and may be watered by the waves of divine knowledge, and so that purified by them all we may be made worthy to enter the promised land'.[53]

The most famous metaphor of faith as a journey is captured by John Bunyan in *The Pilgrim's Progress*.[54] Bunyan, a seventeenth-century Puritan writer, served in the parliamentary army from the age of 16 and was twice imprisoned for his puritanical preaching and views. It was in his first imprisonment in 1671 that he began writing his famous allegory that challenges particular aspects of non-Puritan forms of Christianity. Bunyan wrote some 60 other texts, mostly sermonic in nature. *The Pilgrim's Progress* describes Christian as *leaving behind the City of Destruction* and setting out for the Celestial City. Along this journey, Christian experiences a moment of regression when he falls into *the Slough of Despond* and then, after this hiatus, begins his journey again. At other points, the journey is used as a way of talking about the various kinds of engagement with practices of faith through time at *the Interpreter's House*, and indeed in experiencing challenges and temptations from the likes of *Worldly Wiseman*, who suggests a 'good life' free of religion, and *By-ends*, who uses religion as a means to societal advancement, the people of the town of *Vanity* and their Fair, or other low moments in *the Valley of Humiliation, the Valley of the Shadow of Death* and *Castle Doubt*.

After the final temptations and traps of characters named Ignorance, Flatterer and Atheist, Christian makes it to the *Celestial City*. This is essentially a heroic journey of overcoming various trials. Although there are clear stages to the journey (including significant moments of hiatus), it is not clear that the sequence of them is significant. Christian meets Ignorance (who suggests that faith is not necessary to a good life) towards the end of the journey, whereas this might be considered more apt for an earlier stage if the encounters were in a logical sequence of Faith Development.

There are two other models that also use journeys in rather different ways and we will explore each of these in depth.

Teresa of Avila

Teresa de Cepeda y Ahumada was born in 1515 to a family that included a grandparent who had been forced to convert from Judaism to Christianity. She lived for 18 months at the Augustinian Convent of St Mary of Grace in Avila from when she was 16, and at the age of 21 entered the Carmelite Convent of the Incarnation at Avila as a novice, professing her vows in 1537. She suffered from severe illness in her early 20s for three years, with recurring symptoms for over a decade. Her visions began around 1555. She wrote the first draft of her autobiography in 1562.[55] In the 1560s she spent some time at St Joseph's, Avila, which was to be part of the reformation of the Carmelites, of which she was a significant part. She wrote several books, including *The Way of Perfection*, *Exclamations of the Soul to God* and *Foundations*. She founded many new houses of the Discalced Carmelites. In 1580, shortly after she suffered a stroke and a couple of years before her death, the Discalced Carmelite order was finally recognized as separate from the main order.

Teresa of Avila used the metaphor of a castle to describe the deepening experience of faith moving ever inwards into the interior castle, having started out through the door of prayer and meditation.[56] She compares these various dwelling places to the leaves of a palmetto (similar to an artichoke), so that they are not so much in a prescribed order of waymarks on a journey but nested within each other. As she says:

> You mustn't think of these dwelling places in such a way that each one would follow in file after the other, but turn your eyes toward the center which is the room or royal chamber where the King stays, and think of how a palmetto has many leaves surrounding and covering the tasty part that can be eaten. (1.2.8)[57]

Gillian Ahlgren describes Teresa's work as 'first and foremost a descriptive and prescriptive itinerary toward union with God, a God encountered, discovered and revealed gradually in the innermost recesses of the soul'.[58] She describes each of Teresa's seven dwelling places in the castle as 'representing a further stage of development in the realization and integration of the fullness of the human being'.[59] *The first dwelling places* are about inhabiting stillness and recognizing God within us.[60] This primitive experience of faith is the simple acknowledgement of creatureliness and a refusal to conform to the demands of worldliness (1.2.11–14).

The second dwelling places are where the individual hears the voice of God, though on hearing it can be troubled and regress to the first dwelling places of the temptations of worldliness (2.1.2). Individuals seek to understand their true self, which they had thought they had understood, yet hearing the voice of God raises further their awareness of their own flaws. Teresa encourages the individual to seek support for this stage from someone with wisdom and experience (2.1.6). In *the third dwelling places* an invitation is offered to move from 'A constructed identity [to] ... a new, relational identity with God.'[61] This requires humility (3.2.9) and the alignment of the individual's will to the will of God, not subjugation but alignment or union of wills. Without humility, an individual will go no further than this dwelling place. Hence it is a place of transition or hiatus.

After this transition, *the fourth dwelling places* are nearer the centre; places where the Holy Spirit becomes more important as a guide than the doing of right actions or right thinking. It is a place of 'an expansion or dilation of the soul' (4.3.9). As Wahlgren describes it, 'the soul learns, experientially, a more fully subjective way of being, made possible by its dedication to a more integrated, affective way of knowing'.[62] This leads to a deeper self-knowledge from which the individual is able to enter *the fifth dwelling places*, a place of union with God which gives the individual assurance of the union by 'a certitude remaining in the soul that only God can place there' (5.1.9). Here Teresa includes another much briefer metaphor for Faith Development, the story of the silkworm (5.2.2–8). The building of a chrysalis is all the work so far of the previous dwelling places, and the appearance of the moth the completion of this union with God: 'In the delightful union, the experience of seeing oneself in so new a life greatly helps one to die; in the other union, it's necessary that, while living in this life, we ourselves put the silkworm to death' (5.3.5).

She also uses the metaphor of a dove in her description as the stage is difficult to put into words any other way. She is not explicit, though there is an air of intimacy in this stage, not uncommon in mystical writing, alluding to the language of courtship and the Song of Solomon.[63] *The sixth dwelling places*, as Rowan Williams has described them, are an intensification of what has preceded.[64] Here, Teresa explores many 'paramystical phenomena' that typify the growing partnership with God.[65] *The seventh dwelling places* are the dwelling places of God. As a mystical stage of Faith Development this can best be described as theosis. Here Teresa completes the courtship metaphors at which she had earlier hinted:

> When our Lord is pleased to have pity on this soul that He has already taken spiritually as His Spouse because of what it suffers and has suffered through its desires, He brings it, before the spiritual marriage is consummated, into His dwelling places which is the seventh. (7.1.3)

Teresa also points out that this is the place where the individual truly comprehends the unity of the Holy Trinity as three persons.

John of the Cross

John of the Cross was a Spanish Carmelite of the sixteenth century. He was born in 1542 to parents who married for love, rejecting the wealth of his father's family (who may have been Jewish). Consequently, on the death of his father, John's mother and her children were destitute. John was placed in a school for impoverished boys to teach him a trade. He worked in a hospital from the age of nine. There he encountered the Jesuits who taught him Latin and rhetoric. Despite being offered ordination and the role of chaplain to the hospital at the age of 21, John instead joined the Carmelite order. After his novitiate, he studied theology and philosophy at the university in Salamanca and the Carmelite college of San Andrés. During his studies he was ordained and soon thereafter met Teresa of Avila. He followed her to support her in the establishment of her new order. He spent time with her community at Valladolid before founding a similar house for friars at Duruelo. It was then that he took the name Juan de la Cruz.

Later, tensions arose surrounding this breakaway order. Consequently, John was imprisoned and ordered to recant the order. He refused and was punished with beatings, a strict diet of bread and water, and being locked in a small cell with only a tiny window for nine months. There he composed in his head *The Spiritual Canticle*.[66] This experience had a powerful impact on the imagery he chose for his spiritual writings.

Eventually, John escaped from his cell and found refuge with a group of Teresa's Carmelites in Toledo. On reconciliation between the Carmelites and Teresa's Discalced Carmelites as a separate province, John became vicar at a house in Calvario, teaching at a new college of Discalced Carmelites. He then served as vicar provincial and later prior of the order for Andalusia. During these years (1580s) he wrote most of his works. His final years were plagued again by controversy and he died in 1591.[67]

John produced two major works which deal with the development of faith. In each, he uses the same poem as the springboard of his reflections, 'passing through the dark night of faith, in detachment and purgation of itself, to union with the Beloved'.[68] John explored this poem first in the *Ascent of Mount Carmel* but found himself drawn into many diverting topics, so began *The Dark Night of the Soul* to return to the original topic.[69] The poem is powerful, with strong overtones of the Song of Solomon and deeply intimate descriptions of the soul's relationship with God, upon which John never fully expands. He comments extensively on the first half of the poem though not on the latter section, which contains what could be described as detailed spiritual ecstasy of the soul in connection with God. This leaves interpretation of this section of the poem quite open. Some have considered it to be indicative of something more than an allegorical description of his faith's journey and suggested it as an example of medieval Queer Theology.[70] One writer suggests that this voice is such a fundamental part of John's approach to theology that it cannot be ignored:

> To do theology sanjuanistamente is to be seduced by divine love. For Juan de la Cruz mysticism provides a way of knowing God via a love in which one not only knows but also savors the beloved, 'no solamente se saben, mas justamente se gustan'.[71]

Other commentators, more disturbed by the tone of the poem, have chosen to suggest, due to the heightened language of the piece, that it portrays the character of a 'lovesick girl' despite there being no suggestion of such personification.[72] One Carmelite commentator proposes that the allegory is simply that and any suggestion of a Queer Theology is simply a modern interpretation rather than an authentic reading of the text:

> Whether or not John was gay, and this is a question that today vexes some scholars and readers, is actually beside the point. The poet is

using a convention of the first-person subject, that is when he says 'I' he means you and me, whoever the person is reading the poem. We identify with the 'I' of the poem. Our assumption that it has to be John is a mere assumption of modern reading practice, where we wish to believe that the poem is autobiographical, an insight into this person's personal experience of passionate love, a confession of erotic desire and fulfilment.[73]

So that readers can form their own view on this somewhat controversial debate, I include the full poem here:

On a dark night, Kindled in love with yearnings – oh, happy chance! –
I went forth without being observed, My house being now at rest.
In darkness and secure, By the secret ladder, disguised – oh, happy chance! –
In darkness and in concealment, My house being now at rest.
In the happy night, In secret, when none saw me,
Nor I beheld aught, Without light or guide, save that which burned in my heart.
This light guided me More surely than the light of noonday,
To the place where he (well I knew who!) was awaiting me – A place where none appeared.
Oh, night that guided me, Oh, night more lovely than the dawn,
Oh, night that joined Beloved with lover, Lover transformed in the Beloved!
Upon my flowery breast, Kept wholly for himself alone,
There he stayed sleeping, and I caressed him, And the fanning of the cedars made a breeze.
The breeze blew from the turret As I parted his locks;
With his gentle hand he wounded my neck And caused all my senses to be suspended.
I remained, lost in oblivion; My face I reclined on the Beloved.
All ceased and I abandoned myself, Leaving my cares forgotten among the lilies.[74]

This, then, whatever you make of it, is the founding text of John's further writings which are expressed as commentaries upon this poem.

In addition to presenting the stages by which he believes an individual draws closer to God, John talks about the reasons why faith develops rather than happens instantly. In *Ascent of Mount Carmel*, he associates three scriptural passages with describing how God works in developing people's faith. He cites St Paul's description of God's works being well ordered (Rom. 13.11), and the book of the Wisdom of Solomon's description of the gentleness of the spirit in ordering things as surely as night follows day (Wisd. 7.30 and 8.1). Finally, he cites Thomas Aquinas' idea that 'God moves each thing according to its mode'.[75] According to these texts, John suggests three qualities of the development of faith: first, it is ordered; second, it is gentle; third, it is according to the nature of the individual. Thus, John argues, there are various stages by which faith develops as an individual moves from the human/external/sensory world towards the divine/internal/spiritual realm:

> He must gradually bring the soul after its own manner to the other end, spiritual wisdom, which is incomprehensible to the senses ... Therefore God perfects people gradually, according to their human nature, and proceeds from the lowest and most exterior to the highest and most interior.[76]

John defines the aim of Faith Development as the growth of spiritual wisdom towards unity with God and uses the powerful image of a dark night, no doubt inspired by his physical incarceration, as a vital catalytic aspect of that process. In *Ascent*, he describes the 'dark night' as 'this darkness and these trials, both spiritual and temporal, through which happy souls are wont to pass in order to be able to attain to this high estate of perfection'.[77] He makes clear that his account is based 'neither [on] experience nor [on] knowledge, since both may fail and deceive', but rather informed by scripture.[78] Though scripture is definitely a strong feature of his work, John's model is highly informed by his own experience. Although his work is later more expansive on each part of the journey, John summarizes much of his work in his opening chapter:

> Into this dark night souls begin to enter when God draws them forth from the state of beginners – which is the state of those that meditate on the spiritual road – and begins to set them in the state of progressives – which is that of those who are already contemplatives – to the end that, after passing through it, they may arrive at the state of the perfect, which is that of the Divine union of the soul with God.[79]

It is therefore a journey of five stages: the stage of beginners, the dark night of the senses, the stage of progressives or contemplatives, the dark night of the soul, which leads ultimately to union with God. John describes himself as being at 'the state of perfection, which is the union of love with God',[80] because he has already passed through the trials which he describes as necessary to reach that point. The pinnacle of his model might otherwise be considered only achievable in the afterlife.

The stage of beginners is typified by much spiritual devotion and yet also tinged with pride in devotions.[81] These beginners are inclined to reticence about their failings because admitting failings would suggest they were not as perfect as they consider themselves to be through their great devotions. It is humility that determines movement to the second stage:

> not only thinking naught of their own affairs, but having very little satisfaction with themselves; they consider all others as far better ... These souls ... being far from desiring to be the masters of any, are very ready to travel and set out on another road.[82]

Their destination then is *the dark night of the senses*, which involves the individual no longer being able to experience things as they had previously: 'they suffer, as of the fear which they have of being lost on the road, thinking that all spiritual blessing is over for them and that God has abandoned them'.[83] This is a stage of contemplation and waiting and potentially experiencing a void; a hiatus. From this sensory-deprivation stage, the soul, purged of physical desires, is then able to move to the third stage:

> its passions being quenched and its desires put to rest and lulled to sleep by means of this blessed night of the purgation of sense, the soul went forth, to set out upon the road and way of the spirit, which is that of progressives and proficients, and which, by another name, is called *the way of illumination* or of infused contemplation, wherein God Himself feeds and refreshes the soul, without meditation, or the soul's active help. (my emphasis)[84]

He calls people in this stage 'proficient' because of the experience they have gained through the dark night of the senses. However, he is also careful to point out ways in which these individuals are not perfect: 'The habitual imperfections are the imperfect habits and affections which have remained all the time in the spirit, and are like roots, to which the purgation of sense has been unable to penetrate.'[85] He attributes pride and vanity as potential pitfalls for this stage, suggesting that individuals consider themselves superior to those who have not passed through the dark night of the senses. This explains the necessity for John's fourth stage, *the dark night of the soul*. John links the necessity of the second dark night with the first:

> In this night following, both parts of the soul are purged together, and it is for this end that it is well to have passed through the corrections of the first night, and the period of tranquillity which proceeds from it, in order that, sense being united with spirit, both may be purged after a certain manner and may then suffer with greater fortitude.[86]

The experience of this second dark night of the spirit can sound like a positive experience: 'God secretly teaches the soul and instructs it in perfection of love without its doing anything, or understanding of what manner is this infused contemplation.'[87] Though this stage is also one of deprivation and loss. John refers to many passages from scripture that talk about how this darkness relates to the Divine Light. He pulls no punches in describing, over several chapters, the sufferings of this stage:

> As a result of this, the soul feels itself to be perishing and melting away, in the presence and sight of its miseries, in a cruel spiritual death, even as if it had been swallowed by a beast and felt itself being devoured in the darkness of its belly, suffering such anguish as was endured by Jonas in the belly of that beast of the sea. (Jonas 2)[88]

The result of this second dark night is a soul purified, as the senses had been purified in the first, resulting in happiness:

> the spirit that is purged and annihilated with respect to all particular affections and objects of the understanding ... is fully prepared to embrace everything to the end that those words of Saint Paul may be fulfilled in it: Nihil habentes, et omnia possidentes [Having nothing and possessing everything (2 Cor. 6.10)]. For such poverty of spirit as this would deserve such happiness.[89]

John devotes no chapters to the final unitive stage, focusing mostly on the preceding dark nights. From the commentary on these stages, though, it is clear that the ultimate stage of *union with God* is one in which love is the defining value and where there is abandonment of temporal, physical and sensual concerns:

In this way the soul gradually becomes wholly spiritual; and in this hiding-place of unitive contemplation its spiritual desires and passions are to a great degree removed and purged away. And thus, speaking of its higher part, the soul then says in this last line: My house being now at rest.[90]

This use of the image of the house harks back to the founding poem on which John has based all his reflections. In this poem, he has left the house at night. The house therefore could symbolize daily life or, alternatively, the self.

This brief survey of some models from the tradition shows that Christians have been charting the development of faith for centuries. For a fuller survey, the reader may wish to engage with the work for Evelyn Underhill (1875–1941), a British writer from an Anglo-Catholic tradition. She was influenced by Friedrich von Hügel and interested in art and mysticism. Her own model is based on a wide reading of the mystics and summarizes much of the wisdom of these models we have explored (and others for which we have not had space). According to Underhill, the individual experiences Awakening, Purgation, Illumination, the Dark Night until finally Union with God.[91]

Notes

1 Hugh of St Victor, 1962, *Selected Spiritual Writings*, London: Faber and Faber p. 185.

2 Hugh of St Victor, *Selected*, p. 185.

3 https://d.lib.rochester.edu/teams/text/gallacher-cloud-of-unknowing, Chapter 1, line 229, accessed 09.05.2025.

4 *The Cloud of Unknowing*, 1981, ed. Walsh, James, New York: Paulist Press, Chapter 1, pp. 116–17.

5 *Cloud*, p. 38.

6 *Cloud*, p. 38.

7 *Cloud*, p. 38.

8 Field, Sean L., 2017, 'Debating the Historical Marguerite Porete', in Terry, Wendy R., and Stauffer, Robert, eds, *A Companion to Marguerite Porete and the Mirror of Simple Souls*, Leiden: Brill, p. 9.

9 Porete, Marguerite, 1993, *The Mirror of Simple Souls*, trans. and Introduction by Babinsky, Ellen L., New York: Paulist Press, p. 5.

10 Porete, *Mirror*, p. 24.

11 Robinson, Joanne Maguire, 2017 'Marguerite's Mystical Annihilation' in Terry et al., *Companion*, p. 50.

12 From the Introduction in Porete, *Mirror*, p. 27. Echoing St Paul's 'mirror', cf. 1 Corinthians 13.11 quoted above.

13 Hackett, Jeremiah M., ed., 2013, *A Companion to Meister Eckhart*, Leiden: Brill, pp. 7, 15, 16 and 19.

14 Hackett, *Eckhart*, pp. 50–76.

15 Hackett, *Eckhart*, p. 77.

16 Hackett, *Eckhart*, pp. 85–95.

17 Eckhart, Meister, 2009, *The Nobleman* in *The Complete Mystical Works of Meister Eckhart*, trans. and ed. Walshe OC, Maurice, revised with a Foreword by McGinn, Bernard, New York: Crossroad Publishing, p. 559.

18 Eckhart, *Complete*, p. 559.

19 Eckhart, *Complete*, p. 559.

20 Eckhart, *Complete*, p. 559.

21 Eckhart, *Complete*, p. 559.

22 Eckhart, *Complete*, p. 559.

23 Eckhart, *Complete*, p. 559.

24 Eckhart, Meister, 1981, 'The Book of Benedictus: Of the Nobleman' in *Meister Eckhart: The Essential Sermons, Commentaries, Treatises and Defense*, trans. Colledge OSA, Edmund, with an Introduction by McGinn, Bernard, London: SPCK, p. 47; cf. Sermon 52, p. 203.

25 Eckhart, *Complete*, Sermon 74, p. 376.

26 Eckhart, *Complete*, Sermon 84, p. 415.

27 https://www.newadvent.org/fathers/310243.htm, accessed 09.05.2025.

28 https://www.newadvent.org/fathers/240183.htm, accessed 09.05.2025.

29 Canlis, Julie, 2010, *Calvin's Ladder: A Spiritual Theology of Ascent and Ascension*, Grand Rapids: Eerdmans.

30 Augustine, *On the Greatness of the Soul*, 33; see also *On True Religion*, XL; and *On Music*, VI.

31 John Climacus, 1959, *The Ladder of Divine Ascent*, 2.7, trans. Moore, Archimandrite Lazarus, London: Faber and Faber, p. 58.

32 Cullen, Christopher M., 2006, *Bonaventure*, New York: Oxford University Press, p. 14.

33 Cullen, *Bonaventure*, pp. 16–17.

34 Cullen, *Bonaventure*, p. 20.

35 *Itinerarium mentis in Deum*, Prologue 1.6 translation from CCEL, https://www.ccel.org/ccel/b/bonaventure/mindsroad/cache/mindsroad.pdf, accessed 09.05.2025.

36 St John of the Cross, 1959, *The Dark Night of the Soul*, trans. and ed. Peers, E. Allison, Grand Rapids: Christian Classics Ethereal Library, p. 110.

37 John of the Cross, *Dark Night*, p. 112.

38 John of the Cross, *Dark Night*, p. 113.

39 John of the Cross, *Dark Night*, p. 114.

40 John of the Cross, *Dark Night*, p. 116.

41 John of the Cross, *Dark Night*, p. 117.

42 Hilton, Walter, 1957, *The Ladder of Perfection*, trans. Sherley-Price, Leo, London: Penguin.

43 Hilton, *Ladder*, p. 3.

44 Hilton, *Ladder*, p. 5.

45 Hilton, *Ladder*, pp. 7–8.

46 Scott, Mark S. M., 2012, *Journey Back to God: Origen on the Problem of Evil*, Oxford: Oxford University Press, p. 103.

47 Scott, *Journey*, p. 105.

48 Origen, *Homilies on Numbers*, 27.4 in Origen, 1979, *An Exhortation to Martyrdom, Prayer and Selected Works*, trans. and Introduction by Greer, Rowan A., New York: Paulist Press, p. 252.

49 Origen, *Homilies*, 27.2 and 3, p. 249.

50 Origen, *Homilies*, 27.5, p. 252.

51 Origen, *Homilies*, 27.9, p. 257.

52 Origen, *Homilies*, 27.12, p. 268.

53 Origen, *Homilies*, 27.12, p. 268.

54 Bunyan, John, 1984, *The Pilgrim's Progress*, ed. Keeble, N. H., Oxford: Oxford University Press.

55 Teresa of Avila, 2014, *Autobiography of St. Teresa of Avila*, ed. and trans. Peers, E. Allison, Mineola, NY: Dover Publications.

56 Teresa of Avila, 1979, *The Interior Castle*, ed. Kavanaugh, Kieran, London: SPCK p. 35.

57 Avila, *Interior*, p. 42. The bracketed references here and that follow are to Teresa of Avila, *The Interior Castle*, as cited in note 56 above.

58 Ahlgren, Gillian T. W., 2005, *Entering Teresa of Avila's Interior Castle*, New Jersey: Paulist Press, p. 21.

59 Ahlgren, *Entering*, p. 21.

60 Ahlgren, *Entering*, p. 24.

61 Ahlgren, *Entering*, p. 40.

62 Ahlgren, *Entering*, p. 50.

63 Ahlgren, *Entering*, pp. 63–5.

64 Williams, R., 1991, *Teresa of Avila*, Harrisberg: Morehouse, p. 136.

65 Ahlgren, *Entering*, p. 79.

66 https://www.ccel.org/ccel/john_cross/canticle.ii.html, accessed 10.06.2025.

67 St John of the Cross, 1987, *Selected Writings*, ed. Kavanagh, Kieran, The Classics of Western Spirituality, New York: Paulist Press, pp. 8–38.

68 St John of the Cross, 1962, *Ascent of Mount Carmel*, trans. and ed. Peers, E. Allison, Grand Rapids: Christian Classics Ethereal Library, Book 1, Ch. 1, p. 61.

69 John of the Cross, *Selected Writings*, p. 157.

70 https://queeringthechurch.wordpress.com/2009/12/14/st-john-of-the-cross/, accessed 09.05.2025.

71 Díaz, M., 2022, *Queer God de Amor*, New York: Fordham University Press, p. 1, citing John's commentary, 'The Spiritual Canticle', meaning, 'They not only know each other but justly love each other.'

72 https://www.spainthenandnow.com/spanish-literature/san-juan-de-la-cruz-noche-oscura, accessed 09.05.2025.

73 Harvey, Philip, 2012, *The Matrix Poems of St John of the Cross*, http://the-carmelitelibrary.blogspot.com/2012/12/the-matrix-poems-of-saint-john-of-cross.html accessed 09.05.2025.

74 John of the Cross, *Ascent*, p. 61.

75 John of the Cross, *Ascent*, Ch. 17, p. 122, citing Thomas Aquinas, *De Veritate*, 12.6.

76 John of the Cross, *Ascent*, Ch. 17, p. 123.

77 John of the Cross, *Ascent*, Prologue, p. 62.

78 John of the Cross, *Ascent*, Prologue, p. 66.

79 John of the Cross, *Dark Night*, Book 1, Ch. 1, p. 17.
80 John of the Cross, *Dark Night*, Prologue, p. 14.
81 John of the Cross, *Dark Night*, Book 1, Ch. 2, p. 19.
82 John of the Cross, *Dark Night*, Book 1, Ch. 2, pp. 20-1.
83 John of the Cross, *Dark Night*, Book 1, Ch. 10, p. 40.
84 John of the Cross, *Dark Night*, Book 1, Ch. 14, p. 54.
85 John of the Cross, *Dark Night*, Book 2, Ch. 3, p. 61 and Ch. 2, p. 59.
86 John of the Cross, *Dark Night*, Book 2, Ch. 3, p. 61.
87 John of the Cross, *Dark Night*, Book 2, Ch. 5, p. 64.
88 John of the Cross, *Dark Night*, Book 2, Ch. 6, p. 67.
89 John of the Cross, *Dark Night*, Book 2, Ch. 8, p. 77.
90 John of the Cross, *Dark Night*, Book 2, Ch. 7, p. 128.
91 Underhill, Evelyn, 1913, *The Mystic Way: A Psychological Study in Christian Origins*, London: J. M. Dent and Sons, pp. 53-6.

2

Progressive Stages

Among the theories of Faith Development, those that identify a series of stages are the most common. This is largely due to James Fowler (whose model we will explore first) as his work has influenced many other models (including my own). However, not all of these progressive models owe a particular debt to Fowler. Other theorists have independently come to similar conclusions, through their own work, that faith grows and develops over time, and has certain markers that can be said to indicate various distinguishable stages. At a similar time to Fowler's initial research, Oser and Gmünder were independently developing a progressive theory of Faith Development through interview-based research.[1] Progressive models fall into two distinct sets: those that are purely progressive, and a subset that are progressive but include elements of regression. The first group are models that not only chart stages but do so with a confident assumption that the development of faith is on a trajectory ever moving towards some kind of perfection. Unlike many of the models from the Christian tradition, few of these modern models suggest a stage after death. The two models by Fowler, and Oser and Gmünder have certain commonalities and a similar number of stages. The next model we will explore was patterned on Fowler by Peck but varies from Fowler's in consideration of Peck's critique of his model. Moving away from this group of Fowleresque models, we will turn our attention to Jamieson's model, which offers a far more creative narrative than the functional stages described by the others and has more in common with the models from the Christian tradition.

James Fowler

James W. Fowler (1940–2015) was the son of a Methodist minister, who himself became a Methodist minister and studied at Duke University before moving to Drew Theological Seminary and ultimately to Harvard for doctoral studies.[2] Fowler describes his own lived experience, including his role, during his PhD research, at Interpreters' House (a 'center for personal and vocational self-examination and growth for clergy and laity') where he was associate director during 1968–69.[3] There, he was supporting people in explorations of their vocations and lecturing on the life-cycle theory of Erik Erikson alongside his own studies on 'the theological ethics of H. Richard Niebuhr'. From Interpreters' House, he returned to Harvard where he taught, 'theologically from Niebuhr and Tillich; psychologically ... from Erikson, Freud, Jung, and others ... [and] began to draw on the hermeneutical work of Ricoeur, Polanyi, and Barfield'.[4] Through his Harvard students Fowler encountered Kohlberg's work and through Kohlberg he discovered Piaget. From Harvard he moved for a year to Boston College before going to Emory in 1977 where he continued at the faculty for almost 30 years, working mostly with those preparing for ministry. He describes the impact of this context:

> The M.Div. students were often older than those I had taught at Harvard. By and large, they were more interested in the church and the practices of ministry than many at Harvard had been. This altered setting and my returning to the South, which has strong storytelling traditions, both permitted and demanded an increased attention to narrative.[5]

Fowler talks about the enthusiasm of working with his students on Faith Development interviews, thereby acknowledging the origins of his work in the highly educated adult world of academia.[6]

Fowler's seminal work *Stages of Faith*, and the model it propounds, is arguably the foundation stone of the modern study of Faith Development. This text contains not only the model itself but also Fowler's description of the method he used to establish the model, including the pattern for the interview and the content of various interviews that he and his team conducted. It recounts how they dealt with the resulting data, including guidance on coding the texts of respondents' interviews according to seven aspects used to determine their stage of faith. Fowler further explored his model in a series of subsequent texts with a variety of particular applications including vocation and adult development,[7] pastoral care,[8] public faith,[9] education,[10] and postmodernity.[11] Finally, he looked back over three decades of the influence of his model.[12] Fowler has also revisited his model in collaborations with other academics in the field. Most notably with those who have disagreed with him or sought to critique him, such as James Loder[13] and his former student and colleague, Heinz Streib.[14] His graciousness in response to critique is evident in these collaborations. For example: 'John McDargh's thoughtful and constructive article asserts that despite the usefulness and influence of FDT, it lacks an adequate account of the development of the self.'[15] Such is the regard in which Fowler's work is held that few texts exploring Faith Development would not make reference to it. It is the model that is (or at least was, until Streib's recent but lesser-known work) the most established in empirical research. This does not mean that the model is perfect. Being the best known, it is also the most critiqued with the most well-known weaknesses as well as well-known strengths.

Fowler and his team undertook a substantial research project to establish his model. They interviewed 359 people, using an interview guide that touched on four aspects, namely Life Review, Life-shaping Experiences and Relationships, Present Values and Commitments, and Religion.[16] The team analysed the data from each interview, first through three readings and then using a review by a second researcher. *Stages of Faith* consistently uses interview extracts from individuals in chapters about each of the stages (a practice echoed by later writers), which gives a richness to the text and firmly roots the model in the lived experience of a range of individuals. The model itself is based on the complex interweaving of seven lenses onto the world of an individual's faith: form of logic, perspective taking, moral judgement, bound of social awareness, locus of authority, form of world coherence, symbolic function.[17] Slee connects these clearly to his sources:

> The development of logical thinking according to Piaget (1929, 1962); the construction of social perspective according to Selman (1980); the development of moral judgements according to Kohlberg (1981, 1984); the understanding of social reference points; the interpretation of what legitimates commitments; the ways of unifying meanings as found in Erikson (1980); the understanding of symbols, and the stages of self as elaborated by Kegan (1982).[18]

Fowler presents faith as 'a way of seeing our everyday life in relation to the holistic images of what we may call the ultimate environment'.[19] He also defined faith as

> People's evolved and evolving ways of experiencing self, others and world (as they construct them) as related to and affected by the ultimate conditions of existence (as they construct them) and of shaping their lives' purposes and meanings, trust and loyalties, in light of the character of being, value and power determining the ultimate condi-

tions of existence (as grasped in their operative Images – conscious and unconscious – of them).[20]

As the major theologian in this field, we do not only have Fowler's own description of what he considers he means when he talks of faith. Heinz Streib suggests that Fowler in his definition of faith provides a 'demarcation between the "logic of conviction" ("constitutive knowing") that characterizes "faith," as opposed to Piaget's "logic of rational certainty"'.[21]

Fowler in his later work describes faith both as 'a relation of trust in and loyalty to one's neighbors, maintained through trust in and loyalty to a unifying image of the character of value and power in an ultimate environment'[22] and as 'the process of composing an image of the ultimate environment'.[23]

Fowler explores not just the nature of faith but the nature of the way it changes. He delineates certain stages to any change in faith that are: '(1) Disengagement, (2) disidentification, (3) disenchantment, and (4) disorientation'.[24] Fowler goes on to add a further stage to these, adopting William Bridges' term 'the neutral zone' which ultimately leads to a new beginning. In his first iteration of the model, Fowler suggested that there were six stages of faith, namely Intuitive-Projective, Mythic-Literal, Synthetic-Conventional, Individuative-Reflective, Conjunctive and Universalizing. In later texts his original three pages devoted to 'Infancy and Undifferentiated Faith' are re-termed 'Primal Faith' and given something more of an equal footing with the original six.[25] Fowler's exploration of faith from birth to approximately 18 months incorporates data from his extensive interviews alongside theoretical works by Erikson, Piaget, Daniel Stern, William James and Ana-Maria Rizzutto.[26] These latter three are new conversation partners for Fowler and introduce new aspects of the development of the individual. Rizzutto's work focuses on three aspects of faith, namely God, Belief and Unbelief, as related to the way that a child interacts with parents and the wider world.[27] Other developments in his thinking centred on engaging with more narrative, such as exploring the idea of 'the dance of faith development', alongside the idea of seasons in our faith, saying, 'faith involves a process of maturation and growth as we move from one season of our life to the next'.[28] He refers to faith stages themselves as images, describing them not as 'snapshots in a photo album' but 'connected scenes in an unfolding drama'.[29]

In his exploration of *(0) Primal Faith*, Fowler focuses on the foundational importance of the 'triadic ... covenantal pattern' between self, others and 'Shared Center(s) of Power'.[30] He traces this covenantal triad through different age ranges and in combination with Stern's four overlapping themes in the development of self, namely the emergent self, the core self, the subjective self and the verbal self.[31] The first three of these Fowler maps as fitting Primal Faith (prizing the verbal self as part of Intuitive-Projective Faith).[32] First, a child from birth to two months experiences coherent otherness and has particular connection to other human beings over objects.[33] Then between two and sixth months a child becomes more aware of their body and their core self, which Fowler links to the beginnings of ritualization.[34] The next phase is that of subjective self, whereby a child begins to sense the emotions of others, her own emotions and the sense of fitting in to a climate of emotions alongside pre-verbal communication via sign or intention. Somewhat heterodoxically, Fowler terms this the 'birth of the soul'. It is the place where his triadic covenant really takes hold.[35] So, although Fowler has sought here to correct a lacuna in his model which, as we shall see later, has been critiqued by the likes of Miller-McLemore, he has nonetheless fallen short. It is only in going on to talk about the verbal self that Fowler begins to really discuss a child's sense of God rather than just relationship to others. This should not be too surprising in a model that has been critiqued for prizing intellectualism over other expressions of faith.

The first stage in Fowler's original configuration of stages is that of early childhood, *Intuitive-Projective Faith*, specified as ages two to six or seven (though his interviews involved those aged four and upwards). He bases his work on observable cognitive operations in those of this age, examining how children construct the world from their own understanding of it without awareness that others understand the world in a different way.

Fowler's description might be viewed as rather pejorative of this age of children. He focuses on the abilities they do not have – 'deductive and inductive logic' – and speaks of them having 'cognitive egocentrism'.[36] In this stage, the individual's faith is based on what they gain from others and intuit from those around them. Symbolization is key in this stage as this is when imagination begins to arise in the individual. Children form their world, their questions, their understanding and therefore also their faith through daydreaming and imagination. Some ideas, though, can take hold and prove formative for ideas of morality and taboo in positive and negative ways.

One danger at this stage is that children can grasp hold of ideas that make them afraid and hold on to them into adulthood. So those with carers and teachers preaching/teaching about the power of the devil, human sinfulness and the dangers of hell can hold on to those in later faith through 'a very rigid, brittle and authoritarian personality'. Conversely, children hearing about love, faith and courage can carry these into adult faith too. Fowler emphasizes 'the tremendous responsibility for the quality of images and stories we provide as gifts and guides for our children's fertile imaginations' and the importance of 'an atmosphere in which the child can freely express, verbally and nonverbally, the images she or he is forming'.[37] In this stage, a person's faith can be strongly influenced by those around them. Faith is fluid and full of new experiences, ideas, images and stories that feed a continuously imaginative process of meaning-making which might tend to involve ritual, religious and otherwise. This stage is rather distinctive within his model; Fowler is clear both about what initiates it and what leads to its end. The birth of imagination is the point at which a child enters this stage of faith, and the beginning of concrete operational thinking ends it.

The *Mythic-Literal* stage follows naturally from the Intuitive-Projective as a child takes the images and ideas that they have heard from those around them and imagined for themselves and begins, as concrete operational thinking develops, to sort between those things that are either real or not real and to develop a sense of patterns, order and narrative. This involves taking on 'the stories, beliefs and observances that symbolize belonging to his or her community'.[38] Although these symbols and stories are eagerly received, retold and adopted, the person at this stage of faith tends to take these things at face value without depth or nuance. These narratives are not without merit, as they begin to offer the individual a sense of coherence for their experience of the world within and around them. This is linked to other changes from the previous stage, namely a nascent awareness of the difference of the other, paired with a sense of fairness and reciprocation. Within the stories of a person's faith life here, there is a clear distinction between me and other, between good and bad, and also a sense of justice that those who do bad things in stories or in an individual's life face consequences. One of the key factors in transition from this stage is the realization that this simple concept of fairness and the idea of clear lines between good and bad, reward and punishment is not coherently observable in the world.

The third stage in Fowler's model, *Synthetic-Conventional Faith*, can be summed up with the opening words of the Nicene Creed, 'We believe'. Though some occasionally view this stage pejoratively or talk about people being 'stuck' in this stage, it is a place of genuine commitment. Following the Mythic-Literal stage of sorting the real from the unreal, a person comes to a point where they make a decision about what it is they believe by aligning themselves to a belief system espoused by trusted individuals around them. It is no longer easy to say that good always triumphs and the evil are punished. The world has evidently demonstrated that it does not work that way, so the individual seeks for a rationale for how the world is working from those who seem to have reconciled themselves somehow to the inconsistencies of life. For people in this stage, 'Faith must synthesize values and information; it must provide a basis for identity and outlook.'[39] Within a place of religious practice, such as a church, this might well be to join in with those words of the Creed.

For regularly maturing individuals, Fowler seems to locate this stage's beginnings quite firmly in adolescence. This transition stems from a combination of increasing spiritual and mental maturity and the impact of a teenager's wider connections afforded by the greater independence they are allowed because of their age. This wider social circle of trusted individuals might include a religious leader, friends, a teacher or even God. Parents may be included in this circle of trusted authorities but may also fall in and out of the circle or be rejected from it entirely at this stage. With the strength of the conviction that is shared by others, this stage can be one of great confidence in a set of beliefs and one in which interpersonal relationships are very important.[40]

Some, Fowler says, stay in this stage for a considerable time. This should not be viewed negatively. Estep and Kim seem to suggest this perception is because there are stages beyond this one. I suspect that the title of this stage, intended to describe the combination of the process of synthesis and joining with a set of beliefs, has often been heard in a different way because of the alternative meanings of the words synthetic and conventional. This misunderstanding could suggest a faith that is 'fake and ordinary', which was certainly not Fowler's intention. Fowler himself argues: 'it becomes a long-lasting or permanent equilibrated style of identity and faith', and, 'in many ways, religious institutions "work best" if they are peopled with a majority of committed folk best described by stage three'.[41] For those that do transition from this stage, it is through examining their faith and questioning not simply their own beliefs but the whole system of faith that they affirmed at the start of it. Fowler suggests that reflective practice is a natural means by which someone would begin this transition.[42] He goes further to theorize that a certain amount of disillusionment is required to transition to Stage 4.[43] This can involve disinvestment in the symbolic nature of certain images or practices, and clashes with those sources of authority who have previously been trusted. Developmentally, some might link this stage with 'leaving home' and Fowler does use this phrase, though, as many adults remain in this stage, the link is not absolute.[44]

Fowler describes the transition to Stage 4, *Individuative-Reflective*, as 'the critical distancing from one's previous assumptive value system and the emergence of an executive ego'.[45] At this stage each individual works out their own sense of faith for themselves, which may share similarities with more than one group or set of beliefs but represents an individual worldview.[46] By its very essence of individuality, this stage is therefore difficult to pin down. Fowler describes it as a point when an individual focuses on 'self-fulfillment or self-actualization' in tension with connection and mutual dependence on others.[47] This stage might be typified by a rise in critical thinking in terms of one's own faith and in the structures within the communities of their experience.

The corollary of this is that symbolism can become a source of skepticism. Where a child might have heard in school that we light a candle because Jesus is the light of the world, someone in Stage 4 could be more likely to say, 'It's just a candle!' This tendency towards the prosaic can, Fowler suggests, be a source of pain and regret for those who have previously valued a sense of the transcendent. The disconnection between symbol and concept can lead those at Stage 4 to gain a richer understanding of the concept represented by a symbol that must be inherently simpler than the concept itself.[48] This is the first stage in Fowler's original model where the timeline steps away from something normative. He associates Stage 4 with emergent adulthood, yet at the same time identifies that it may not happen until a person's mid-30s/40s and may not happen at all. Arguably, some at this stage may reach a personal worldview that bears close resemblance to one of the next two stages, so it is possible that an individualized faith might present as Conjunctive or Universalizing, simply because of the particular individual form that person's faith has taken.

Although he puts no precise marker on transition from Stage 4 to Stage 5, Fowler does suggest that *Conjunctive Faith* is 'unusual before mid-life'.[49] He says it is prompted by a disillusionment with the rigidity and logic of Stage 4 that cannot account for the complexity of the world. This echoes the transition from Stage 2 to Stage 3. Originally, Fowler expressed some concern about the nature and even the existence of this faith stage, saying that he struggled to define it but attributes this to a lack of research rather than to the nature of the stage itself.[50] Though he used the term 'dialogical knowing' originally, in later works he seems more confident to talk about this as a dialogical stage.[51] This dialogue is not simply with others of different faith perspectives but 'with reality'.

Fowler characterizes this stage as showing 'what the mystics call "detachment"', which nonetheless retains conceptual clarity in its fluidity. There is a move from Stage 4's focus on either/or to a both/and position.[52] A person is more aware of the plurality of meaning systems and the multi-layered nature of meaning. 'The person at Stage 5 seeks understanding rather than explanation ... is less interested in defending a worldview.'[53] Fowler describes them as having 'a radical openness to the truth of the other'.[54] Those at Stage 5 regain their sense of mystery and once more appreciate the power of symbols, though now with an appreciation of a greater number of meanings and of ambiguity. To offer my own example here, the candle can once again represent Jesus as 'the light of the world' but with awareness also that God is not only to be found in places of joy and gladness, for 'even the darkness is not dark to you; the night is as bright as the day, for darkness is as light to you' (Ps. 139.12). Conjunctive Faith is aware of polarities and respects their particularity. Someone at this stage is aware of their own position in relation to others while being self-critical, even questioning, of themselves, or self-doubting.[55] Fowler distinguishes Stage 5 and previous stages by comparing them to the difference between Ignatian approaches to studying scripture and source or form criticism.[56] He also associates Stage 5 with Paul Ricoeur's concept of second naivety, which he terms a 'postcritical desire to resubmit to the initiative of the symbolic'.[57]

Fowler says that those in Stage 5 can only move to Stage 6, *Universalizing Faith*, through a selfless engagement with the two great absolutes of existence, 'the imperatives of absolute love and justice', as universalizing people's 'felt sense of an ultimate environment is inclusive of all being'.[58] There are echoes here of the Buddhist concept of Nirvana or oneness, or the mystics' descriptions of their deepest connections with God, verging on theosis. Fowler is keen to hold back from this ultimate claim that individuals become one with God, focusing instead on individuals becoming fit for the kingdom. He says those at Stage 6 are not perfect in a 'moral, psychological or leadership sense'.[59] Despite critique that his model overvalues academic and cognitive factors, Fowler is clear to say that those at stage six typify a significant level of humility, 'born out of radical acts of identification with persons and circumstances where the futurity of being is being crushed, blocked or exploited'.[60] In describing this stage, Fowler does not follow his usual pattern of tracing through the faith life of an individual identified through his interview data because only 0.3% of the 359 people he interviewed are described as having been in Stage 6 and none as in a transitional stage between five and six.[61] In fact, this 0.3% is just one person. The patterns explored in previous stages were not so clear in this one person's interview. Fowler chooses instead to explore famous individuals whom he has 'identified' as likely to have been Stage 6: Mahatma Gandhi, Mother Teresa and Martin Luther King.[62] I think this weakens Fowler's argument for the existence of this stage and papers over the fact that his model has attempted to define a stage of faith based on the observation of one person.

The terms for the individual stages in Fowler's model are not the most accessible to the general public as they are so rooted in sociological and psychological terminology. His model remains the benchmark against which any other model is measured, so a basic understanding of it is important before explaining any others. These seven stages, 0–6, can be summarized as follows:

0 Primal faith – beginning to find our self.
1 Intuitive-Projective Faith – finding our self in the world.
2 Mythic-Literal Faith – entering the story of our faith.
3 Synthetic-Conventional Faith – committing to be one among a community of believers.
4 Individuative-Reflective Faith – owning one's faith for oneself.
5 Conjunctive Faith – entering a dialogue with reality.
6 Universalizing Faith – self-emptying openness to the ultimate.

Charles McCollough offers alternative titles for each of the stages, which are also more accessible to a non-academic audience though they present the stages with a certain prejudice; McCollough terms them as the Innocent, the Literalist, the Loyalist, the Critic, the Seer, the Saint.[63] Reading those stages, Stage 3, Synthetic-Conventional, sounds the most normative though possibly more positive than it can sometimes be presented; Stages 1 and 2 sound as if they are lacking somehow; Stage 4 sounds very negative; and Stages 5 and 6 sound frankly unattainable.

One of the key factors in terms of the usefulness of this model in parishes is in understanding the potential worldviews in a diverse congregation. This helps plan for intergenerational worship, discipleship and missional activity. The love of symbolism at stages two and five explains why young children and older people can bond so well (as has been demonstrated in various projects pairing nursery schools with day centres for the elderly). Mark Chater has suggested that Fowler's model could be useful in assisting whole churches that might be stuck in a particular stage.[64] It is also key in thinking about mission; where might people who are not part of church be in their faith? A significant focus in recent years has been placed (though it has not often been presented through the lens of Fowler) on the transition of individuals from Stage 3 to Stage 4. This can be perceived by some churches as people 'losing faith' because they step outside of the 'we believe' culture and begin to question, or can be seen as being challenging or difficult. Research has focused on those leaving the church,[65] and projects such as Doubt and Proud in Birmingham have been established to support those who find themselves questioning and no longer as confident in the 'we believe'.

No model of Faith Development has been as thoroughly critiqued as Fowler's. The critique covers various areas, including research design (notably the selection of his participants and their lack of diversity), the structuring of his model (and whether his stages fully account for experience at each stage), his definition of faith, and the relationship of his model particularly to Christianity. For some the model is questioned fundamentally on the validity of his concept that faith has stages at all.

In terms of research design, Richard Osmer critiqued Fowler for 'structuralism' because of his strong reliance on developmental models, making the model inadequate to encompass human faith.[66] Mary Ford-Grabowsky argued that his fundamental principles for exploring Faith Development were flawed because of his confusion between systems of understanding the self and his focus on purely cognitive ego questions rather than addressing the whole person:

> Although Fowler purports to be studying the stadial growth of the human ego, he in fact quite inadvertently stumbles, as it were, into the life of the self. While his faith stages 1 through 4 do concentrate on the structures of the ego, as intended, stages 5 and 6 point to the self, so that Fowler's work on his first four stages belongs to the literature of ego development, his work on the next two stages to the literature of spiritual development.[67]

She also argued that his work had 'a quadruple bias toward (1) the ego (which neglects the self); (2) cognition (which neglects affect); (3) consciousness (which neglects unconsciousness); and (4) positivity (which neglects negativity)'.[68] Ford-Grabowsky uses the theology of Hildegard of Bingen and her concept of the '*homo exterior* or outer person and the *homo interior* or inner person',[69] alongside the work of Jung, to demonstrate the weakness of Fowler's interviews which focus on only one aspect of a person:

Jung envisions spiritual growth as 'circumambulation about the center,' an image that would appeal to Hildegard. The 'center' would have a different meaning for each of them, of course: for Jung it is archetypal, and has the face of the individual; for Hildegard, it is mystical, and has the face of Christ.[70]

Heinz Streib also points to Fowler's own self critique of the original model as not fully taking the relational aspect into account:

> In his foreword to the German translation of *Stages of Faith*, Fowler admitted that his theory and methodology had not dealt adequately with the relational style of faith, a style that is possibly preferred by women. Fowler thus self-critically accepted the criticism expressed by Gilligan and others. Referring to work by Belenky et al., Fowler said he would like to expand his stages of faith, especially Stage 4, to include the style of 'connected knowing'.[71]

In defence against this criticism that his model does not fully reflect the development of the self, he further argues,

> faith, and the development of faith, has a triadic structure. There is the self, there are the primal and significant others in the self's relational matrix, and there is the third center of relational engagement – the ultimate Other, or the center(s) of value and power in one's life structure.[72]

This expanded, relational understanding of faith is most likely based on Fowler's engagement with Richard Niebuhr and his focus on understanding faith as having its highest meaning in relationship to the Ultimate One. This means faith and our understanding of life can be

> Illuminated by the awareness of One whose knowledge and love meet persons/searchings; the chaotic and mutually conflicting ends feverishly sought fall into intelligible focus, and the potential meaninglessness of human existence is subverted by a developing trust in the One who is trustworthy above all others.[73]

There is also critique of his interview methods. Slee critiques Fowler for using fully structured interviews rather than a mix of structured and open interviews, saying that his interview design was therefore unable to take account of experiences outside his rigid pattern.[74] Fowler was also critiqued for the people he selected for interview. Estep and Kim question the validity of Fowler's interview sample and the lack of record regarding the educational level of any of his interviewees, which might mean that the model is not relevant to all people but only to the population living within the vicinity of a university campus.[75] Furushima points to the data sampling for Fowler's research, which was heavily weighted towards white Christians: 'Of the total respondents to date, 97.8% are white, 81.5% are either Protestant or Catholic, 11.2% are Jewish, 3.6% are Orthodox, and 3.6% are of other orientations.'[76]

Furushima's critique from a cross-cultural perspective suggests that the model essentially has Christian bias and does not reflect the lived experience of those in a different cultural setting. When using Fowler's research model with 12 Hawaiian Buddhists, Furushima found that individuals exhibited a variety of characteristics from across several stages, which suggested that the distinction between Fowler's stages were not as clear for a different cultural context.

Fowler is further critiqued for the way he handled the data that the interviews generated. Echoing earlier concerns from Ford-Grabowsky,[77] Slee critiques Fowler for his model's treatment of the data from women's interviews, arguing that inherent flaws prejudice a woman's life experience in favour of the male normative model that Fowler has essentially commended.[78] Slee's critique includes Fowler's construction of what faith is, failing as it does to take account of 'intuitive knowing, imaginative, metaphoric and concrete forms of thinking'.[79] She gives examples of the different experiences of men and women at the transition from Stage 3 to Stage 4 reflecting the difference between the crisis of middle age for men and women.[80] Essentially, women's tendency towards self-sacrifice for the care of others would probably have reduced their score in terms of individualization to no more than Stage 3, despite evidence of high tolerances of ambiguity that could have leaned towards Stage 5. Ford-Grabowsky reinterpreted the data that Fowler had collected in the interview with Mary, to whom Fowler dedicates a whole chapter. Ford-Grabowsky demonstrated not one but two conversions in Mary's life.[81] Mary, she says, does not simply convert to faith: 'In the first conversion experience, there is a transition from ego to self; in the second, a transition from self to Christian self.'[82] Reflecting on the development of Christian virtues as drawn from Hildegard, she suggests a significant flaw in Fowler's model, as 'it can be shown that Mary occupies not only stage 3 on his scale, but simultaneously stage 5: which is of course impossible. The paradox is due to her being at stage 3 in terms of ego development, at stage 5 in terms of spiritual development.'[83]

Critics have suggested that, even based on the data as it was discovered, the model that Fowler extrapolates from it is flawed. His colleague Heinz Streib critiques Fowler for trying to do too many things in one model and ultimately not achieving a coherent model that is usable: 'Fowler's terms, "constitutive-knowing" or the affectedness by "the ultimate conditions of existence" are examples of concepts that are rather difficult, if not impossible, to operationalize in the empirical framework of scientific psychology.'[84] Mary Ford-Grabowsky critiqued not just his use of theory but also the model itself on four counts, each of them rooted in aspects of faith and religion.[85] The conversation between Fowler and Loder emphasized the issue of whether the model was a specifically Christian one or not. Fowler had always suggested it was a model of faith rather than specifically Christian Faith Development. Loder suggests that Fowler's model is not sufficiently biblically based, summarizing Fowler's model as 'a sensitive, insightful study of the ego's competence in structuring meaning, and it is only potentially but not necessarily related to faith in a biblical or theological sense'.[86] This is an argument picked up by Estep and Kim who question both whether a maturing faith necessarily involves increasing pluralism and whether Fowler's model measures Christianity at all.[87] Fowler's later work reflects on how his model echoes scripture, saying 'maturity in faith involves reclaiming some childlike dimensions of faith'[88] (cf. Matt. 18.3). Stephen Parker's review article critiques the empirical evidence for the determination of Fowler's stages of faith.[89] Edward Piper has identified a significant flaw in the design of Fowler's model. Even though it is based on interviews with a large number of people, 'the fact that nearly one-third of his subjects could not be assigned to a specific stage raises questions about the construct validity of the stage descriptions'.[90] Streib also critiques Fowler for suggesting that the distribution of stages across the age range of his participants evidenced progression in general, pointing out:

> Because the sequence, especially in the age groups of children, adolescents, and early adults, indicates a stage-like, upward movement from age group to age group, it could be taken as indication for the progressive development of stages of faith. Closer inspection of the age groups in adulthood and old age, however, indicates an up and down of frequencies in the age groups, especially of stage three and stage four assignments. Thus, Fowler's frequency statistics could be interpreted as conflicting with his own assumption of an exclusive upward direction of faith development.[91]

There is also critique of the model for what it is not able to explain or explore. Another former colleague, Sharon Parks, claims that Fowler's Stage 4 does not quite sufficiently account for this stage. Fowler himself interpreted some individuals' interview data as demonstrating 'an interesting and potentially long-lasting equilibrium in a transitional position between stages three and four'.[92] Fowler accounts for this transitional stage as being a result of an individual completing only one of the two essential tasks of transitioning to Stage 4; either they don't sufficiently critically distance themselves from the structures that fed them at Stage 3, but they do establish an individual worldview, or they critique their previous beliefs but do not replace them with a coherent new worldview of their own. Parks suggests that there is an in-between phase, a Stage 3/4 for which Fowler's model does not properly account.[93] Similarly, Slee critiques the lack of accounting for stalling or regression, in that the movement between stages is irreversible.[94] She also questions his account of what prompts movement between stages, saying he places too much emphasis on 'critical reasoning and analytical thinking, especially in the movement to stage 4'.[95]

In a joint article with James Loder, Fowler engages in a 'critical friend' discussion about his model in the light of Loder's work on Christian education and human transformation. Essentially, Loder's issue is that the model is normative rather than descriptive, and Fowler admits that, on reflection, by presenting a model 'it has become clear that we are trying to do both descriptive and normative work'.[96] In other words, Fowler conflated two pieces of research into one. Rather than first discussing the details of patterns he found from his sample, he does this while also trying to suggest that these details indicate a model. This critique of normativity is echoed by Jeff Astley who has critiqued Fowler's model for 'rushing people through the stages' rather than simply describing where people are in their experience of faith.[97]

Some critics go as far as to offer their own models. A reworking of Fowler's model by Benjamin Jones has suggested that instead of seven stages, the model genuinely reflects four stages with the first three stages conflated into a combined first stage and the dubious sixth stage omitted. This then becomes a model defined by the processing of faith in four modes: Religious Socialization (Primal, Intuitive-Projective and Mythic-Literal), Early Questioning, (Synthetic-Conventional), Exploration (Individuative-Reflective) and Engagement Refinement (Conjunctive).[98] Although this proposed model solves some of the criticisms of others, it exacerbates the adult-centric issue of Fowler's early stages. Piper also offers a reworking of Fowler's model. He cites the work of Daniel Batson et al., suggesting that while Fowler's model has merit in its early stages, in the latter stages what Fowler identified were three distinct styles:

> Rather than Stages 3, 4, and 5 being hierarchically ordered, one following the other, these three forms of faith may lie alongside one another ... Overall, then, the results suggest that for adults it may be more appropriate to speak of styles of faith, as Fowler sometimes has, not stages.[99]

Piper suggests that this results from a focus on vertical growth, which he calls 'an intrapsychic process', rather than also incorporating horizontal growth, the 'dimension of interpersonal relationships'.[100] Drawing on the work of Fowler's contemporary Carol Gilligan, he demonstrates that moral development is not properly attended to in Fowler's model.[101] Piper offers his own model, which places the person at the centre and faith developing not in a staged scale but outwards in what he calls regions, 'arranged from inner to outer rather than from lower to higher'.[102] These regions are not distinct but permeable, and working outwards from the self in concentric circles they are values, principles, sources of wisdom and ultimate reality. Likewise, Slee's work, as we shall see in the next chapter, is a corrective of Fowler's model.

Yet not all the criticism rests on the detail of the model. Some challenge Fowler on more philosophical grounds. David Heywood has argued that Fowler's model is insufficiently responsive to a postmodern mode of thought. He suggests that Faith Development theory is

> an example of a paradigm reaching the end of its life [because] the basic explanatory tenet, the idea of sequential, hierarchical stages of development, is an erroneous description of the rich complexity of personal knowing. The attempt to fit this complex pattern into six or seven stage descriptions may in fact do violence to the manifold variety of the paths by which people arrive at the meaning of their lives.[103]

Heywood's point is fair in terms of Fowler's model, though does not respond to the breadth of the field of Faith Development which includes more nuance than he seems to credit. Fowler did later explore his 1980s model in the light of postmodernism, recognizing not this particular issue that Heywood raises but factoring in the increased interaction with media which could lead to what he terms 'the "saturated self" [that] likely becomes the scattered self'.[104] John Hull (with whom I was fortunate enough to study at Queen's in Birmingham) critiqued Fowler from a rather different perspective, suggesting that the model panders too much to the capitalist ideal of continual progress.[105] The main critic of

Fowler in terms of progression is Heinz Streib, who suggests that Fowler merely identified certain faith styles and never demonstrated through empirical research that any individual had previously inhabited another stage or progressed from one to another.

As we have seen, some of the key criticisms of this well-established model of Faith Development have been its failure to account fully for the faith lives of all, but instead presenting essentially white, male, western, Christian, liberal, educated faith lives as normative. Using this model within the parish, ministers would need to be mindful of the biases present. I would suggest, however, that using the theory of Fowler to reflect on the make-up of a congregation or plan for mission would be useful, without necessarily using the terms Fowler uses for each stage, which can be off-puttingly technical.

Sharon Parks

Sharon Parks worked with Fowler and has collaborated on works exploring the implications of his work. She has also constructed her own model of Faith Development with particular reference to young adults. As an educational psychologist, Parks' work is focused on young adults and particularly on the experience of nascent adulthood and higher education. She founds her model on three distinct strands, each of which she traces through four stages and from which she then construes a form of faith for each. Her three strands are cognition, dependence and community. Focused on the journey to adulthood, Parks pays no attention to the spiritual development of those under 18 and focuses her work on developmental theories such as those by Erikson, Piaget and Kegan. She reflects on the relational value of the work of Gilligan.[106] Parks also summarizes Fowler's work as a precursor to her own, then references the work of William G. Perry on the intellectual development of those in young adulthood.

Much like Fowler, Parks distinguishes faith from religion and belief, arguing that

> if we are to recover a more adequate understanding of human faith in the context of present cultural experience, we must be clear that when we use the word faith, we are speaking of something quite other than belief in its dominant contemporary usage. Faith is not simply a set of beliefs that religious people have; it is something that all human beings do.[107]

She considers faith in the sense of meaning-making and defines it as the 'activity of composing and being composed by meaning', and 'the ongoing dialogue between self and world, between community and lived reality [from which] a robust pattern of faith takes form'.[108] She explores how individuals make sense of the world and of themselves, and also in relation to the divine. She says, 'Until this point we have spoken of faith without speaking of "God" per se. In the dynamic activity of composing the meaning of life, the pattern we ultimately depend upon for our existence functions as "God" for us.'[109] This might not endear Parks to anyone who holds to rather more specific credal beliefs. However, she is clear to draw on theological thinkers such as Richard Niebuhr when she talks about the function and dynamics of faith: 'When Professor Neibuhr reflects on human faith, he does so, in part, with the metaphors of "shipwreck, gladness and amazement." These metaphors connote the subjective, affective, dynamic, and transformative nature of faith experience.'[110] She considers these movements as part of the meaning-making process:

> Mature adult faith composes meaning in a self-conscious engagement in the repeated shipwreck and repatterning of one's perceptions of the fabric of life, the dynamic shifting of the assumed connections between persons, things, ideas, events, symbols, the natural order, the social order, space and time.[111]

For Parks, faith, as meaning-making, is the combination of a variety of sources in her three strands of cognition, dependence and community. She tracks each of these in turn, exploring them in four different stages of development. First, she offers a simple model of four stages whereby cognition begins as something that is authority-bound and dualistic. Individuals then develop their own cognition with what she terms 'unqualified' relativism, before the final two stages of commitment in relativism and convictional commitment, or 'the complexity on the other side of simplicity', which Parks clearly relates to Fowler's Conjunctive faith.[112] In terms of dependence, Parks recognizes the four stages of dependence, counter-dependence, inner dependence and interdependence. Her third strand, most likely influenced by Gilligan's work, is community, which Parks charts from Conventional to Diffuse, then to Self-selected and ultimately to Open to Others.

It is the combination of these three stands that leads to Parks' four-stage model of Faith Development. She draws from the story of the people of Israel for these stages of faith, calling them Egypt (God as parent), Wilderness (the far country), Spirit Within, and Promised Land (many members, one body).[113] Having described the three strands in some detail, Parks gives little attention to what the combination of these strands then produces. Neither does she explain how movement in one or more of the strands, but not all, would affect the transition or stability of a stage. She seems to suggest instead that the stage of cognition drives the stages of dependence and community.

Later, she reconsiders her model in the light of the young-adult experience of those she has worked with in higher education, ultimately to offer a model that has four stages of Adolescent, Young Adult, Adult, and Mature Adult, which she maps against Fowler's model as Adolescent (3), Young Adult (3/4), Adult (4) and Mature Adult (5). She makes no reference to Fowler's Stage 6, for which she does not think there is sufficient evidence. For this ultimate model, she moves to conflate her first two stages in each of the strands and replaces Fowler's Stage 3 with two divided stages based on what she has observed as follows for each strand. Cognition moves now through Probing Commitment (ideological) to Tested Commitment (Explicit). Inner dependence splits to become Fragile Inner Dependence and then Confident Inner Dependence, while in Community she adds the new stage of Ideologically Compatible Groupings (mentoring).[114]

This model is particularly apt for those working with large numbers of university students. Parks writes about young adulthood in general, though her model is strongly linked to those in higher education so I am not sure this model would have the same relevance to those young adults who move into employment rather than higher education. This is something of a middle-class bias. Nonetheless, the tasks of meaning-making that Parks identifies remain for those not in university, though the location of solutions to those questions of dependence and community will find different expressions for those in first jobs, living inside or outside the parental home and discovering new modes of independence.

Fritz Oser and Paul Gmünder

Fritz Oser and Paul Gmünder were working independently of Fowler, though at a similar time to him, developing a progressive theory of the development of religious judgement.[115] Oser was a Swiss academic who studied education at Solothurn and worked as a teacher for many years. He later studied musicology (aspiring to be an orchestral conductor), literature, philosophy and theology, then specialized in education. He spent time as a researcher at UCLA and studied with Lawrence Kohlberg at Harvard, serving alongside him as a research fellow.[116] Oser and Gmünder mention Kohlberg's work and frequent discussions with him.[117] Gmünder was born and educated in Zurich, studying philosophy and theology at the Theological Faculty of Lucerne and Tübingen. He went on to become Oser's research assistant for three years before returning to Lucerne, first to the theology department and then to the newly formed philosophy department. He co-founded a publishing house (Edition Exodus) focused on enabling the spread of Liberation Theology in the German-speaking world.[118]

Though influenced by Kohlberg, Oser and Gmünder consciously disassociated themselves from his model. As their research indicated, there were similarities at the earlier stages of their respective models but thereafter they differed. They consider their model to be 'terminologically precise and empirically validatable'.[119] They credit influences from Piaget, Kohlberg (on moral judgement) and George Herbert Mood, as well as Broughton, Döbert (on communicative competence), Selman and Keller (on social perspective taking), Goldman, Elkind and Rosenberg.[120] Using semi-structured interviews, they developed a similar though not identical model to Fowler. It is founded on an initial research project into religious judgement, during which they discovered that participants tended to speak of their current religious judgements with reference to previous religious judgements. This led them to hypothesize a model of stages of religious judgement that they then tested 'with new cross-sectional data' (note the contrast in research method to Fowler here).[121] Their model is based on the principle of there being seven dimensions to religious judgement that comprise a spectrum from one state to another at the polar extremes. Religious judgement, they suggest, is to be found in the equilibrium or disequilibrium of each of the following dimensions: sacred vs profane; transcendent vs immanent; freedom vs despondency; hope vs absurdity; trust vs anxiety; eternity vs ephemerality; and functional transparency vs opaqueness (magic). These dimensions were derived from their pilot study, from 'carefully mining the responses to our dilemma texts given by persons of various ages'.[122] They describe the ways that these dimensions differ in different stages as individuals have 'to establish an equilibrium between these poles ... which is personally valid and satisfactory to them'.[123]

Oser and Gmünder do not describe themselves as writing on faith but on religious judgement. They distinguish this from moral or intellectual development as being founded on a different set of understandings: 'the development of *intelligence* rests mainly on subject-object relations, the development of *morality* on the subject-subject relations, and *religious* development on the relation person-person-Ultimate'.[124] They therefore define not faith but religion as: 'a person's interpretative struggle with reality in light of an Ultimate which transcends the given reality. This is experienced as the establishing of "absolute" reality.'[125] Their research focuses on the way people describe their constructs and concepts of God, distinguishing themselves from Fowler whom they critique as basing his model too much on ego-development.[126] Instead they focus on 'structures of religious meaning [undergoing] a process of progressive construal'.[127] They observed from the participants that just as 'different chronological ages lead people to make different religious judgements', 'their relationship to an Ultimate obtains different qualities as well'.[128] They therefore place rather more emphasis on age for their stages than others. As part of their description of how faith grows, they reference St Paul's identification of maturing understanding in 1 Corinthians 13.11. They use the story of a successful man who then faces misfortune to delineate how individuals at different ages and stages would interpret the story.[129] In discussing how their model is formed, Oser and Gmünder are clear about a hierarchy of stages as they assert that no developmental model can be anything but hierarchical. They indicate that higher stages are an improvement upon previous stages, though not in a way that particularly denigrates the earlier stages: 'a new and higher structure features increased differentiation of certain characteristics ... as well as a broadened integration of the relational dimension'.[130] Though they focus on individuals' conceptions of God, they assign significance to 'autobiographical experiences' which naturally involve the interrelation with others and reflection on the self.

They set out a schema by which they say all developmental models must abide: 'The formal qualities which describe the individual stages are; qualitative differentiation, sequentiality, holism and the incorporation of lower stages into higher ones.'[131] In other words, they argue that each stage needs to be located in a particular place in the sequence and cannot be skipped or taken out of order. They say that each stage should be distinct from any other stage, that the model, as a whole, has to have a sense of fitting together as one and that higher stages must reflect what went before in some way. For Oser and Gmünder there must be progression, expressing 'patterns of religious reasoning which possess a higher degree of organization and a greater equilibrium from those patterns which possess these characteristics to a lesser degree'.[132]

As a person's religious judgement is 'based on the increasing autonomy and differentiation of the perception of the relation between persons and the Ultimate', they argue that 'this relationship is not at all regressive' because people tend to 'select the highest possible available degree of problem-solving strategies'.[133] They do not seem to account for the potential that trauma or crisis might lead people to regress to earlier less developed strategies. Change from one stage to the next is not about increased knowledge or a deeper understanding of something, but 'complicated and constitutes, in any case, a discontinuity'.[134] This may sound as if change means that there is some kind of disruption but in fact they suggest that progression between stages 'is not substantive change i.e. a change in content but a change in the way the elements which determine the religious judgement are interrelated. The different ways in which the elements are coordinated at each stage are significant in a different manner at each stage.'[135] Individuals need to confront conflicts in each stage in turn, resolving that conflict in a new way in a higher stage. They also suggest that each stage is distinguished by 'integrating a new element into an existing structure'.[136] In their model, each stage is defined by a 'prevailing principle' that directs how the seven elements of their model interrelate. Progression represents a greater equilibrium within each of their seven polar pairs. These prevailing principles make use of the word 'I' to indicate the necessary externalization and internalization work of religious judgement.

Oser and Gmünder conceptualize the model as a double helix; at each progression between stages there is a double action related to conceptions of the world in relation to our inward identity and conception of the Ultimate and of others outside ourselves. This means there is 'both an integration and a differentiation' at each transition.[137] By this process, Oser and Gmünder distinguish their model from others, suggesting that stages can be viewed as a constant journey between focusing in turn either on the self or the other. Their model does not posit that transition happens when a person's focus switches from focus on the self to focus on the other, but rather when a new equilibrium is found between those two foci in a necessary process of 'continual decentration and integration'.[138]

Oser and Gmünder suggest five firm stages and two putative stages at each end of their scale.[139] Their model describes each stage as having a particular worldview or 'orientation'. Much like Fowler's later revision of his model, Oser and Gmünder include a stage 0 in their model for the pre-critical child or, as they describe them, the 'pre-religious' child. In this *Pre-Religious: I am me and you are other* stage, children operate from the 'perspective of the dichotomy between interior and exterior', knowing when they do something and when someone else does something but not being able to distinguish more than this.[140] The child knows that they influence the other by certain actions of their own such as crying. The description of children in this stage is not exactly negative though it is somewhat dismissive, suggesting that Oser and Gmünder do not think children at this stage really 'count' in terms of Faith Development.

In Stage 1 – *Absolute Heteronomy Orientation also known as Deus ex Machina: the Ultimate affects everything* – individuals, or children, can distinguish between adults and an Ultimate that guides everything and is behind everything. They view God as all-powerful and humans as mere responders. Oser and Gmünder use the example of children describing people as being 'punished' by God if they fail to do what God wants them to do. The transition out of this stage to the next is prompted when this way of understanding the world is no longer tenable; when it becomes clear to a child that the weather is influenced by certain atmospheric conditions not God turning on a tap, or when the child begins to see that their model means that humans can influence God by behaving one way or another so the relationship is not as one-way as they first construed it. Layered on top of that is the complexity of humans seemingly being sometimes able to influence God by their prayers and sometimes not.[141]

Stage 2 is called *do ut des*[142] *orientation: the Ultimate effects everything if we ...* Here, God remains all powerful and external, but now with newly gained recognition that humans are able to influence God. This shifts the relationship between the individual and others to one in which the individual is in relationship to the Ultimate as other or 'absolute subject'. This shift in relationship also affects the way that the individual understands their own self as having autonomy and influence. The transition to Stage 3 is 'a major shock', that humans do not have the power to influence the Ultimate. This might result from evidence experienced in their own life or in patterns of life in the world seen on the news, or from an individual achieving something by their own efforts without asking God for it in prayer. This shift makes an individual more conscious of their own ability and their own responsibility for actions and consequences. The logic there is that if it is not God doing it, then my own role has significance.

Stage 3 – *Absolute Autonomy Orientation also referred to as Deism: The Ultimate and human beings act independently of each other* – has a worldview that separates God from the world where individuals are autonomous. This can be experienced in two extremes: an atheistic one where God is not relevant, and a religious one in which the dichotomy between the sacred and the secular is emphasized.[143] Rainer Döbert suggested that this can be a place where many get stuck in 'a developmental impasse, a vicious circle in which most young people find themselves lodged'.[144] This echoes Fowler's Stage 3, at which many individuals can stay for some time, though the next transition differs as, according to Oser and Gmünder, the transition from this stage tends towards a negation of the separation of the Ultimate and a re-embracing of the idea that things happen for a reason, nuanced by a sense of an individual's own responsibility. In terms of the pairs of dimensions, this transition is hinged on the rebalancing between the immanent and the transcendent. Oser and Gmünder refer to this transition as a crisis (what I have termed a hiatus) because, 'at least initially, persons consider it a regression'.[145] They suggest this might be prompted by an encounter with someone successful who attributes their success, at least in part, to God-given gifts rather than their own efforts.

Stage 4 – *Mediated Autonomy and Salvation-Plan Orientation: Human beings are able to act, because of the a priori existence of the Ultimate* – reflects the complexities described in the transition from Stage 3. God is perceived as having a relationship to the world but in a new way. The Ultimate is seen as the foundation of existence though not necessarily active in the world. God is still acknowledged though often in a series of symbols and available through many different religious practices. Those in Stage 4 'view themselves in a decisive role, while being located in a universal plan that constitutes the conditions of life'.[146] A considerable issue for those in this stage is the fixation on their own freedom, which is acknowledged as being made possible by the Ultimate though is not fully reconciled to the relationship with the Ultimate who is somewhat distanced by the symbols used to represent it. This lack of resolution is key to the lack of transition to Stage 5.

Stage 5 – *Intersubjective Religious Orientation Autonomy by Means of Intersubjectivity* – sees the individual feel utterly accepted by God in a universal joining of the world and the Ultimate.[147] The freedom of the individual is viewed in the context of the absolute freedom that is the Ultimate. This is a freedom not for the individual but a freedom to act for others, not just for self. This is a shift across the last three stages, as Oser and Gmünder explain: 'At stage 3, freedom *from* the Ultimate was dominant; at stage 4 it was freedom *by means of* the Ultimate. Now at stage 5 freedom is viewed always for others and is postulated for them.'[148]

Oser and Gmünder suggest a putative Stage 6 – *Universal Orientation: Human beings act through the actions of the Ultimate which itself is con-*

tingent upon the acts of human beings – which they inferred 'deductively from theological and philosophical models'. They could not validate this by their empirical data. In strong contrast to Fowler's model, which suggests just such a stage on the basis of one participant's interview, Oser and Gmünder do not include this stage and even suggest that their own construction of it without such data would lack objectivity as it could be 'related a bit too closely to our cultural sphere'. This putative stage 'tends towards universal communication and solidarity'.[149] It is a stage at which there is an essence of self-negation and simultaneously a total acceptance of the self and an awareness of unconditional love by the Ultimate.

In terms of using this model in the parish setting, there is one aspect of the basis of the model that might be particularly informative. Oser and Gmünder used a single story that people at different stages responded to in differentiated ways. This is an excellent exemplar of how the same scripture or sermons might be received at different levels in varying ways. The best example of this in modern culture is the way that Pixar films are enjoyed by both children and adults for different reasons. However, the model as it is presented shares in common with Fowler's model the rather inaccessible names of stages, so might not be so suitable for a wider audience without translation.

M. Scott Peck

M. Scott Peck was an American psychologist best known for his book *The Road Less Travelled* (sometimes called the first self-help book), which stayed on the *New York Times* bestseller list longer than any other book.[150] He wrote it two years before he was baptized as a Christian in 1980.[151] Peck describes his spiritual journey from upbringing in an essentially secular household to calling himself a Zen Buddhist at the age of 18, exploring Hasidic Jewish teaching and Islamic Sufism at the age of 30, and finally meeting Christ through reading the Gospels in his forties.[152] He sees the strength of what he calls 'great religions', namely Christianity, Judaism, Islam, Taoism, Buddhism and Hinduism, as encompassing those of institutional faith and those of more mystical faith.[153]

Peck's academic background is somewhat circuitous. He studied for two years as an undergraduate at Middlebury, then for two further years at Harvard before a year of pre-med (without biology) at Columbia. He was accepted to a further year of pre-med at Columbia.[154] Peck married fellow student Lily Ho, a Singapore-born daughter of Chinese parents. Interracial marriage was rare in the 1950s and both sets of parents objected to the marriage. There was a brief hiatus in Peck's studies before his father restored his financial support for tuition, no longer at Columbia but at Cleveland Western Reserve.[155] Peck's cultural outlook was deeply impacted by his interactions with 1950s America, as the husband of a non-white woman, in ways he had not previously experienced. On graduating medical school, he entered military service, serving in Hawaii, San Francisco and then as a psychiatrist in Okinawa and Washington.[156] Later he worked as a psychiatrist in West Connecticut.[157] His focus as a psychiatrist was on practice rather than research.[158] In both his practice and writing, he drew from a diverse range of psychological schools.[159] In *The Road Less Travelled*, he also drew from Buddhist teaching and asserts that spiritual development and the development of the mind are not separate but one unified path.[160]

He describes each individual, whether or not they follow a particular creed, as having a religion, which he also calls worldview or a growing understanding 'of what life is all about', based on how individuals 'grow ... or fail to grow in discipline, love and life experience'.[161] This is essentially Peck's initial construction of faith. Peck's idea of Faith Development is one in which growth in faith is a matter relating to a whole person and whole life, not restricted to someone who has declared themselves as a believer in a certain faith. Peck talks about the important tasks and lessons of self-discipline that any person needs to complete in order to mature. He also describes growth as a matter of needing to 'constantly revise and extend our understanding to include new knowledge of the larger world'.[162] Following the enormous success of his first book, he travelled the US speaking to groups and co-founded the Foundation for Community Encouragement.[163]

Peck sets out a model of Faith Development in another book, *The Different Drum: Community Making and Peace*. He talks about Fowler as 'the expert in Faith Development' and says of his own revision of Fowler's model, 'I simplify them a bit.'[164] He describes his model (together with a development model for how communities are formed) and does so again in the later follow-up book.[165] He says of his work:

> All my work can be traced back to my Harvard college thesis, 'Anxiety, Modern Science and the Epistemological Problem.' I outlined three basic ways to try and look at things. They can be looked at as if they were caused by something external, or they were caused by something internal, or they were caused by relationships between things ... The

answer to understanding this is not one of those three, but all of them simultaneously. It's more than a paradox – it's a triadox.[166]

Although Peck did not conduct his own research, he bases much of his work on the observation of psychological practice with numerous individuals, and his book uses individual stories such as those of 'Kathy', 'Marcia' and 'Theodore' to explicate how a person's faith grows.[167] One might question the ethics of this sharing of clients' stories when they were potentially unaware that their experiences would be included in research; Peck is not clear that he sought suitable permissions.

Peck sees an overarching trajectory of growth in terms of the metaphor of a journey and comments on what triggers transition from each stage. In terms of overall direction of travel, he says, 'Spiritual growth is a journey out of the microcosm into an ever greater macrocosm. In its earlier stages … it is a journey of knowledge and not of faith.'[168] One of the prime forces for change is love, which is essentially 'an extension – that is an expansion – of ourselves'.[169] The other force for change is echoed in the work of Brian McLaren. Peck argues that doubt is a prominent initiator of progress in faith:

> The road of spiritual growth … begin[s] by distrusting what we already believe, by actively seeking the threatening and unfamiliar, by deliberately challenging the validity of what we have previously been taught and hold dear. The path to holiness lies through questioning *everything*.[170]

Peck suggests that his Faith Development model hinges on the key moment of going through difficulty in order to come out the other side:

> You have to go through a phase of doubting. One of the great sins of the Christian church is the discouragement of doubting … If you become really good at stage three doubting, you begin to doubt your own doubts. And that's when you begin to move to stage four.[171]

For Peck, the development of faith is a journey of theosis: 'God wants us to become himself or herself or itself. We are growing towards Godhood. God is the goal of evolution.'[172] Walter Wink critiqued Peck in many ways, particularly Peck's description of this concept, prompting a response from Peck:

There is a paradox here, and that is that we, ourselves, cannot become God except by bumping ourselves off. The process is one that real theologians refer to as kenosis – the process of self-emptying. The goal is imaged by that of the empty vessel, in which there is still enough ego left to comprise the walls of the vessel, but which is otherwise sufficiently empty to be able to become spirit-filled.[173]

He describes the transition from Stage 1 to Stage 2 as being 'as if God literally reaches down and grabs the soul and yanks it up in a quantum leap'.[174] Essentially, he considers this transition an unconscious effort by the individual to rid themselves of the chaos that has governed them. The transition, or conversion as Peck calls it, between later stages is much more gradual.[175]

Peck offers four simple stages, conflating Fowler's earliest stages into Stage 1, which he refers to as 'at the beginning – the bottom, if you wish'.[176] He calls this stage *Chaotic/Antisocial*. His negative description continues as he attributes approximately 20% of the population to this stage and describes them as 'including those whom I call people of the lie',[177] referring to his earlier book of that name on the subject of evil.[178] Within this group, he says, can be found those who 'will frequently be found in trouble or difficulty and often in jails or hospitals or out on the street'. Though this is not true for all at this stage, as some may 'be quite self-disciplined, from time to time, in the service of their ambition and may rise to positions of considerable prestige and power. They may even become presidents or famous preachers.'[179] This is a rather negative view of 20% of humanity and yet recent political history, especially in the US, could be considered to support the latter part of his proposition. He asserts that individuals at this stage are 'utterly unprincipled' and without spirituality. Like Fowler, he typifies this as an egotistical stage in which individuals are self-willed, unwilling to accept a will greater than their own and often unprincipled.

This lack of any guiding set of principles is what characterizes the stage as chaotic. Individuals in this stage also lack empathy, though may be able to feign a loving response while 'actually all their relationships with their fellow human beings are self-serving and covertly, if not overtly, manipulative'.[180] His description of Stage 2 is *Formal/Institutional*. Peck describes this as the stage 'in which the fundamentalists fall'.[181] Streib might agree with this, however, as Peck's first definition of religion as worldview suggests he doesn't restrict the institution by which someone might be governed to faith groups alone. He also talks about prisoners and those in the military who demonstrate strong dependence on an institution, and those who value working for a 'highly organized business corporation'.[182] Nonetheless, he suggests that the 'majority of churchgoers fall into Stage Two' and that they are 'dependent on the institution ... for their governance'.[183] This stage maps against Fowler's Synthetic Conventional stage, though Peck describes it not simply as a place of communal faith but instead of dependence. Individuals at this stage have little sense of God's immanence, only of God as an external being, and 'they generally envisage God along the masculine model' with a sense of being a loving God but also a God with 'punitive power' like 'a giant benevolent cop in the sky'.[184]

Although Peck's description of the first stage of his model may not be especially positive towards children, he does suggest that children brought up in a household governed by those in Stage 2 might, when maturing, reject the institutional faith of their parents and therefore move into Stage 3 ahead of them. Stage 3 for Peck is called *Skeptic and Individual.* This is a stage in which many are atheist or agnostic, after rejecting whatever institution may have previously governed their worldview. Peck asserts that 'they are not religious in the ordinary sense of the word' but, by his own definition they do have a particular worldview.[185] Individuals at this stage are not antisocial (like those in Stage 1), rather they are positive members of society, often including scientists or those who are scientific-minded because this is a stage that involves truth-seeking and serious questioning. Through the truth-seeking of this stage, some may fit together 'enough pieces of truth to catch glimpses of the big picture and see that it is not only very beautiful, but that it strangely resembles many of those primitive myths and superstitions' belonging to Stage 2.[186] Reconciling this conjunction of old truth and new truth leads to progress onwards to Stage 4, his final stage of *Mystical/Communal.* Peck considered himself a mystic from an early age.[187] He described mystics as those who 'have seen a kind of cohesion beneath the surface of things. Seeing that kind of interconnectedness beneath the surface, mystics of all cultures and religions have spoken of things in terms of unity and community ... of paradox.'[188] In this stage, echoing Fowler's Conjunctive stage, individuals are able to hold ambiguities and put behind them the notion of competing camps of belief. It also involves a loss of attachment to ego and a concurrent loving of others as oneself.

As someone whose work gained much acclaim, just like Fowler, Peck comes in for some justified criticism. Wink, known for his work on power, suggests, however, that Peck's position changed radically from his bestseller when he composed the Faith Development model that he based on Fowler's work. Wink writes:

In *Road*, Peck clearly sees himself among a tiny and select group of saints who, by participating in God's omniscience, also 'share His agony,' and who walk ahead, utterly alone. 'As we outdistance our fellow humans our relationship to God inevitably becomes correspondingly close.' This is a curiously elitist view of mystical development, and it is sharply at odds with his understanding of community in *Drum*. He has apparently learned, in the intervening years, that spiritual development means not isolation but the capacity for community.[189]

Wink also suggests that Peck's model might be contextual to the era in which it was composed rather than universal:

What if children were taught to ask questions from the earliest age, especially of the Bible? Then a healthy skepticism would grow up alongside faith, rather than being the destroyer of an inadequate stage two faith. Thus people would not tend to stay caught in stage three skepticism so long, sometimes unable to pass to mature faith.[190]

From my own perspective, Peck suggested that he had simplified Fowler's model. He has also simplified the bias at the heart of Fowler's analysis. Peck's model reveals a staggering elitism and arrogance towards those of the first three stages and makes little to no acknowledgement of the lived experience of children and young people in terms of faith. Although he may have written encouragingly about the need for development, the model he offers is pejorative about those in the earlier stages. I hope I am correct in suggesting that Peck is really referring only to adults in his model and that adults within the first stage have failed to complete some of the essential work of growing to adult maturity. Yet even that interpretation means that Peck's assessment of children is far from positive.

This is not a model that can be usefully applied by those working with children and young people seeking to encourage a sense of a growing faith across the whole of human experience from birth to old age. Peck explores the relationship between people of different stages, suggesting that this is one of the prime reasons for having such a model. He notes that there can be antagonism between people of different stages. Those in Stage 1 tend to distrust anyone at all. People with Stage 2 faith may view those in Stage 1 as 'sinners' to be saved but feel threatened by 'the sceptic individual of Stage Three'. Yet the greatest source of threat for those in Stage 2 are the people in Stage 4 who 'seem to believe in the same things they believe in and yet believe them with a kind of freedom they find absolutely terrifying'.[191] The people in Stage 3 also tend to be threatened by those in Stage 4 as they combine something of their own scientific approach yet also 'believe in this crazy God business' though they have no issue with those in the first two stages.[192] Peck's usefulness in ministry might also be the simplification of the complexities of other models. This might well appeal to a wide audience. However, caution is needed as simplification also leads to the loss of nuance.

Alan Jamieson

One of the few modern models to echo the medieval tendency to use imagery when tracking the life of faith is a work by New Zealand theologian Alan Jamieson, a Baptist minister with a background in the military and sociology.[193] He is currently the general director of the New Zealand Baptist Missionary Society and contributes teaching to courses in Christian spirituality and missional leadership at Carey Baptist College. Previously he has been part of the emergent church blog *prodigal kiwis* and *Spirited Exchanges*, a group established to help support the faith lives of recent church-leavers. His first book is the published version of his doctoral thesis in sociology.[194] It explores the faith lives of those who have left church but continue to explore their relationship with God and the meaning for that in their lives. It was based on interviews with over a hundred individuals who have left the church. He draws from stories of their lived faith experience, mentioning them prominently in his acknowledgement: 'Each journey of faith, told and heard, has opened a sacred space. It is from these stories and from my own story that this account has been shaped.'[195] He is not specific about how these stories were incorporated but the implication is that the work is ethnographic and autoethnographic in its methodology. However, he also drew on other empirical research when recounting survey data that revealed that the proportion of people who expect their faith to grow was 65% of those surveyed.[196]

Jamieson's focus on those who have left the church might indicate that by faith he does not mean simply a credal adherence to a particular denomination. He traces the faith journey from the moment of conversion to Christian faith (rather than from birth).[197] He describes faith as modelled by Jesus being something that:

> involves our whole intellect, our passions, our convictions and our willpower. It is intrinsically a relational endeavour ... far more than

making meaning; it is living fully within the meaning we make ... a life of faith comprised of meaning making and meaningful living.[198]

The way faith changes for Jamieson has three essential movements: 'the primary metamorphosis of adult Christian faith is the move from pre-critical faith through a period of hypercritical faith towards a post-critical faith'.[199]

In presenting his model, Jamieson offers what he calls 'a rough map on which to locate ourselves and the people we accompany in this journey of Christian faith'.[200] He is clear that his model is rooted in scripture. Jamieson writes about the lived experience of faith with a firm and clear awareness not of the great and mighty journey of positive and constant improvement but of the significance of crisis on the shaping of our faith lives.[201] He links his model to the 'wall' described by Hagberg and Guelich, the dark night of John of the Cross, Brueggemann's pit and Parks' shipwreck.[202] This is the determining factor of Jamieson's model. He is convinced that this factor does not feature in the lives of many Christians who instead remain in pre-critical faith most if not all of their lives.[203] He calls Faith Development 'a journey of almost imperceptible growth and radical transformations'.[204] Drawing on Erikson, he describes the stages of faith as nested within each other 'like Russian dolls ... the previous phases of faith are part of us and are alive deep within us'.[205] This is similar to the tree rings offered by Westerhoff's model (see next section).

Jamieson's model draws on an image from nature. He speaks of deliberately choosing an image from nature, having rejected a more laboratory-centred model, and acknowledges influence from the medieval tradition with a mention of Teresa of Avila and John of the Cross.[206] He gives particular credit to Teresa's metaphor of the silkworm.[207] His book *Chrysalis*, as the name implies, uses the imagery of the lifecycle of a caterpillar/butterfly to track the stages of faith, and deals very well with the concept of the hiatus.

The caterpillar stage, *Can't get Enough – Growing*, as Jamieson describes it, is the eager stage of the new convert. He associates it particularly with adolescence and growing into adulthood, drawing on his own life experience in particular and with reference to similar experiences of others.[208] This stage is '"conventional" or "pre-critical"' and largely focused on activity and the rate of growth determined by the quality of teaching and Christian input available (echoing the caterpillar freshly born on the leaf that they will consume). Within this one stage, Jamieson also identifies some sub-stages through 'shedding one layer of skin to expose a soft new skin' as the caterpillar grows. This identification of sub-stages is key as Jamieson locates most adult faith experience in this stage and is keen not to diminish people's lived experience of faith: 'for most of us, our Christian faith journey is a mix of growth and stagnation'.[209] Jamieson identifies the trigger point for leaving this stage as analogous to John of the Cross's work.[210] By his description, this naturally allies to the dark night of the senses. He describes this as an internal process that many experience as a dissatisfaction with their experience of church because, like the caterpillar who has eaten enough and filled out to their last possible skin, those experiencing this dark night need something different. It is not the church getting it wrong. It is something within each person that needs examining and exploring:

> The problem wasn't with my prayer life, the worship services or preaching. My prayer space wasn't changing, the worship services I attended were just as good, if not better than before, and the preaching was undeniably solid and sound. The problem was with me.[211]

Jamieson identifies the stage in his own journey here and also suggests it has been present in the lives of others he has spoken to about their experience of faith.

Jamieson identifies this second stage of faith as *Golden Crucible Cocooning*, in which the caterpillar stops eating and starts building an anchor point for their cocoon and enters it.[212] It happens when a person finds that the things that have always helped them in their faith no longer do so. They need to do something different. He identifies the mode of this change as a deep yearning within, which is rooted in two or more of what he calls dissociative behaviours: disenchantment, disillusionment, disengagement, disidentification or disorientation.[213] These echo Fowler's general modes of change: '(1) disengagement, (2) disidentification, (3) disenchantment, and (4) disorientation'.[214] He uses other analogies to explore this stage, including the story of Job.[215] Jamieson identifies this stage as a time of grief and loss where human agency is not the vital catalyst: 'The chrysalis time is a time of transformation and we cannot transform ourselves. This is the Spirit's work.'[216]

It is in fact in the third stage, *In the dark – Letting Go*, that the spirit really is at work. Jamieson talks about this stage as a meeting with three strangers who have not formed part of our previously very active faith:

> The strangers of darkness, inertia, and loss confront us in our chrysalis of faith and though, at first, we want to ignore them and hide from

them, we find that it is in befriending these strangers that new growth is achieved.[217]

He then uses Parker Palmer's work on engagement with the dark and the five monsters that dwell there: 'insecurity and self-worth that seeks to validate itself by external successes, possessions and confirmations';[218] 'the belief that the universe is a battleground and hostile to our interests;'[219] 'functional atheism' whereby a person believes that it's all down to humanity and God does not act; 'fear of the chaos of life' and 'our denial of death', not just of ourselves or human beings in general but a denial of the ending of things and our unwillingness to let things like groups or projects come to a natural end.[220] Jamieson roots this engagement with the darkness in scripture through the story of Jacob wrestling with the angel, and the Christian understanding of Good Friday's tomb in expectation of the resurrection of Easter.

> Here is the ultimate parable of what the dark night is all about. Though our experience will never embrace the fullness of Christ's, we are challenged to enter into and live our own dark night, with Christ as both model and guide.[221]

After experiencing this darkness, the transition to the fourth stage, *From deep Within – Letting Come*, initializes when 'the chrysalis becomes home'.[222] This does not happen as soon as the caterpillar enters the chrysalis. Like the metamorphosis to a butterfly, this takes time and space. It is a time when we become accustomed to the truth of grace.

> The crucial learning of the chrysalis is that our God becomes a God whose dominant face towards us is one of generosity and compassion: a God who is far more interested in delighting us as a friend than worrying about what we do.[223]

He explores this stage through various references, including Teresa of Avila, and devotes a subsequent chapter to the importance of the support of others during this time, watching over the cocoon from outside.[224] Having discussed the process of the chrysalis with friends who are more scientifically knowledgeable than me, Jamieson's description of this stage as challenging and draining still does not quite come close to the description of the caterpillar becoming 'stew' out of which the butterfly is then recreated. Something happens that unmakes us and then remakes us in our faith. Jamieson indicates that the trigger for the next stage, the bursting out of the chrysalis, is the deep yearning within (after this time of drawing aside) to once again be with people in our faith.[225]

Jamieson describes this post-chrysalis phase, *Going Solo – Emergence*, as a self-owned faith.[226] The stage comes with risks: of sharing our faith with others and re-engaging with the church when it may have been a place of challenge.[227] This stage is about presenting what was within to the outside: 'It is the time when we sense a new way of living; a way of living which is congruent with our deepest sense of ourselves and what we desire to do and be in the world.'[228] Jamieson describes this as the first step into communion, which is followed by a second step into generativity.

Jamieson uses the biological name for the butterfly stage of the cycle – imago – to title his final stage of *Imago – Being*.[229] The story he recounts as typifying this stage is one of someone in midlife discovering a new vocation.[230] He links this with Richard Rohr's concept of the 'second stage of life'.[231] This stage encompasses post-critical faith and is marked with graciousness. He draws on the story of the prodigal son as an exemplar of this stage.[232] Jamieson goes on to explore the distinctiveness of the life of the butterfly from that of the caterpillar, arguing that in this new post-critical faith, the individual finds new ways to pray and worship.

You might argue from Jamieson's rhetoric about it that the church has little role to play in the post-critical faith of individuals willing to experience that chrysalis time. Jamieson cites the work of Kester Brewin in suggesting how churches should reflect this model in their work with individuals who might be entering the chrysalis or considering it. He emphasizes the importance of supporting individuals where they are rather than expecting everyone to be at the same stage.[233] Jamieson acknowledges the importance of spiritual directors and soul friends during the chrysalis stage.[234] This is no sat-nav with directions that must be followed and that churches should insist people follow according to an external timeframe. Rather, as Brewin suggests, 'What is important is that the path is clear for them to travel when they find their way there in their own time.'[235] He explores how churches might be strategic in responding to these processes that are going on outside their control, suggesting that those seeking spiritual support in alternative Christian communities are likely to be 30–35% by 2025. He sees an important role for 'wayfarers', those who have left the church, and waystations, which might be other churches, 'para-church groups, small groups, house churches, web or blogsites'.[236] Finally he presents a vision of not just waystations where butterflies can top up on nectar but butterfly houses designed for them; churches with post-critical faith in mind. The Spirited Exchanges groups that he helped establish in Wellington, seem to have been an outworking of this idea.

Sadly, the implication from their website is that ultimately these groups did not survive in the long term as they no longer seemed to serve the needs of those they were intended to support.[237] However, this model of engagement is still apparent. I am certainly aware of a group of post-critical Christians meeting as Doubt and Proud, reflecting a mix of those still in church, those in ministry and those holding on by their fingertips to membership of a church that no longer reflects their understanding of God, the world or themselves, not because church has changed but because their faith has grown. Indeed, traditional churches without programmatic structures for discipleship might also, by their lack of structure, allow for more individual discipleship if they are willing to be responsive.

Notes

1 Oser, Fritz and Gmünder, Paul, 1991, *Religious Judgement: A developmental approach*, Birmingham: Religious Education Press.

2 https://web.archive.org/web/20160304204245/http://www.myajc.com/news/news/local-obituaries/james-w-fowler-75-theologian-author-embodied-the-f/nn7P7/, accessed 09.05.2025.

3 Fowler, J. W., 2001, 'Faith Development Theory and the Postmodern Challenges', *The International Journal for the Psychology of Religion*, Vol. 11, No. 3, pp. 159–72.

4 Fowler, 'Postmodern', pp. 159–60.

5 Fowler, 'Postmodern', p. 162.

6 Fowler, J. W. and Dell, M. L., 2006, 'Stages of Faith from Infancy through Adolescence: Reflections on Three Decades of Faith Development Theory', in Roehlkepartain, E. et al., eds, *The Handbook of Spiritual Development in Childhood and Adolescence*, Thousand Oaks: Sage, pp. 34–45, p. 35.

7 Fowler, James W., 1984, *Becoming Adult, Becoming Christian: Adult Development and Christian Faith*, San Francisco: Harper.

8 Fowler, James W., 1987, *Faith Development and Pastoral Care. Theology and Pastoral Care*, Philadelphia: Fortress Press.

9 Fowler, James W., 1991, *Weaving the New Creation: Stages of Faith and the Public Church*, San Francisco: Harper.

10 Fowler, James W. et al., eds, 1992, *Stages of Faith and Religious Development: Implications for Church, Education and Society*, London: SCM Press.

11 Fowler, James W., 1996, *Faithful Change: The Personal and Public Challenges of Postmodern Life*, Nashville: Abingdon Press.

12 Fowler, James W., 2004, 'Faith Development at 30: Naming the Challenges of Faith in a New Millennium', *Religious Education*, Vol. 99, No. 4, pp. 405–21.

13 Loder, James and Fowler, James F., 1982, 'Conversations on Fowler's Stages of Faith and Loder's Transforming Moment', *Religious Education*, Vol. 77, No. 2, March–April, pp. 133–48.

14 Fowler, James W. et al., eds, 2004, *Manual for Faith Development Research*, Atlanta: Center for Research in Faith and Moral Development.

15 Fowler, J. W. 2001, 'Faith Development Theory and the Postmodern Challenges', *The International Journal for the Psychology of Religion*, Vol. 1, No. 3, pp. 159–72, p. 163.

16 Fowler, James W., 1995, *Stages of Faith: The Psychology of Human Development and the Quest for Meaning*, San Francisco: Harper, pp. 310–12.

17 Fowler, *Stages*, pp. 244–5.

18 Slee, Nicola, 2004, *Women's Faith Development: Patterns and Processes* London: Routledge, p. 29.

19 Fowler, *Stages*, p. 25.

20 Fowler, *Stages*, pp. 92–3.

21 Streib, Heinz, 2003, 'Religion as a Question of Style: Revising the Structural Differentiation of Religion from the Perspective of the Analysis of the Contemporary Pluralistic-Religious Situation', *International Journal of Practical Theology*, Vol. 7, No. 1, pp. 1–22, p. 6, referencing Fowler, *Stages*, pp. 98–105.

22 Fowler, Becoming, p. 70.

23 Fowler, *Weaving*, p. 28.

24 Fowler, *Faithful*, p. 72.

25 Fowler, *Faithful*, pp. 57–8, 20–53.

26 Fowler, *Stages*, pp. 41–51, 98–114, 129; Fowler, *Faithful*, pp. 22–53, 75–87.

27 Fowler, *Faithful*, pp. 47–53, 59.

28 Fowler, *Weaving*, p. 94.

29 Fowler, *Faithful*, p. 67.

30 Fowler, *Faithful*, p. 21. On reading this, as a Christian I noticed the clear connection with the dominical commandment involving love for God, neighbour and self (Mark 12.30–31). Fowler makes no such connection, and perhaps was seeking to avoid credal connections in order to make his model as universally applicable as possible. However, linking this triadic covenant to The Golden Rule is also possible and would not tie the model just to Christianity.

31 Fowler, *Faithful*, pp. 26–43; cf Stern, Daniel N., 1985, *The Interpersonal World of the Infant: A View from Psychoanalysis and Developmental Psychology*, London: Taylor and Francis.

32 Fowler, *Faithful*, p. 27.

33 Fowler, *Faithful*, pp. 28–30.

34 Fowler, *Faithful*, p. 31.

35 Fowler, *Faithful*, pp. 33–4, 38.

36 Fowler, *Stages*, p. 123.

37 Fowler, *Stages*, pp. 130–3.

38 Fowler, *Stages*, p. 149.

39 Fowler, *Stages*, p. 172.

40 Fowler, *Stages*, pp. 154 and 156.

41 Fowler, *Stages*, pp. 161 and 164.

42 Fowler, *Stages*, p. 160–3.

43 Fowler, *Stages*, p. 163.

44 Fowler, *Stages*, p. 173.
45 Fowler, *Stages*, p. 179.
46 Fowler, *Stages*, p. 178.
47 Fowler, *Stages*, p. 182.
48 Fowler, *Stages*, pp. 180–1.
49 Fowler, *Stages*, p. 198.
50 Fowler, *Stages*, pp. 183–4.
51 Moseley, Romney M., Jarvis, David and Fowler, James W., 1992, 'Stages of Faith', in Astley, Jeff and Francis, Leslie J., eds, *Christian Perspectives on Faith Development: A Reader*, Grand Rapids: Eerdmans; Leominster: Gracewing, pp. 29–57, p. 53.
52 Fowler, *Stages*, p. 185.
53 Moseley, Jarvis and Fowler, 'Stages', p. 54.
54 Fowler, *Stages*, p. 185.
55 Moseley, Jarvis and Fowler, 'Stages', p. 55.
56 Fowler, *Stages*, p. 186.
57 Fowler, *Stages*, pp. 187–8, referencing Ricoeur, Paul, 1978, 'The Hermeneutics of Symbols and Philosophical Reflection', in Regan, Charles E. and Stewart, David, *The Philosophy of Paul Ricoeur*, Boston: Beacon Press, pp. 36–58.
58 Fowler, *Stages*, p. 210.
59 Fowler, *Stages*, p. 202.
60 Fowler, *Stages*, p. 203.
61 Fowler, *Stages*, p. 318.
62 Fowler, *Stages*, pp. 201–3.
63 Modica, Joseph B., 1998, 'Stages, Styles, or Stories? A Brief Guide to Faith Development', *Catalyst*, citing McCollough, C., 1983, *Heads of Heaven, Feet of Clay: Ideas and Stories for Adult Faith Education*, Cleveland: Pilgrim.
64 Chater, Mark, 1994, 'In Stages or on Wings?', *New Blackfriars*, Vol. 75, No. 888, December, pp. 569–75, p. 574.
65 See Jamieson, Alan, 2002, *A Churchless Faith: Faith Journeys Beyond the Churches*, London: SPCK, and Aisthorpe, Steve, 2016, *The Invisible Church: Learning from the Experiences of Churchless Christians*, St Andrews: St Andrew Press.
66 Osmer, Richard R., 1990, 'Faith Development', *Harper's Encyclopedia of Religious Education*, New York: Harper and Row, pp. 252–3.
67 Ford-Grabowsky, Mary, 1987, 'Flaws in Faith Development Theory', *Religious Education*, Vol. 88, No. 1, Winter, pp. 80–93, p. 85.
68 Ford-Grabowsky, 'Flaws', pp. 80–1.
69 Ford-Grabowsky, 'Flaws', p. 83.
70 Ford-Grabowsky, 'Flaws', p. 85, citing Jung, C. G., 1967, *Alchemical Studies, The Collected Works*, Vol. XIII, Princeton: Princeton University Press, par. 38f.
71 Streib, 'Religion as a Question', p. 10, referencing Fowler, James W., 1991, *Stufen des Glaubens*, Gütersloh: Gütersloher Verlagshaus, 18f; cf. also his comment on this in Fowler, James W., 1993, 'Response to Helmut Reich. Overview or Apologetic?' *International Journal for the Psychology of Religion*, Vol. 3, pp. 177f.
72 Fowler, 'Postmodern', p. 163.

73 Holbrook, C., 1965, 'H. Richard Niebuhr', in Marty, M. and Peerman, D., eds, *A Handbook of Christian Theologians*, New York: World Publishing Company, p. 384.

74 Slee, *Women's*, pp. 166–7.

75 Estep, J. and Kim, J. eds, 2010, *Christian Formation: Integrating Theology and Human Development*, Nashville: B. and H. Academic, p. 176.

76 Furushima, Randall Y., 1985, 'Faith Development in a Cross-Cultural Perspective' *Religious Education*, Vol. 80, No. 3, Summer, pp. 414–20, p. 414.

77 Ford-Grabowsky, 'Flaws', p. 80.

78 Slee, *Women's*, pp. 31–2, 35–7.

79 Slee, *Women's*, p. 165.

80 Slee, *Women's*, pp. 35–6.

81 Ford-Grabowsky, 'Flaws' pp. 80–93 pp. 86–93 (See Fowler, *Stages*, Ch. 22).

82 Ford-Grabowsky, 'Flaws', p. 87.

83 Ford-Grabowsky, 'Flaws', pp. 91–2.

84 Streib, H., 2010, *Conceptualizing and Measuring Religious Development in Terms of Religious Styles and Schemata New Considerations and Results*, paper for the Conference 'Psychologie du dévelopement religieux: Questions classiques et perspectives contemporaines', Lausanne, p. 2.

85 Ford-Grabowsky, 'Flaws', p. 80.

86 Loder and Fowler, 'Conversations', p. 135.

87 Estep and Kim, *Christian Formation*, pp. 189, 183, 163, 166–7.

88 Fowler, *Weaving*, p. 92.

89 Parker, Stephen, 2010 'Research in Fowler's Faith Development Theory: A Review Article', *Review of Religious Research*, Vol. 51, No. 3, pp. 233–52. See also Parker, Stephen, 2006, 'Measuring Faith Development', *Journal of Psychology and Theology*, Vol. 34, No. 4, pp. 337–48.

90 Piper, E., 2002, 'Faith Development: A critique of Fowler's model and a proposed alternative', *Journal of Liberal Religion*, Vol. 3, No. 1, p. 7.

91 Streib, H., Chen, Z. J. and Hood, R. W., 2021, 'Faith Development as Change in Religious Types: Results from three-wave longitudinal data with faith development interviews', *Psychology of Religion and Spirituality*, Vol. 15, No. 2, pp. 298–307, p. 300, citing Fowler, *Stages*, p. 323.

92 Fowler, *Stages*, p. 179.

93 Parks, S., 1986, *The Critical Years: The Young Adult Search for a Faith to Live By*, San Francisco: Harper and Row, pp. 41, 73, 82.

94 Slee, *Women's*, p. 40.

95 Slee, *Women's*, p. 165.

96 Fowler, *Stages*, p. 199.

97 Astley, J., ed., 1991, *How Faith Grows: Faith Development and Christian Education*, London: National Society and Church House Publishing, p. 40.

98 Jones, Benjamin, 2022, 'Reimagining Fowler's Stages of Faith: Shifting from a seven-stage to a four-step framework for faith development', *Journal of Beliefs and Values*, pp. 1–13, p. 4.

99 Batson, C. Daniel, Schoenrade, Patricia and Ventis, W. Larry, 1993, *Religion and the Individual*, New York: Oxford University Press, pp. 74–5.

100 Piper, E., 2002, 'Faith Development: A critique of Fowler's model and a proposed alternative', *Journal of Liberal Religion*, Vol. 3, No. 1, p. 8.

101 Gilligan, Carol, 1982, *In a Different Voice: Psychological Theory and Women's Development*, Cambridge, MA: Harvard University Press, https://www-fulcrum-org.ezproxy-prd.bodleian.ox.ac.uk/concern/monographs/gb19f658d, accessed 09.05.2025.

102 Piper, 'Faith Development', p. 10.

103 Heywood, David, 2008, 'Faith development theory: A case for paradigm change', *Journal of Beliefs and Values*, Vol. 29, No. 3, December, pp. 263–72, p. 270.

104 Fowler, 'Postmodern.', p. 169.

105 Hull, John, 1991, 'Human Development and Capitalist Society', in Fowler, J., Nipkow, K. and Schweitzer, F., eds, *Stages of Faith and Religious Development: Implications for Church, Education, and Society*, New York: Crossroad, pp. 209–23 p. 214.

106 Parks, *Critical*, p. 38.
107 Parks, *Critical*, p. 12.
108 Parks, *Critical*, pp. 14, 19.
109 Parks, *Critical*, p. 17.
110 Parks, *Critical*, p. 24.
111 Parks, *Critical*, p. 27.
112 Parks, *Critical*, p. 51.
113 Parks, *Critical*, p. 70.
114 Parks, *Critical*, p. 95 and Appendix B, p. 208.
115 Oser and Gmünder, *Religious Judgement*.
116 https://sites.bc.edu/ipal-rd/in-memoriam/, accessed 09.05.2025.
117 https://www.amenetwork.org/remembrances/fritz-oser, accessed 09.05.2025.
118 Interview with Paul Gmünder by Doris Rudin, in *Schweizer Heimwesen Fachblatt VSA*, January 1987, No. 58, pp. 505–10, https://www.e-periodica.ch/, accessed 09.05.2025.
119 Oser and Gmünder, *Religious Judgement*, p. 4.
120 Oser and Gmünder, *Religious Judgement*, pp. 38–40.
121 Oser and Gmünder, *Religious Judgement*, p. 3.
122 Oser and Gmünder, *Religious Judgement*, pp. 23–4.
123 Oser and Gmünder, *Religious Judgement*, pp. 26–32, 23.
124 Oser and Gmünder, *Religious Judgement*, p. 57.
125 Oser and Gmünder, *Religious Judgement*, p. 3.
126 Oser and Gmünder, *Religious Judgement*, p. 40.
127 Oser and Gmünder, *Religious Judgement*, p. 4.
128 Oser and Gmünder, *Religious Judgement*, p. 9.
129 Oser and Gmünder, *Religious Judgement*, pp. 10–11.
130 Oser and Gmünder, *Religious Judgement*, p. 18.
131 Oser and Gmünder, *Religious Judgement*, p. 63.
132 Oser and Gmünder, *Religious Judgement*, p. 58.
133 Oser and Gmünder, *Religious Judgement*, pp. 64–5.
134 Oser and Gmünder, *Religious Judgement*, p. 63.
135 Oser and Gmünder, *Religious Judgement*, p. 57.
136 Oser and Gmünder, *Religious Judgement*, p. 65.
137 Oser and Gmünder, *Religious Judgement*, pp. 82–5.
138 Oser and Gmünder, *Religious Judgement*, pp. 85.

139 Oser and Gmünder, *Religious Judgement*, pp. 68, 85.
140 Oser and Gmünder, *Religious Judgement*, p. 69.
141 Oser and Gmünder, *Religious Judgement*, pp. 70–1.
142 Meaning in Latin 'I do so that you would do'.
143 Oser and Gmünder, *Religious Judgement*, p. 73.
144 Streib, 'Religion as a Question', p. 8, citing Döbert, Rainer, 1991, 'Oser and Gmünder's stage 3 of Religious Development and Its Social Context: A "Vicious Circle"', in Fowler, James W., Nipkow, Karl Ernst and Schweitzer, Friedrich, eds, *Stages of Faith and Religious Development*, New York: Crossroads, pp. 162–79.
145 Oser and Gmünder, *Religious Judgement*, p. 74.
146 Oser and Gmünder, *Religious Judgement*, p. 76.
147 Oser and Gmünder, *Religious Judgement*, p. 68.
148 Oser and Gmünder, *Religious Judgement*, p. 79.
149 Oser and Gmünder, *Religious Judgement*, pp. 80–1.
150 https://www.guinnessworldrecords.com/world-records/67373-most-weeks-on-best-seller-list, 598th week in 1995, accessed 09.05.2025.
151 'After many years of vague identification with Buddhist and Islamic mysticism, I ultimately made a firm Christian commitment – signified by my non-denominational baptism on the ninth of March 1980', Peck, M. Scott, 1988, *People of the Lie: The Hope for Healing Human Evil*, London: Century Hutchinson, p. 11.
152 Epstein, Robert, 2002, 'Interview of M. Scott Peck', *Psychology Today*, November–December, p. 70.
153 Peck, M. Scott, 1993, *Further Along the Road Less Traveled: The Unending Journey Toward Spiritual Growth*, New York: Simon and Schuster, p. 110.
154 Jones, Arthur, 2007, *The Road He Travelled*, London: Random House, p. 75.
155 Jones, *Road He Travelled*, pp. 78–80.
156 Jones, *Road He Travelled*, p. 82.
157 Jones, *Road He Travelled*, pp. 111f.
158 Epstein, 'Interview', p. 70.
159 Peck, M. Scott, 1990, *The Road Less Travelled*, London: Arrow Books, p. 10. Original edn, New York: Simon and Shuster, 1978.
160 Peck, *Road Less Travelled*, p. 9.
161 Peck, *Road Less Travelled*, p. 199.
162 Peck, *Road Less Travelled*, p. 205.
163 https://www.fce-community.org/about, accessed 09.05.2025.
164 Epstein, 'Interview', p. 70.
165 Peck, M. Scott, 1987, *The Different Drum: Community Making and Peace*, New York: Simon and Schuster; Peck, *Further*.
166 Epstein, 'Interview', p. 72.
167 Peck, *Road Less Travelled*, pp. 222–36.
168 Peck, *Road Less Travelled*, p. 207.
169 Peck, *Road Less Travelled*, p. 207.
170 Peck, *Road Less Travelled*, p. 207.
171 Epstein, 'Interview', p. 70.
172 Peck, *Road Less Travelled*, p. 288.

173 M. Scott Peck, letter appended to Wink, Walter, 1991, 'Walking M. Scott Peck's Less-Travelled Road', *Theology Today*, Vol. 48, No. 3, pp. 279–89, p. 288,
174 Peck, *Further*, p. 106.
175 Peck, *Further*, p. 111.
176 Peck, *Further*, p. 105.
177 Peck, *Further*, p. 105.
178 Peck, *People*.
179 Peck, *Further*, p. 105.
180 Peck, *Further*, p. 105.
181 Epstein, 'Interview', p. 70.
182 Peck, *Further*, p. 106.
183 Peck, *Further*, p. 107.
184 Peck, *Further*, p. 107.
185 Peck, *Further*, p. 108.
186 Peck, *Further*, p. 109.
187 Epstein, 'Interview', p. 70.
188 Peck, *Further*, p. 109.
189 Wink, 'Walking', pp. 282–3, quoting Peck, *Road Less Travelled*, pp. 288–9.
190 Wink, 'Walking', p. 287.
191 Peck, *Further*, p. 111.
192 Peck, *Further*, p. 111.
193 Jamieson, Alan, 2007, *Chrysalis: The Hidden Transformation in the Journey of* Faith, Milton Keynes: Paternoster.
194 Jamieson, *Churchless Faith*.
195 Jamieson, *Chrysalis*, p. ii.
196 Jamieson, *Chrysalis*, p. 5.
197 Jamieson, *Chrysalis*, p. 11.
198 Jamieson, *Chrysalis*, pp. 5–6.
199 Jamieson, *Chrysalis*, p. 96.
200 Jamieson, *Chrysalis*, p. 3.
201 Jamieson, *Chrysalis*, pp. 2–3.
202 Jamieson, *Chrysalis*, p. 96; see Parks, *Critical*, pp. 24–7. Brueggemann uses the idea of the pit as the place of disorientation in his orientation/disorientation/reorientation model. See Brueggemann, W., 2007, *Praying the Psalms: Engaging Scripture and the Life of the Spirit*, Eugene: Wipf and Stock, pp. 32–42.
203 Jamieson, *Chrysalis*, p. 98.
204 Jamieson, *Chrysalis*, p. 8.
205 Jamieson, *Chrysalis*, p. 9. See later for reference to nested dolls in the description of my own model.
206 Jamieson, *Chrysalis*, pp. 1, 6–8.
207 Teresa of Avila, *Interior Castle*, Fifth Mansions, Ch. 2.
208 Jamieson, *Chrysalis*, pp. 11–14.
209 Jamieson, *Chrysalis*, pp. 15–16.
210 Jamieson, *Chrysalis*, pp. 16, 6–8.
211 Jamieson, *Chrysalis*, p. 17.
212 Jamieson, *Chrysalis*, p. 20.
213 Jamieson, *Chrysalis*, pp. 21–2.

214 Fowler, *Faithful*, p. 72.
215 Jamieson, *Chrysalis*, pp. 25–7.
216 Jamieson, *Chrysalis*, p. 33.
217 Jamieson, *Chrysalis*, p. 43.
218 Jamieson, *Chrysalis*, p. 47.
219 Jamieson, *Chrysalis*, p. 33.
220 Jamieson, *Chrysalis*, p. 48.
221 Jamieson, *Chrysalis*, p. 50.
222 Jamieson, *Chrysalis*, p. 54.
223 Jamieson, *Chrysalis*, p. 57.
224 Jamieson, *Chrysalis*, pp. 62–70.
225 Jamieson, *Chrysalis*, p. 71.
226 Jamieson, *Chrysalis*, p. 61.
227 Jamieson, *Chrysalis*, p. 73.
228 Jamieson, *Chrysalis*, p. 74.
229 Jamieson, *Chrysalis*, p. 81.
230 Jamieson, *Chrysalis*, p. 82.
231 Jamieson, *Chrysalis*, p. 87; Rohr, Richard, 2012, *Falling Upward: A Spirituality for the Two Halves of Life*, London: SPCK, p. vii.
232 Jamieson, *Chrysalis*, pp. 86–7.
233 Jamieson, *Chrysalis*, p. 108.
234 Jamieson, *Chrysalis*, pp. 62–70.
235 Jamieson, *Chrysalis*, p. 33, citing Brewin, Kester, 2004, *The Complex Christ: Signs of Emergence in the Urban Church*, London: SPCK, p. 15.
236 Jamieson, *Chrysalis*, pp. 102–3.
237 https://www.spiritedexchanges.org.nz/, accessed 09.05.2025.

3

Progressive/Regressive Stages

Among the Faith Development models that can be corporately described as staged models, there are some that do not offer a simply linear progression towards an ultimate perfection. Some acknowledge that faith does not always develop in a direction of improvement but sometimes stalls or regresses. This is evident in five models that tend to reflect a faith development not of becoming but of being. These thinkers suggest that we are not simply striving towards some perfect icon of ourselves or gradually training to get fitter until we are at peak performance. Rather, we are on something that might be called a journey that is very much not a straight line and can involve doubling back, going round in circles or even simply sitting down at the side of the road and going nowhere for a while.

The models in this category come from somewhat different perspectives. The first is from American educationalist John H. Westerhoff III, the second from British feminist theologian and poet Nicola Slee. The third is a model by authors Janet O. Hagberg and Robert A. Guelich which comes from the popular sector of theological writing. The fourth comes from world-renowned Franciscan writer/activist Richard Rohr. The one with which we will start, perhaps unexpectedly given what I suggested in the Introduction about the reticence of certain parts of the church about Faith Development, comes from the American evangelical Willow Creek church network. Although these might sound rather distinct sources, there are commonalities. For Westerhoff and Willow Creek there is a sense of faith being deeply connected with community and both use organic imagery. The Willow Creek model echoes Westerhoff's tree-based analogy in *Reveal: Where Are You?*, using words like 'growth' and 'rooted'.[1] Slee's work, in *Women's Faith Development*, in part responds to Fowler's model with a feminist critique based on research into the faith lives of women and girls,[2] while in *Will Our Children Have Faith?*, Westerhoff acknowledges the influence of Fowler even if he moves away from the model as his work progresses.[3] Slee and Westerhoff also both have experience in ecumenical theological education institutes and therefore have lifelong learning as a key lens on the subject. Both Rohr's and Westerhoff's models come, as they describe them, from observation of their own Faith Development and that of others. Similarly, although Hagberg and Guelich do not demonstrate empirical research clearly, they do include the voices of different (sometimes unnamed) individuals talking about faith, as well as their own faith lives. Slee and Willow Creek both draw from qualitative research with individuals, if on rather different scales and with significantly different approaches to data. Slee's is drawn from in-depth semi-structured interviews with a number of Christian women. Willow Creek's model results from a large-scale survey of hundreds of members of their congregations.

Willow Creek

Willow Creek is a non-denominational mega-church based out of Chicago with multiple congregations. Their contribution to the literature of Faith Development predates the public revelation of sexual misconduct within the church and the attendant resignation of their founder Bill Hybels in 2018 (and the simultaneous resignation of the entire senior leadership and board of elders). The texts we explore to study their work on Faith Development were written by two people who were not named in connection with the scandal.

In the Introduction to *Reveal: Where Are You?*, the book that first contained their model, Willow Creek church leaders describe the motivation for the book as rooted in reflection that their members were not flourishing spiritually as much as they had hoped. They commissioned research to find out the reality of the Faith Development of their members. Their first book rather stands out from other sources on Faith Development as it has a magazine style and seeks to appeal to a broad readership.[4] This research was undertaken to help them plan how best to respond in terms of mission and discipleship to the current church membership. Nonetheless, the quality or style of production should not negate the fact that this model is founded upon some substantial research, possibly one of the largest surveys of people about their faith in recent years, albeit within a particular expression of the church and using not specifically theological or sociological models of research. The results are further explored in a much more substantial text, *Move*, written by the same authors, Greg Hawkins and Cally Parkinson.[5]

The Willow Creek research was conducted along the lines of market research.[6] It involved a series of preliminary surveys with 6,000 people attending Willow Creek, 300 surveys of those who had recently left Willow Creek, and then a qualitative phase with 68 congregation members in individual interviews covering 15 topics such as spiritual life history, personal spiritual practices, spiritual attitudes, church background, and so on.[7] This was followed up with a quantitative phase involving nearly 5,000 people completing a survey that covered topics including:

> attitudes towards Christianity and one's personal spiritual life; personal spiritual practices, including statements about frequency of Bible reading, prayer, journalling, solitude etc; overall satisfaction with the church and specific church attributes; most significant barriers to spiritual growth; participation and satisfaction with church activities such as weekend services, small groups, youth ministries and serving.[8]

This focus on 'satisfaction' does rather belie the market research foundations of the model, which is particularly clear when compared to the questions used in interviews for both Fowler's and Slee's models, which focus more on aspects of identity.[9] The group also included the 'study of scripture and more than one hundred books and articles on spiritual formation and human development', as well as consultation with experts in spiritual growth.[10] However, the authors don't specify which texts or experts these were. The first book opens with an explanation of the origins of the project and a brief description of what it calls 'The Church Activity Model for Spiritual Growth', namely that on which many churches found their concept of mission and discipleship. Essentially the premise is 'the more a person far from God participates in church activities, the more likely it is those activities will produce a person who loves God and loves others'.[11] Of course we would hope that being a member of a church would promote the development of faith more than not being part of the church; however, there is clearly something about the quality of the experience in a church in worship, community and mission that can help or hinder a person's development in many areas of their life, including faith. Nonetheless, faith is not just about presenteeism, as their research found. Involvement did not 'predict or drive long-term spiritual growth. But they did infer a "spiritual continuum" that is very predictive and powerful.'[12] They suggest that this discrepancy is 'because God "wired" us first and foremost to be in a growing relationship with him [sic] – not with the church'.[13] They found that the role of the church was more important in early stages of faith and less so for those further advanced in their spiritual growth, for whom personal spiritual practices rather than corporate activity promoted growth.[14] The group set various hypotheses to test via their data. These were: 'There is a migration path for spiritual growth based on church activities. The most effective evangelism tool is a spiritual conversation. Spiritual relationships are a key driver of spiritual growth.'[15] Statistically they make three demographic observations that gender and age had 'no significant impact on spiritual growth' and found no distinction between the experience of different churches.[16] Of course, if this research were extended beyond the Willow Creek network and churches rather different from this particular family of congregations were included, this latter observation might change.

In the subsequent and more substantial text, there is an exploration of what it means to 'measure the heart'. It is here that they come closest to defining faith in terms of what it is that they are seeking to describe as growing in their model. Essentially for Willow Creek, faith is about 'disciples who obey Jesus by loving God and loving others', and growing in faith means 'the people in our congregations are truly growing in love with God and extending that love to other people'.[17] The nature of this model makes it clear that it only seeks to measure the Christian faith of those within a congregation. Unlike Fowler and others, this model sees faith as a particular Christian commitment rather than the personal framework for understanding ultimate reality, transcendent of credal factors. The authors also identify modes of spiritual leadership that ensure the growth of individuals within congregations.

They explore what they call Spiritual Movement, the way people move from one stage to another, identifying three spiritual movements that rely first on teaching about faith, second on spiritual practices, and third on personal sacrifice. The authors describe spiritual growth that 'is not linear or predictable. It is a complex process as unique as each individual, and it progresses at a pace determined by each person's circumstances and the activity of the Holy Spirit.'[18] The research also identified people at various stages who had stalled or, in other words, who were stuck at one stage without progressing to the next. This concept of a hiatus is not explored in quite the same way as it is in other models. The tone of the descriptions of this stalling is not compassionate or exploratory, but rather problematizing. For those stalling within each stage, *Move* offers 'a solution'.[19] Within this model, it is clear that stages one to three are simply necessary steps to get to the stage desired, rather than valuable in their own right.

Willow Creek offers a model of people's faith growing in four stages, which they call the spiritual continuum. These are very clearly framed as coming to faith, and specifically a Christian faith, rather than an expression of faith throughout life. This is slightly different from other models we explore in this book. Researchers based the model on their dataset, which showed a clear distinction between people according to 'his or her personal relationship with Jesus Christ'.[20] This is predicated on adult conversion and does not seem to take age or psychological constructions of developmental stages into account, or pay particular attention to the spiritual life of children and young people. For each of these stages, the researchers established common behaviours and identified the needs of people in that stage. Using the market research model of drivers and barriers, they explored what might promote movement between stages.[21]

Their model therefore involves four stages and three movements between stages:

Exploring Christianity
    Movement 1
        Growing in Christ
            Movement 2
                Close to Christ
                    Movement 3
                        Christ-Centred

In the first stage, *Exploring Christianity*, the individual has some sense of the divine, or of there being something more to life, but may not see faith as a significant part of their lived experience. They do not adhere to any particular creed and are not engaged with scripture. They may seek God's guidance in times of need, or seek the help of others to interpret and understand the spiritual aspects of their lives. Willow Creek identified that the primary needs of those at this stage are seeker services and 'opportunities to connect with others'.[22] Although those at this stage were less likely to state that they read scripture or set aside time to listen to God, almost half of them said that they prayed and half of those prayed to confess sins.[23] This group showed high satisfaction with church services. Over 75% stated that the church provided compelling worship services, and 50–75% agreed with statements that the church helps them 'understand the bible in greater depth' and 'challenges me to take next steps'.[24]

What takes people to the next step is a change in spiritual behaviour and attitudes or, more accurately, an increase in engagement through activities like tithing, serving and evangelism. The researchers highlight that people in this stage, who have attended church for longer, are more likely to be stalled. In *Move*, the description of the 'stalled' is slightly more negative, saying that their spiritual growth is 'sluggish'.[25] The spiritual movement needed from this stage to the next is focused on what they term 'Christian basics', namely belief and some practices.[26] Their research identified 13 key catalysts for Movement 1, centred on four categories: Spiritual Beliefs and Attitudes, Church Activities, Personal Spiritual Practices, and Spiritual Activities with others. Of the 13, six fall within the first category, namely that an individual believes in salvation by grace, the Trinity, a personal God, that Christ is first, and the authority of the Bible. In terms of church activities, catalysts include serving the church, attending weekend services and small groups. Personal spiritual practices that help movement to the next stage are reflection on scripture, Bible reading, prayers to seek guidance, and prayers of confession. The one spiritual activity with others, which promotes movement to the next stage, is spiritual friendship.[27]

The next stage, *Growing in Christ*, is comprised of those who are still new to church but have committed to believing in Christ.[28] They are described as discovering faith and still needing others to help them in this exploration of spiritual issues, but in comparison to those in the first stage they 'willingly participate in small groups', serve in the church in other ways and sometimes read Christian books. Willow Creek identifies their key needs as small group opportunities, basic personal spiritual practices, increased involvement at church and also the incorporation of spiritual practices into normal routines outside of church.[29] There is a distinct rise in the number who read scripture in this stage in comparison to the previous one, as well as in prayer and confession, though there is only a slight increase in numbers of those who set aside time to listen to God.[30] Those who move from this stage to the next continue on this trajectory of involvement with church, but it is their engagement with personal practices that is most significant. *Move* characterizes those Growing in Christ as in the difficult adolescent phase yet also the most active in church life.[31] The research demonstrated that being active in the church was not what drives spiritual growth. This depends firmly on the growth of personal spiritual practices.[32] It is these practices that underpin Movement 2 towards the next stage

Those at the *Close to Christ* stage consider the Bible provides them with direction and that prayer is central for their lives. Small groups are less important, but spiritual friends increase in importance. This group tends to serve the church regularly, though, conversely, weekend services become less important to them. Their presenting needs are opportunities for service and advanced personal spiritual practices.[33] The number at this stage who tithe is double that at the previous one, Growing in Christ, and more than one in five agreed with the statement, 'I have six or more meaningful spiritual conversations per year with non-Christians.'[34] Where other models, such as Fowler's, have been critiqued for the fact that maturity in faith is linked to increased liberalism, those at this stage are described as demonstrating 'an increasing spiritual certainty – a growing confidence in the existence, dependability, and power of God's presence in their lives'.[35]

Within the spiritual continuum it was at this stage, at first, that the authors discovered a following intermediate stage of being stalled. In subsequent research, this category was evidenced at all stages and not specifically explored at Stage 3, so we will explore this category at the end of the model, where Willow Creek now places it.[36] Instead, the Movement 3 that they identify is the need of individuals to 'replace secular self-centredness with Christ-like self-sacrifice'.[37]

The pinnacle stage of the Willow Creek spiritual continuum is *Christ-Centred*, including those who might say, 'God is all I need in my life.'[38] They show increased levels of tithing, evangelism and serving,[39] and the highest levels of prayer and reading scripture. Indeed, prayer becomes a constant conversation with God. There is a significant rise in those who set time aside to listen to God. For this group, the church's primary role is to offer opportunities for service. Service to the poor is particularly significant.[40] They also mentor others and see service as a way of life.[41] Their primary needs are opportunities for service. This is the ultimate stage of the spiritual continuum. In *Reveal* the researchers identified a further group who have a similar status to the stalled group, whom they term 'the dissatisfied'. In *Move* they talk instead about the gap between what they say and what they do. In other words, they score highly on love for God but much less so on stewardship, serving and evangelism.[42]

The most startling discovery from the research is that many respondents described themselves as feeling stalled and others as dissatisfied. This concept of stalling in faith echoes the hiatus of other models.[43] In fact the *stalled* represented a quarter of those originally surveyed. The originally identified location of this stalling, between the final two stages of the continuum closely matches the mystics' models of the dark night of the soul or the critical stages of Westerhoff, Slee and Fowler. Those surveyed described themselves as, 'I believe in Christ but I haven't grown much lately.' As this data was based on the model of market research, this sector is identified as significant. If this data related to customers, a market researcher would be assessing how to keep them. The Willow Creek research echoes this approach and notes that a quarter of the stalled are considering leaving the church. No surprise then that the researchers took a closer look at those in this stage. Their engagement in some personal spiritual practices like reading scripture and setting time aside to listen to God dips back to levels of those at Stage 1. They also identify some negative practices that are 'significant barriers to spiritual growth', such as addictions (27% of the group), inappropriate relationships (16%) and emotional issues including anger and depression (48%). The largest common factor was the crowding out of spiritual life by spending more time on things such as TV, the internet, shopping (89%).[44] However, in *Move* they present rather different data, which suggests that those who are stalled 'come primarily from the less spiritually mature segments'.[45] They go on to identify three characteristics of those who are stalled, namely that they invest little effort in their faith, they are less connected with and more disappointed in the church, and they say they are too busy. Yet this group is complex. While others are very dissatisfied, some remain highly satisfied with church. The researchers suggest that 'a tool like a personal spiritual growth plan might address some of these needs'.[46] Otherwise, though, in *Reveal* they are not very specific about how those who are stalled get to the next stage. This is covered in *Move*, with the identification of the three movements between stages.[47]

In *Reveal* the dissatisfied are identified as demonstrating qualities of those who are Christ-Centred, such as the centrality of faith to their lives. They also express an eagerness to continue growing but feel 'my church is letting me down'. They noted that 'the people who are most dissatisfied with their church tend to come from the segments that are more Christ-focused'.[48] In *Move*, researchers observe that there is a significant overlap between the dissatisfied and the stalled and that the dissatisfied actually fall evenly across the four stages.[49]

My reflection on this model, returning to it a few years after I first encountered it, is to question whether the indicators of the stages are outworkings of the Faith Development of those at that stage or in fact if they are the instrumental factors that enable them to grow into or out of that stage. The Willow Creek team present them as characteristics, but where is the causality to be located? Is it through serving the poor that the Christ-Centred become so or is it, as Willow Creek seem to suggest, the Christ-Centred who tend to serve the poor? Although this research is clearly rooted in a church community, it is a very particular expression of church. If your church shares some characteristics with

Willow Creek, then this research would be fairly instructive and could well help a church reflect on its growth. Indeed, *Move* includes a section on Spiritual Leadership which addresses how to use their model to help leaders reflect on what it is that particular members of congregations need.[50] Willow Creek has also since produced two further texts, *Follow Me* (Hawkins and Parkinson, 2008) and *Focus* (Parkinson, 2015), in the more magazine style of the original book targeted at church leaders applying the learning to congregations.[51] However, if your church is not like Willow Creek, there may be some distinctive characteristics of such a substantial corporate or leader church[52] that would not accurately represent your local congregation.

Cally Parkinson has since written about different characters of churches and how they might best grow, which might have more to offer a range of churches.[53] The most important aspects of their research might be the reflection on the differing needs of new and long-established members of a church. If your church does not have many new members, this might be because you are resourcing the presenting needs of more established churchgoers. For your established members, consider what you are doing to offer them resources to develop those personal spiritual practices (which Willow Creek's research discovered were more important for them than church attendance). If we accept the researchers' first interpretation of their data, that the dissatisfied number highly among those who are Christ-Centred, it might be worth reflecting on Fowler's assessment of some churches being stalled at a particular stage. One could consider whether the church is stalled at, as Fowler might suggest, Stage 3 but that there are individuals who are ready to progress forwards but feel unable to do so in this particular church.

John Westerhoff

Westerhoff was an authority on Christian religious education. He grew up in a Christian home in New Jersey and, with his family, worshipped first in a Presbyterian and later a Dutch Reformed Community church. He took a Bachelor of Science in psychology at Ursinus College before studying for a Bachelor of Divinity at Harvard. His first role was on the United Church Board of Homeland Ministries, where he was the founding editor of the journal *Colloquy: Education in Church and Society* in which he published multiple articles on the place of education in church communities and, to a slightly lesser extent, the role of social justice in church life. He later lectured at Harvard, and received a doctorate in education from Columbia University before moving to Duke University's Divinity School as Professor of Theology and Christian Nurture. There, he was ordained by The Episcopal Church. After retiring from academia, he continued in ministry to three successive churches and established the Institute for Pastoral Studies. In one obituary, his self-description said his 'core identity was priest, pastor, and teacher ... [and] said he wrote like a painter, with flow from one question to the next without adherence to systemic thinking'.[54]

Westerhoff has written about catechism,[55] the role of Sunday school,[56] the parenting of children for faith,[57] the place of learning both in liturgy[58] and preaching,[59] and the nature of being Episcopalian.[60] The roots of his work are both catechetical and anthropological. He explores faith formation through what he terms a 'cultural anthropology'[61] and, as implied by the focus of much of his other published works and the title of his seminal book, *Will our Children have Faith?*, the concern for religious education of the young. Westerhoff's particular approach to Faith Development reflects his motivation for exploring it. He was concerned, as his title suggests, not simply with delineating the stages of a growing faith for the sake of mapping it. He was motivated by an investment in the religious education of children and of Christian communities. His perspective is one not of cognitive knowledge acquisition but of 'a developmental-interactional view of education' drawn from the likes of John Dewey.[62]

Westerhoff himself acknowledges the influence of Fowler's model on his own.[63] However, he differs significantly from Fowler and indeed increasingly, throughout his academic exploration of Faith Development, he moved away from the psychological school of faith formation: 'The process of spiritual growth is the development of consciousness and the wholeness of human life in moral community.'[64] Westerhoff offers us additional models to the tree-ring model of Faith Development (for which he is best known), one of which we shall explore in this chapter and, though I will mention another here, we shall explore it more fully in the chapter on cycles. His models form something of a family of interrelated ideas, each encompassing some element of story and rooted in common understandings of what it means to grow in faith.

Westerhoff's understanding of faith is certainly not purely cognitive nor derived from a set of psychological lenses. He describes it as

> the expression of meaning revealed in a person's life-style, or that foundation upon which persons live their lives, that point of centeredness or ultimacy that underlies and is expressed abstractly in a world view

and value system or, more concretely, in the ways persons think, feel, and act.[65]

Later he describes faith as 'a verb ... a way of behaving which involves knowing, being and willing'.[66] Westerhoff talks of faith as an expanding belief and in terms of individual maturity as demonstrated by actions and motivations:

> emotional and spiritual maturity begin when we give love without expecting anything in return. Only when we forget status, reverse roles, and wash each other's feet; only when we forsake ambition, pride, and greed and give ourselves to acts of unselfish love can we experience a life that is whole and holy.[67]

He places significance on the outworking of faith not simply as a sign of faith but as an indication about the nature of that person's faith. Westerhoff's view of faith prizes the location of an individual within a community:

> No one can determine another's faith and no one can give another faith, but we can be faithful and share our life and our faith with another. Others, regardless of age, can do the same with us, and through this sharing we each sustain, transmit, and expand our faith.'[68]

His model explores individual Faith Development but does so from the perspective of individuals bound together by ritual forming a worshipping community.[69] 'A community of faith is essentially a community interaction with a living tradition.'[70] It is through the experience of this community, not through the acquisition of knowledge gained by teaching, that a person grows in faith.[71] Within these communities of faith, Westerhoff suggests that individuals gain experience in terms of their faith in three stages: 'Persons learn first inactively through their *experience*, then by *imaging* (stories), and last of all through *the use of signs* (conceptual language).'[72] It's clear that Westerhoff's four styles of faith echo this process of experiencing faith, telling one's own stories of faith and shaping that faith in conceptual language. Across each of his models, faith is about inhabiting an unfolding story rather than assessable factors of cognitive and psychological development. He considers story to be at the heart of the Christian faith and therefore a story of faith to be the most apt model to track any sense of development in that faith.

> The Bible is a symbolic narrative. That is why it enlightens us about ourselves and fosters our growth. It offers meaning on varying levels and enriches our lives in countless ways. The means of each story will change at different times in our lives, insights will vary, depending on our needs and experiences at the moment.[73]

As Ronni Lamont has observed, one of the key differences between Fowler and Westerhoff's model is that, with Fowler, a person's faith moves on from one stage to the next whereas with Westerhoff a person's faith expands to encompass something new, always keeping the previous stage within it.[74]

Westerhoff described *Will our Children Have Faith?* as 'my first and perhaps most significant effort. All my other books either prepared me for writing it or have been in some sense commentaries on or expansions of thoughts in this seminal book.'[75] The model in this text is simpler than Fowler's, based not on empirical research but 'after reflection on my own and other's faith pilgrimages'.[76] His model appears in this section on staged models, though, when first describing it, he describes it as 'four distinctive styles of faith' that he had observed in himself and others. However, in the description of his model the styles are clearly described as stages, using the image of faith as tree rings building up in layers, with each previous stage contained within subsequent stages as a person's faith expands to encompass a new style: from Experiencing, to Joining, to Searching, to Owning faith. As we explore these, you'll see how they echo Fowler's stages up to Individuative-Reflective. Westerhoff deliberately does not go beyond this stage, acknowledging that his model is an 'attempt to distance myself from the faith-development paradigm with its cognitive understanding of faith and its preferential higher stages'.[77] He explores this further elsewhere, saying: 'Psychology, for the most part, assumes that human development leads naturally and rightfully to a final state of scientific thinking. Perhaps we need in our study of our own humanness, a greater awareness of the limits of cognitive theory.'[78] Westerhoff explores imagination not as 'a particular faculty of the mind, but a posture of the whole person toward experience'.[79] As his model's particular purpose was to help churches respond more appropriately to people in their communities, he does not chart the totality of the faith journey but instead focuses on enough to understand those coming to faith and those in early discipleship. In this respect, this four-stage model has something in common with Willow Creek's model.

Westerhoff saw the root of what he termed a 'crisis' in local church religious education for children because of the increasing problem of theological diversity. This theological crisis meant that 'the local church cannot develop an adequate educational ministry when the pluralism with which it lives lacks agreement on theological essentials'.[80] Westerhoff's solution was to look to a Liberation Theology approach, offering as it does a coherent 'unification' of attention to both the Christian tradition and social justice. He suggests that combining these two factors offers a hope of unity of approach to disparate parts of the church (via tradition for the conservatives and social justice for the liberals).[81] Westerhoff develops this further citing the concept of *via media*, which he calls 'a theological conviction that truth is comprised of two opposite truths held in tension'.[82] For Westerhoff, this 'being held in tension' includes the relationship between the individual and the community, where 'a community of faith has a common story, and its life is shaped by that story'.[83] Westerhoff offers two models in this progressive/regressive mode: the pilgrim pathway and his better-known tree-rings model with which we shall start

Westerhoff's model begins with the image of a tree and the rings it grows each year. He affirms the validity of a tree with only one ring as equal to that of a tree with three rings. Rings are added one after the other; without skipping or eliminating a ring but building upon the previous rings, 'we do not leave one style behind to acquire a new style ... we do not outgrow a style of faith and its needs but expand it by adding new elements and new needs'.[84] He describes it as a 'long pilgrimage',[85] expanding this in his later update that involves three paths: the Experiential Way, the Reflective Way and the Integrative way.[86] Westerhoff describes each style. The first is *Experienced Faith*, which he links firmly with children and the shared experience they and adults have with 'other faithing selves in a community of Christian faith',[87] by hearing stories, retelling stories and imagining. This stage is 'foundational to faith' and is not abandoned as other styles of faith grow:

> A person first learns Christ not as a theological affirmation but as an affective experience. For children and adults, it is not so much the words we hear spoken that matter most, but the experiences we have which are connected with those words.[88]

Westerhoff links this style of faith with James' comment on faith and works (James 2.18) and to *missio Dei* – God being active in making Godself known in the world through Christ (and, I would add, through the Holy Spirit). Westerhoff's second style, *Affiliative Faith,* is dependent on an adequate satisfaction of needs during the first stage. This suggests that Westerhoff's model is trickier to apply to those who come to faith later in life. Perhaps Westerhoff's roots in Christian education have influenced his model's alignment to a specifically Christian faith and community. In the Affiliative stage a person has a sense of wanting to belong to the group that they have experienced at the first stage and to contribute to the life of the community. Westerhoff also places 'religious affections' in this stage, citing the arts, awe, wonder and story as important aspects of faith. Westerhoff's earlier three-stage model is clearly echoed here. The Christian who has experienced faith in the first stage, in this second stage then goes on to story that faith. This storying is combined with a need for authorship, authenticity and authority. That is, the community needs to affirm the story told by the individual. Evidently the first and second stages connect closely. Only one who has experienced the community in the first stage of faith can retell the story they have been told in a way that can be recognized by the community. This is not mere recitation of cognitively acquired facts but a story of the heart retold by one who has been told the story and lived it alongside others. Westerhoff sees this as particularly vital for those in early adolescence:

> We need to belong and participate in an identity-conscious community of faith. We need to act in ways that nurture our religious affections. And we need to act to internalize, rehearse and personally own the story which undergirds the community's faith.[89]

Westerhoff links *Searching Faith* to late adolescence, saying it can only be entered if the previous two stages have been experienced. This is a time of the 'religion of the head', when questioning or 'doubt and/or critical judgment' are the prime modes of engaging with faith.[90] Again, this maps on to Westerhoff's three-stage model whereby concepts and signs are the final means of engaging with faith. He identifies experimentation as the logical outworking of this questioning stage. Although he identifies this stage with late adolescence, Westerhoff acknowledges that some adults will not have entered this stage. He describes the inevitable complications that arise in a community where those who do reach this stage are in conflict with those who have not, as 'they are often frightened or disturbed by adolescents who are struggling to enlarge their affiliative faith to include searching faith'.[91] This stage is a crucial one for the church, during which individuals will need the support of the community:

perhaps most crucial, we must acknowledge that learning is a process that goes from the inside to the outside ... we need to encourage people to trust their questions, to be open about them and to follow their own maturation or hatching process.[92]

Once these three stages have been completed, the individual, perhaps in early adulthood, moves into *Owned Faith*. This may be experienced, after the darker experiences of Searching Faith as 'a great illumination or enlightenment', which may well lead to social action and witness. Westerhoff states clearly that this personal owned faith does not mean that the community is no longer needed. Rather, 'persons with owned faith want and need the help and support of others in sustaining and putting their faith to work'.[93]

Westerhoff's own conclusions about the implications of his tree model are framed in terms of the duties of church educators. This has been expanded by Pete Maidment and Susie Mapledoram in their excellent work *Reconnecting with Confirmation*. One chapter considers at what stage the church should be encouraging confirmation. They acknowledge that the earlier stage of Affiliative Faith might be a more comfortable time to prepare young people for confirmation as they would be affirming the faith and re-storying it for themselves, but argue that the time of Searching Faith, though more challenging, would be more logical as a place for preparation with the actual confirmation echoing the transition to Owned Faith.[94] The danger here, of course, is that some in the Searching Faith stage might experiment with new ideas to the extent of leaving the church before confirmation. We would do well to reflect whether this is worse than people being confirmed, later regretting it, and then leaving the church. Westerhoff also acknowledges that the adult congregation may not all be at the stage of Owned Faith, so confirmation might sit less well in adolescence for many.

Westerhoff's reconfigured model using the image of three pathways for the same pilgrimage abandons his tree image, which he had originally described as 'the best I've found though still inadequate'.[95] For this new image of the pilgrimage, Westerhoff suggests that each pathway can be travelled at any time but that 'it is natural and wise for persons of all ages to begin with the first'.[96] This is the *Experiential Way*, which he calls a 'slow easy path' of participation in the community of intuition. The second path is the *Reflective Way*, which presents more challenges, such as 'traversing over rocks'. Although this way includes the support of others, Westerhoff describes it as a way of individuation and assuming 'responsibility for their own faith and life'.[97] The third path is the

Integrative Way, which seeks to 'resolve any dissidence that may have been experienced by traversing the other two ways, by bringing them into creative tension or integration'. This is a rather different model from Westerhoff's original. The three stages blur the boundaries of his four-stage model, with parts of Experiential and Affiliative to be found in the Experiential Way, and yet part of the Affiliative Faith and Searching Faith combined in the Reflective Way, and Searching Faith and Owned Faith combined in the Integrative Way. It is sketched much more briefly than his tree model and, as described above, the sequential nature that he formerly described as expanding gives way to a seemingly more disconnected model. Elsewhere, Westerhoff uses the image of pilgrimage through the embodiment of the Christian story by the church community as mapped against the church's liturgical year, beginning with Holy Week and Easter.[98] We will explore this more fully in the chapter on cycles.

Nicola Slee

Nicola Slee is a feminist theologian and poet with a diverse range of publications including poetry and writings on poetry, as well as other subjects such as rest, prayer, liturgical ministry, Feminist Theology and Faith Development. Slee's work on women's faith lives is founded upon a research project from 1994 to 1998 which was first explored in her doctoral thesis of 1999.[99] An article detailing her key findings was published in 2000,[100] and her book followed soon afterwards in 2004.[101] She has continued to work with other scholars exploring this subject through a project entitled 'The Faith Lives of Women and Girls', aspects of which have also been published in subsequent texts.[102]

Slee acknowledges that she builds on and challenges Fowler's theory,[103] offering a modern interpretation and a counterfoil to it and its strong association with theories of cognitive development. To correct the 'imbalance' that she identified in Fowler's model, she deliberately turned to 'the work of feminist psychologists and theologians and studies of women's moral and identity development, as well as feminist pastoral theology texts'.[104] One of the key distinctive characteristics she identifies for women's Faith Development (a corrective to Fowler's model, useful not only for women but for all) is the focus on the self. Fowler's sources for his analysis of development follow the 'classic pattern of male development', focusing on development as 'a process of individuation via separation from the other', whereas, Slee argues, 'women's spirituality is essentially relational in character, rooted in a strong sense of connection to others and an ethic of care and responsibility'.[105] She locates her work firmly in the field of feminist practical theology specifically as a subset of Feminist Theology.[106] She identifies her other sources as developmental psychology (for theory) and qualitative research (for her use of empirical data).[107] Slee interviewed 30 women about their faith lives. From this qualitative study she established ground for her model of Faith Development.

Slee identifies gaps in Fowler's model in three main areas: relationality, apophatic faith, and any analysis of people being stalled in a stage. She cites Robert Kegan in arguing against the very concept of faith being something that is constantly moving onwards and upwards to some kind of perfection in regimented and identifiable stages; too often such models tend to privilege the particular characteristics of a certain group or groups.[108] She identified that participants regularly offered metaphorical descriptions of faith:

> Whilst for many persons faith comes to expression and accountability through the symbols, rituals and beliefs of particular religions and traditions, many other persons in our time 'weave and paint' their meaning-canvases in communities other than religious.[109]

She records interviewees using powerful images in describing their faith lives. The women placed emphasis not so much on what happened in their lives as what meaning the events had. Slee's feminist critique of Fowler asserts that there are

> serious limitations in his work at a number of different levels. The sources drawn upon, the images and metaphors of faith employed, the models of mature faith adumbrated and the theoretical understanding and operationalization of faith and the account of stage development can all be critiqued for their inbuilt androcentric bias.[110]

In the construction of her own model, Slee categorizes certain schools of Faith Development based on what they each map. She describes lifespan theories, (e.g. Erikson, Levinson and Spencer),[111] structural stage theories (Piaget, Kohlberg, Fowler and Loevinger)[112] and models that fell outside the scope of Fowler in the formation of his theory, namely relational psychodynamic theories (Jean Baker Miller and Carol Gilligan)[113] and Dialectical theories (Belenky et al. and Orr).[114] Although Slee expressed reservations about calling her work a model of Faith Development, elsewhere she describes one aspect of her findings, her three movements, as a 'rudimentary model'. Slee identifies her work as not an alternative but a corrective to Fowler as she sees correlation between some of her findings and his model. For example, she connects the transition from Fowler's Stage 3 to Stage 4 with her own description of patterns of alienation and finds echoes of her descriptions of awakening and relationality with Fowler's Stage 5.[115] Her distinction between her findings and Fowler's is around the individuation he asserts necessary for owned faith at Stage 4:

> Many of the women's stories suggest the movement towards a more flexible and self-consciously owned faith, not in separation or critical distance from the relationships and commitments in which their lives are embedded but precisely in and through those relational ties.[116]

Slee describes her definition of faith as echoing Fowler's. She says faith is 'a lifelong dynamic process of meaning-making and patterning', though she adds her own hypothesis of faith as being 'an orderly and patterned deep structure in women's lives which integrates and gives coherence to all the disparate events of their lives'.[117]

Distinct from Fowler's model, she 'rejects the traditional image of the spiritual life as a lonely epic quest',[118] suggesting instead that, especially for women, faith is 'being in relation with God and/or the other'.[119] She calls for 'a more dialectical type of faith development theory' than has been offered by Fowler and others.[120] Much of her work focuses on what prompts faith to develop or recounts how faith has moved and changed in the women's lives. Slee's research explored key movements involved in women's faithing:

> I use the looser terminology of 'patterns' in preference to that of 'stages' deliberately, since, whilst there was some evidence of a developmental process at work in the accounts, my findings do not allow me to hypothesize a developmental sequence with any certainty.[121]

The patterns of faith that Slee suggests consist of two different elements. First, she identified the processes that women described as shaping their faith. Slee calls these processes of faithing, identifying six distinct processes: conversational faithing, metaphoric faithing, narrative faithing, personalized faithing, conceptual faithing and apophatic faithing.[122] Alongside these processes, Slee also identified three recurrent themes in the way women described their faith. From these themes she has delineated three movements of faith, namely alienation, awakenings and relationality.

Slee originally termed her first movement 'paralysis' though later called it *Alienation*.[123] She identifies an experience particular to pre-teen girls and fundamental to the later development of those individuals as women: girls realize they must choose between conformity to societal (especially patriarchal) stereotypes or authenticity to themselves and subsequent exclusion.[124] She supports this via a number of feminist academics who have identified this crisis moment.[125] It could be argued that this is the experience of all adolescents (not only girls). Slee identifies the intersectionality of this crisis and goes on to expand this idea to include the greater impact this would have on those from working-class or deprived backgrounds or those of GMH.[126] Whatever the cause of alienation, Slee recounts the stories of various interviewees who experienced 'powerlessness, alienation, impasse and fragmentation'. Slee connects this pattern with the concept of the desert experience, noting that though it may be bleak it can also enable growth to happen: 'The wilderness may, indeed, be a place of sterility and dark, but it can also be a place of vision, renewal and choice.'[127] This potentiality in the wilderness can therefore lead to the next pattern that Slee identifies.

Slee links *Awakening* with the first stage in Maria Harris's model (which we explore in the chapter on styles).[128] Slee's research identified different common sources for awakening including some that would match Fowler's idea of individuation, such as separation, leaving home or travel to a new country.[129] However, she also identifies sources that involve closer engagement with others rather than separation, such as motherhood, caring for a vulnerable other or coming home to oneself.[130] She also identifies the discovery of one's own creative voice and the experience of illness or bereavement as key patterns for Faith Development.[131]

Slee suggests that the women in her research demonstrate patterns of *Relationality* of faith as expressed within relationships but also that faith for them spoke of connectedness in a wider sense.[132] For participants, faith was about patterns, connections and an interwovenness of creation and humanity.[133] This sense of connection has implications for how we meet the other in terms of empathy. It was demonstrable in the way that women's patterns of faith found expression in the ordinary and the everyday.[134] This challenges the sense of Fowler's model as one that prizes individuation and suggests instead that integration not separation is the aim of Faith Development.[135]

In terms of how this model can be useful in ministerial practice, Slee makes her own suggestions in her conclusion. She is reticent about the very concept of models of Faith Development and sees them as 'useful heuristic tools' but

> more or less adequate ways of organising, relating and interpreting observed behaviour ... The very strengths of stage development theory – the suggestion of order and coherence in apparently random behaviour; its intuition of pattern across great diversity; its description of movement towards increasing flexibility, integration and complexity; its amenability to educational and pastoral application through the description of a normative pattern of development – are also its weaknesses.[136]

She identifies spheres in which her model would have particular relevance as theological education and the formation of people for ministry, preaching, liturgy in churches and other settings such as schools and prisons and in women's networks.[137] She suggests that the patterns and processes of faith that she identified can help inform the practice of encouraging and supporting women's spirituality by taking into account the importance of the everyday experience of women and not insisting that spiritual growth is only to be found in separation from their lived experience. She argues that current spiritual practice has 'prized the flight from the mundane, the denial of the body and the passions and the prioritizing of religious ideals of the demands of connection'.[138] To support women in learning and spiritual development, pastors and teachers should enable women to be rooted in experience and adopt models not of the usual 'banking teacher', who controls all the knowledge and hands it out, but as a midwife teacher who enables the learner to identify what they already know and assist them in bringing forth the potential within them. Slee asserts the importance for women as they grow in faith of the 'affirming other' and potentially the importance of women-only groups to enable this.[139] She suggests that an awareness of the experience of women in apophatic faithing, of defining their faith by what it is not, and those experiencing alienation would need such accompaniment.[140] The metaphorical nature of the way women described their patterns of faith in their interviews also suggests to Slee that engaging women creatively in acts of imagination in a local church would be fruitful.[141]

Janet Hagberg and Robert Guelich

In 1989, just after Fowler had conducted his research, Janet Hagberg and Robert Guelich collaborated on *The Critical Journey*,[142] which presents a model of Faith Development that was intended for popular consumption. Seven stages come with exercises and questions for reflection and there are links in the back of the book to a Spiritual Life Inventory, which readers are encouraged to access and complete and is still available on Hagberg's website. Though they mention Fowler and others in the field, they give no references and, though they include quotations from people they spoke to, there is no suggestion that this was as part of formal research but more in a supervisory, discipleship or formational mode. The model is presented to support the reader in understanding their own Faith Development, or support them as a leader with pastoral care of others' Faith Development. Hagberg and Guelich give good insight into their own backgrounds through their prefaces and the descriptions of their own personal spiritual journeys.[143] Hagberg grew up in a Lutheran family; her previous interests were in Christian leadership, social work and psychology.[144] She now describes herself as an 'artist, mentor, healer'. Guelich was the son of a businessman turned Baptist minister, with a BA from Wheaton College, an MA from the University of Illinois, an STB from Fuller Theological Seminary, connections to both the Universities of Aberdeen and Tübingen, and a doctorate in theology from the University of Hamburg.[145] He served as Professor of New Testament at Fuller Theological Seminary before becoming theologian in residence at the Colonial Church, Edina, Minnesota.[146] He wrote a book on the Sermon on the Mount and the first volume of a commentary on Mark, before his sudden death in 1991.[147] Hagberg had spoken at a conference that Guelich attended and he asked her to talk to his church about how people relate to God and to each other. From this conversation a collaboration grew to look at the relationship between spirituality and the world.

Their Faith Development model, *The Critical Journey*, was inspired by engagement with writers from the Christian tradition and modern writers on Faith Development. They mention Augustine, Aelred of Rievaulx, Julian of Norwich, Francis of Assisi, Ignatius of Loyola and Sören Kierkegaard, as well as James Fowler, Gerald Heard, Elizabeth O'Connor and Scott Peck.[148] They support their descriptions with references to scripture, though, somewhat frustratingly, without any referencing to non-biblical texts. Faith is a journey that they describe 'some people' as undertaking. Their model is designed for those who have made a conscious decision to acknowledge the place of God in their lives. It is not linked to any age brackets. Anyone starting out in faith, either as a child of parents who take them to participate in a worshipping community or an adult who decides to go to church, begins at Stage 1.[149] That said, much of their description seems to focus on adult conversion. They talk about a 'childlike faith' in Stage 1 (an odd description if this is the stage for children).[150] Like other models, theirs does not fully account for children's spirituality. Their model is further restricted as it does not cover faith life outside a relationship with God or indeed outside Christianity.[151]

In addition to the model of Faith Development, Hagberg and Guelich present a model for the Stages of Power:

Stage 1: Powerlessness.
Stage 2: Power by Association.
Stage 3: Power by Achievement.
Stage 4: Power by Reflection.
Stage 5: Power by Purpose.
Stage 6: Power by Wisdom.[152]

This gives a new perspective to what might prompt development in our faith and how different faith stages might reflect a different relationship with power. Hagberg went on to write further on spiritual development,[153] and about these stages of power,[154] echoing *Rollo May's earlier work on the spectrum of power*.[155] But here Hagberg has brought power and faith together in a way that others have not.

Hagberg and Guelich speak about spirituality more than faith, describing spirituality as 'the way in which we live out our response to God'.[156] They explore various ways in which the word faith can be used as a noun or verb and, recognizing the active nature of the word, come to a working definition in general as 'the process by which we *let God direct our lives or let God be God*'.[157] They also offer a definition for what faith is at each stage. Brian McLaren picks up on this for his model, which we will explore later. So, faith, depending on your stage, can be: 'Discovering God', 'Learning about God', 'Working for God', 'Rediscovering God', 'Our will facing God's will', 'Surrendering to God', or 'Reflecting God'.[158]

They speak about the factors that determine development in faith from one stage to another and whether there is a need for the specific help of others in initiating this movement. They conclude that at some stages it is vital as the stage is all about the relationship with others (e.g.

the movement from Stage 1 to Stage 2) or because it takes the support of a skilled professional, that is, from Stage 4 to 5 whereas other stages can be done alone.[159] They identify key moments in life that operate as a catalyst for movement to another stage. Their model is divided into two halves with development outwards in the early stages and inwards in the latter stages.[160]

They reject the idea that stages with a higher number are superior to previous stages,[161] portraying the stages as 'very fluid ... we can experience more than one stage at a time'.[162] This is rather distinctive, though bears some similarity to the work of Harris. It could suggest that these are more like styles of faith rather than stages, yet this is clearly not the case as, though there can be movement backwards and forwards, this movement, they suggest, is still within the framework of a 'home stage' (or even two home stages).[163] Like Westerhoff, these stages are nested expansions upon previous stages, not replacements:

> Each one builds on the others, and those we have experienced are readily available to us. Sometimes we revisit them by choice because we have a renewed need for community or because we sense again the awe of God in a deeper way.[164]

This means that,

> once you have moved to Stage 2, for instance, you can move back and forth from 1 to 2 frequently or be both at the same time. When you have experienced Stages 3 and 4, you can move fluidly among all four stages experiencing them simultaneously.[165]

This revisiting is always back into stages that have been previously occupied and can be fruitful as people are then able 'to experience them often in a deeper or more personal way than they did the first time'.[166] Hagberg and Guelich clearly allow space for the concept of regression and talk about people getting stuck so that a stage becomes a cage. These cage stages can occur when people become too comfortable in one stage or frightened of the next. Being stuck can lead to complex interactions with others because of an entrenched defensiveness, and a 'sign of stuckness is having to be right and convincing others of our rightness, at any stage in our journey of faith'.[167] The authors point out ways in which certain stages will interact with each other, especially those in different halves of the journey where the focus is inward rather than outward or vice versa. In the two distinct halves to the journey of development, they point out the similarity between pairs of stages: Stages 1 and 4, Stages

2 and 5, and Stages 3 and 6. These can be seen as echoing each other.[168] Stages 1 and 4 focus on our sense of worth but in different ways; Stages 2 and 5 involve letting go of something; Stages 3 and 6 include giving something away. Yet the most obvious distinction about this six-stage model is an additional stage that is not numbered. This is *The Wall* which stands between Stages 4 and 5. Hagberg and Guelich compare this to the idea of the dark night of the soul, though they make no reference to John of the Cross's work on it.

Stage 1: Recognition of God is initiated by the person making an active connection with God as significant in their life. It is characterized by a 'sense of awe' and a 'sense of need' for God.[169] People at this stage demonstrate a 'natural awareness' of God's presence and a 'sense of innocence'.[170] The authors cite the story of Zaccheus as an example of finding the 'greater meaning of life' at this stage.[171] However, it is also possible for individuals to get caged in this stage if they do not complete the movement that instigates the progression to Stage 2, whereby an individual experiences a sense of worthlessness and a failure to live up to the expectations of God and others.[172] The authors also describe 'spiritual bankruptcy', 'martyrdom' and 'ignorance' as characteristics of being stuck in this stage. It's a rather bleak portrayal (liberation from which is to be found in an acknowledgement of self-worth and a sense of belonging within a community of faith or under the care of a charismatic leader).[173]

Stage 2: The Life of Discipleship offers an individual a sense of meaning from belonging in a worshipping community.[174] This is accompanied by a 'sense of rightness', echoing the stories of the first disciples like Philip rejoicing on finding the Messiah (John 1.45).[175] This stage also involves 'security in our faith' as it is reinforced by the shared creed of the community, just as Ruth rejoiced in following faithfully with Naomi (Ruth 1.16).[176] Those who become caged in Stage 2 can be 'rigid in righteousness' with an unhealthy 'we against them position'.[177] Others caged in this stage might be characterized as the misplaced; they are either 'swtichers', constantly changing worshipping communities once they become disappointed in them, or 'searchers', who may be seeking to escape churches they have grown up in and outgrown or found, perhaps rightly, unhelpful. The movement from Stage 2 to Stage 3 is to be found in self-development and in identifying individual uniqueness and gifts and being ready to offer them.[178]

From this realization of their unique ability to contribute, those at *Stage 3: The Productive Life* identify their uniqueness within a community and take on a sense of responsibility to follow the call just as others in scripture listened to and acted on God's call.[179] This stage is 'closely allied' with the symbols of a productive life – responsibility, authority and recognition by others – though is also characterized by a deeper level of spirituality that might be explored and recognised through training or study.[180] Those caged at Stage 3 can be 'overly zealous', which can lead them to being 'weary in doing good' and lose heart when not appreciated or not achieving some unclear goal of 'making it happen', whatever 'it' might be. Another way of being caged at this stage is arrogance or self-centredness about uniqueness – no one else could possibly do what I do. Allied with this is a sense that life is all about what we do, so that life becomes a performance. The transition to Stage 4 can be a tough one. Hagberg and Guelich say it usually involves a loss of some kind; a loss of a 'sense of certainty', a 'personal crisis' of faith or a sense of being abandoned. A more positive route can be looking for direction. The catalysts of movement from Stage 3 to Stage 4 are ultimately 'letting go of success' and 'accepting vulnerability'.[181]

Some might characterize *Stage 4: The Journey Inward* as the 'life or faith crisis' and our individual response to it. Whatever the crisis might be (a crisis of faith or upheaval in our personal life), Hagberg and Guelich describe it as a time of 'loss of certainties in life and faith'.[182] This is a time not of searching for answers but of searching for direction, expressed in a 'pursuit of personal integrity in relation to God'.[183] It can also be a time when we let God out of the box of our former preconceptions. To some it might seem like an apparent loss of faith but it is, in fact, a necessary realignment. Hagberg and Guelich reference the story of Elijah fleeing to the desert after he was condemned by Jezebel (1 Kings 18—19).[184] It is a difficult stage and yet still one in which people can get caged if they are 'always questioning' or 'consumed by self-assessment', or through isolation.[185] Instead of being caged at this stage, an individual might prefer to regress to a more comfortable stage from Stages 1 to 3. The way out of Stage 4 to Stage 5 is enabled through letting go of 'spiritual ego' and accepting 'God's purpose for our lives', or through 'seeking wholeness through personal healing and pilgrimage', which means being 'willing to commit to whatever it takes'. The catalysts for this movement are 'finding peace through giving up the search for self' and instead 'allowing for new certainty in God'. For this, an individual must be 'open to the cost of obedience'.[186] This is where individuals on their critical journey of faith hit what Hagberg and Guelich call *The Wall*. This is not strictly a stage of its own but a key part of Stage 4. Hagberg and Guelich use this image of The Wall (reminiscent of those who have trained for long-distance running or other high-level sports) as an indication that of all the transitions this one is the most complex and difficult. They discuss various ways in which people resist The Wall. There are those without a true sense of self, 'strong egos' or, conversely, 'self deprecators' and those bearing a weight of shame and unable to truly accept forgiveness. Others who struggle with The Wall might be 'high achievers' or 'intellectuals' who cannot reconcile their worldly worth with the person they need to be with God. The authors also talk about those of extreme liberal or conservative theology who seem unable to reconcile God with their perspective. Special mention is also given here to those who are ordained or in a position of leadership in the church and feel a sense of responsibility to hold on to the faith of the church on behalf of those in their care rather than take the next step in relying on God.[187]

In order to go through The Wall, an individual must experience discomfort, surrender and healing as such a hiatus requires. This cannot be done without solitude and reflection. It also requires a four-phase process involving an awareness of our 'shadow sides', forgiveness of ourselves and others, acceptance of ourselves as we are and, through all that, the emergence of love for ourselves, others and God. Following this four-phase process there is a new closeness to God and a fresh discernment through 'melting, molding', reminiscent of the hymn 'Spirit of the living God'.[188] Going through The Wall as part of the journey inward is a necessary precursor to the journey outward, which is Stage 5.

Following the intense experience of breaking through The Wall, an individual has a renewed sense of God's acceptance and love, which also enables a new sense of what Hagberg and Guelich call the 'horizontal life' of *Stage 5: The Journey Outward*. This encompasses our care for others, either as individuals or through work for the greater good, and a renewed sense of vocation or a call to something new. This includes an abandonment of a need for achievement and a focus instead on the process of how things are done and the best interests of others or indeed of the world as a whole. This is accompanied by a sense of 'deep calm or stillness' whereby an individual lets 'God be God from the inside out instead of from the outside in'.[189] As saintly as this stage sounds, Hagberg and Guelich still suggest it is possible not so much to be caged at Stage 5 but to present to others in a way that is unhelpful. People can become 'seemingly out of touch with practical concerns' or 'apparently careless about "important" things' in the eyes of others. Of course, this is complex for a stage in which the needs of others are important to someone. It is possible to stay in this stage yet not be caged. It is also possible, of course, to transition to Stage 6. The movement to Stage 6 is a gentle evolution through the 'still small voice' of God and the catalysts for transition are a sense of satisfaction in a vocation and a feeling that 'being whole seems enough'.[190]

Stage 6: The Life of Love is characterized by 'Christ-like living in total obedience to God' and enriched by 'wisdom gained from life's struggles'. The outworking of this stage is 'compassionate living for others' and 'detachment from things and stress'. Individuals at this stage are equally comfortable being the leader and highly successful or undertaking menial tasks for others. This can seem as if an individual has abandoned their own life and yet can also present to others in such a way that 'others sense that God is very much at work' in the person's life in a way that will benefit many. As with Stage 5, no one really becomes caged in Stage 6 but the 'separation from the world' can appear to others as a neglect of the self or even an 'apparent waste of life', as the potential for greatness as regarded by others is seemingly lost.[191]

Due to its intended audience, this text could be quite useful in a parish, though the language of 'The Wall' and being 'caged' might be alienating for some. The model is accessible and relatively neutral as it references problems with both being too liberal and too conservative. It could certainly appeal to those who have a strong connection to sports such as running. There is a clear indication of the need for the support of others for some transitions, which could guide local church communities as to where to focus their energies in ministry. In some churches, the sense of there being a task to complete in order to progress could help them plan support targeted at these tasks, such as promoting self-worth (Stage 1 to Stage 2), helping individuals discern their gifts (Stage 2 to Stage 3) and offering support through trying circumstances (Stage 3 to Stage 4). The Wall could be a substantial focus of offering spiritual development by focusing on forgiveness, awareness of shadow sides (as long as it was in a safe environment) and exploring love for others.

Richard Rohr

Richard Rohr is a Franciscan friar and Roman Catholic priest born in Kansas. He has a master's degree in theology from the University of Dayton. He entered the Franciscan order in 1961 and, a year after he was ordained priest, founded the New Jerusalem Community in Cincinnati, Ohio. He also founded the Centre for Action and Contemplation in Albuquerque where he continues to be a world-renowned speaker and retreat leader as the director and academic dean. The vision for the centre is 'to introduce Christian contemplative wisdom and practices that support transformation and inspire loving action'.[192] The centre offers podcasts, online self-directed learning, one-off events and a two-year course. Daily emails are sent out to thousands of subscribers and Rohr has recorded numerous CDs and written a number of books on the nature of Christian living, scripture, the Enneagram,[193] Franciscan spirituality,[194] contemplative prayer,[195] and the nature of God.[196] He has been a supporter of the LGBTQIA+ community for decades, in 2000 endorsing a group called Soulforce which challenges oppression of that community by the church.[197] He offers radical challenge to the hierarchy of the church.[198] He has also written specifically on male spirituality[199] and collaborated with a feminist theologian, Cynthia Bourgeault, for an eight-hour CD exploring 'the issues of gender, spirituality, and Divine awareness'.[200]

As a devotional writer rather than a Faith Development modeller who uses empirical research, Rohr is not so concerned with specific definitions, thus it can be difficult to pin down what he means when he talks of faith. He comes close to a definition when he talks about the faith we inherit from the apostles. Pointing out how often they got it wrong or failed to understand, he says, 'I indeed share in this faith. We are all and forever beginners in *the journey toward God and truth*' (my italics).[201] He talks about religious faith as

> a vote for some coherence, purpose, benevolence, and direction in the universe ... Faith in any religion is always somehow saying that God is one and God is Good, and if so, then all reality must be that simple and beautiful too.[202]

When he talks about faith growing, it is in the context of greater diversification; faith demonstrates maturity for Rohr when it becomes less certain and more open.[203] He describes change as a 'slow process of transformation' but emphasizes the necessity of a crisis to make the real movement 'upward'.[204]

As a Franciscan friar, much of Rohr's theological underpinnings come from the Christian tradition. He liberally quotes from the likes of Julian of Norwich, Thérèse of Lisieux, John of the Cross and scripture. He also draws on a wide range of modern sources both academic and literary. These are not generally fully referenced as his texts tend to be aimed at a non-academic audience. He also mentions a conversation with Peck (see previous chapter) about the nature of faith journeys[205] and acknowledges the influence of Carl Jung on the idea of there being two halves to life.[206]

Rohr has written in various books on the nature of the faith journey and presents two models. In *Immortal Diamond* he offers Christ as an archetype for every human's movement from the false self to the true self.[207] In *Falling Upward* he talks about the two halves of our life and the need for a 'down-and-then-up perspective' which is necessarily counter-cultural to the success-driven modern world.[208] *The Naked Now* summarizes the teaching on Faith Development that had previously been shared in the CD *The Art of Letting Go*.[209] Here he presents a nine-stage model based on a shifting source of self-identity represented by statements relating the sense of self in relation to others and to God. Most recently, his overarching theme in *The Wisdom Pattern* establishes a basic three-stage pattern of order, disorder and reorder, which he sees reflected in many other models and links to Paul Ricoeur's idea of second naivety.[210] In *The Naked Now* the model he offers is more complex and involves multiple stages. We start by exploring his simpler model.

In his simple two-stage model, Rohr identifies a hiatus in faith. He suggests that the *first half of life* is about ego-structuring and creating a 'container' for your life. This is achieved by establishing boundaries through asking questions such as, 'What makes me significant?', 'How can I support myself?' and 'Who will go with me?' He argues that 'if a person has transcended and included previous stages, he or she will always have patient understanding' of those who have not.[211] Yet at the same time he suggests that those at the first stage will be intolerant of those at the second stage. Rohr here seems to tend towards an elitist construction of the world, which contains two delineated groups. Indeed, he goes on to use the term 'the initiated' and talk about the classic hero/heroine's journey as a pattern for the necessary encounter with trouble and the enlightenment received as a result.[212] This does not particularly honour those in what he calls the first half of life (which would include all children, for example). The *second half of life*, Rohr suggests, is the point at which you are 'led to the edge of your own private resources' through tragedy or an encounter with a particular person.[213] He is clear that an individual must have successfully concluded the task of the first half of life in order to stumble and then get up in this situation.[214]

Though the audio *The Art of Letting Go* covered his second model in more depth, the written description of this model is a brief sketch without substantial exploration or explanation for each stage. However, the titles for each stage are quite descriptive themselves. Rohr does not attribute any of these stages to a particular age bracket. Stage 1, he suggests is 'My body and self-image are who I am', during which an individual focuses on the need for security and safety and demonstrates dualistic or polarized thinking. His Stage 2 is 'My external behaviour is who I am', which echoes the performative Stage 3 of Kohlberg's model. There is a focus on the external reputation, in conflict with an inner shadow. Stage 3 for Rohr shifts the emphasis to 'My thoughts/feelings are who I am', with a concurrent development of intellect and will enabling the individual to control their thoughts and feelings and also hide their own shadow side from themselves. Rohr then inserts a barrier (hiatus) between this stage and those that follow, suggesting that a significant 'defeat, shock or humiliation' is needed to progress beyond Stage 3 to Stage 4, which is 'My deeper intuitions and felt knowledge in my body are who I am'. The revelatory breakthrough that leads to this new connection with these inner feelings can, Rohr suggests, also lead to a self-absorption that locks someone at this stage. In Rohr's model, therefore, there is more than one hiatus.

Stage 5 is the discovery that 'My shadow self is who I am', which he links explicitly with the dark night of the soul in John of the Cross. In this stage, the guidance of another, together with grace and prayer, are necessary to move forward and acknowledge weakness. Without this an individual will move backwards to a previous identity. If, however, an individual progresses, then the statements take on a new form and begin with 'I am'. Stage 6, which Rohr also calls 'God's waiting room', is premised on the statement 'I am empty and powerless'. The individual can acknowledge that they are not their own saviour by good deeds or particular devotion.[215] In this new acceptance, Stage 7 follows as 'I am so much more than I thought I was', in which an individual experiences the death of the false self and the birth of the true self. Rohr links this to John of the Cross's Luminous Darkness. Through this experience of darkness, the individual can come to Stage 8 to say, along with Jesus in John 10.30: 'The Father and I are one.' This stage evidences a humble confidence in a faith that does not need to be proved to anyone, and a focus on unity with God. This identification then leads to the final Stage 9 which, like Fowler before it, offers a seemingly simple construction of faith as 'I am who I am'; a simple 'just me' with no need for pretentions of religious devotion. This echoes the universalist stage of Fowler, having as it does something of a disdain for 'mere religion' though with a clear hint of theosis.[216]

Rohr writes in a popular style and is therefore accessible to many at a parish level. His work offers a choice of simple models or one with greater depth and complexity. His work, therefore, might suit a range of people. His models seem best suited to those who are well established in their faith rather than those who are newer to faith. Though he has clearly offered a great deal to those in later life, he might be a less appropriate choice if you are looking for resources for younger people as his models focus on adult faith.

Notes

1 Hawkins, Greg L. and Parkinson, Cally, 2007, *Reveal: Where Are You?*, Willow Creek: Willow Creek Association, p. 38.
2 Slee, Nicola, 2004, *Women's Faith Development: Patterns and Processes*, London: Routledge, p. 9.
3 Westerhoff, John H., 2000, *Will Our Children Have Faith?* rev. and expanded edn, Harrisberg: Morehouse Publishing, p. 87.
4 Hawkins and Parkinson, *Reveal*.
5 Hawkins, Greg L. and Parkinson, Cally, 2011, *Move: What 1000 Churches Reveal about Spiritual Growth*, Grand Rapids: Zondervan.
6 Hawkins and Parkinson, *Reveal*, pp. 79–88.
7 Hawkins and Parkinson, *Reveal*, pp. 92–3. There is some discrepancy in numbers. In the main text on p. 23 the number given is 120 but the description of the research design gives it as 68.
8 Hawkins and Parkinson, *Reveal*, p. 93.
9 Fowler, James W., 1995, *Stages of Faith: The Psychology of Human Development and the Quest for Meaning*, San Francisco: Harper, pp. 310–12; Slee, *Women's*, pp. 17–27.
10 Hawkins and Parkinson, *Reveal*, p. 23.
11 Hawkins and Parkinson, *Reveal*, p. 13.
12 Hawkins and Parkinson, *Reveal*, p. 33.
13 Hawkins and Parkinson, *Reveal*, p. 39.
14 Hawkins and Parkinson, *Reveal*, pp. 41–4.
15 Hawkins and Parkinson, *Reveal*, p. 30.
16 Hawkins and Parkinson, *Reveal*, pp. 32–3.
17 Hawkins and Parkinson, *Move*, pp. 12, 14.
18 Hawkins and Parkinson, *Move*, p. 26.
19 Hawkins and Parkinson, *Move*, pp. 35–47.
20 Hawkins and Parkinson, *Reveal*, p. 40.
21 Hawkins and Parkinson, *Reveal*, p. 38.
22 Hawkins and Parkinson, *Reveal*, pp. 37–8.
23 Hawkins and Parkinson, *Reveal*, p. 43.
24 Hawkins and Parkinson, *Reveal*, p. 52.
25 Hawkins and Parkinson, *Move*, p. 36.
26 Hawkins and Parkinson, *Move*, p. 22.
27 Hawkins and Parkinson, *Move*, p. 127.
28 Hawkins and Parkinson, *Reveal*, p. 37.
29 Hawkins and Parkinson, *Reveal*, p. 39.
30 Hawkins and Parkinson, *Reveal*, p. 43.
31 Hawkins and Parkinson, *Move*, pp. 49–51.
32 Hawkins and Parkinson, *Move*, p. 53.
33 Hawkins and Parkinson, *Reveal*, pp. 39, 42.

34 Hawkins and Parkinson, *Reveal*, p. 46.
35 Hawkins and Parkinson, *Move*, p. 67.
36 Hawkins and Parkinson, *Move*, p. 37.
37 Hawkins and Parkinson, *Move*, p. 22.
38 Hawkins and Parkinson, *Reveal*, p. 38.
39 Hawkins and Parkinson, *Reveal*, p. 46.
40 Hawkins and Parkinson, *Reveal*, pp. 42–3.
41 Hawkins and Parkinson, *Reveal*, p. 39.
42 Hawkins and Parkinson, *Move*, pp. 89–91.
43 Hawkins and Parkinson, *Reveal*, pp. 47–9; cf. Slee, *Women's*, p. 40.
44 Hawkins and Parkinson, *Reveal*, p. 49.
45 Hawkins and Parkinson, *Move*, p. 173.
46 Hawkins and Parkinson, *Reveal*, p. 53.
47 Hawkins and Parkinson, *Move*, p. 22.
48 Hawkins and Parkinson, *Reveal*, p. 50.
49 Hawkins and Parkinson, *Move*, p. 170–2, 183.
50 Hawkins and Parkinson, *Move*, pp. 193–255.
51 Hawkins, Greg L. and Parkinson, Cally, 2008, *Follow Me*, Grand Rapids: Zondervan and Hawkins; Greg, L. and Parkinson, Cally, 2009, *Focus*, Grand Rapids: Zondervan.
52 See Grundy, M., 1998, *Understanding Congregations: A New Shape for the Local Church*, London and New York: Mowbray, p. 36; Edgell, Becker, P., 1999, *Congregations in Conflict: Cultural Models of Local Religious Life*, Cambridge: Cambridge University Press, p. 14.
53 Parkinson, Cally, 2015, *Rise: Bold Strategies to Transform Your Church*, Carol Stream: Navpress.
54 https://www.gts.edu/latest-news/in-memoriam-john-westerhoff-former-faculty, accessed 09.05.2025.
55 Westerhoff, John H. III and Edwards, O. C., eds, 1981, *A Faithful Church: Issues in the History of Catechesis*, Wilton: Morehouse-Barlow Company.
56 Westerhoff, John H., 1980, 'The Sunday School of Tomorrow: It may be too bound to the past to meet the needs of a new age', *Christian Century* 97, pp. 639–42.
57 Westerhoff, John H., 1980, *Bringing Up Children in the Christian Faith*, San Francisco: Harper and Row.
58 Westerhoff, J., 1978, *Learning through Liturgy*, New York: Seabury Press; Westerhoff, J. and Willimon, W. H., 1980, *Liturgy and Learning through the Life Cycle*, New York: Seabury Press; Westerhoff, John H., 2004, *Living Faithfully as a Prayer Book People*, Harrisburg: Morehouse Publishing.
59 Westerhoff, J., 1994, *Spiritual life: The Foundations for Teaching and Preaching*, Louisville: Westminster John Knox Press.
60 Westerhoff, John H., 2014, *A People Called Episcopalians Revised Edition: A Brief Introduction to Our Way of Life*, New York: Church Publishing.
61 Westerhoff, *Children*, p. 140.
62 Westerhoff, *Children*, p. xiii.
63 Westerhoff, *Children*, p. 87.
64 Westerhoff, John H. and Eusden, John D., 1982, *The Spiritual Life: Learning East and West*, New York: Seabury, p. 122.

65 Westerhoff, *Children*, p. 40.
66 Westerhoff, *Children*, p. 87.
67 Westerhoff, John H., 2005, *Pilgrim People: Learning Through the Church Year*, New York: Seabury Press, p. 15.
68 Westerhoff, *Children*, p. 91.
69 Westerhoff, *Children*, pp. 54–8.
70 Westerhoff, *Children*, p. 66.
71 Westerhoff, John H., 1985, *Living the Faith Community: The Church that Makes a Difference*, rev. and expanded edition, Minneapolis: Winston Press, p. 69.
72 Westerhoff, *Children*, p. 61.
73 Westerhoff, *Pilgrim*, p. 7.
74 Lamont, Ronni, 2020, *Faith in Children*, Oxford: Lion Hudson, p. 85.
75 Westerhoff, *Children*, p. 80.
76 Westerhoff, *Children*, p. 87.
77 Westerhoff, *Children*, p. 128.
78 Eusden, John Dykstra and Westerhoff, John H., 1998, *Sensing Beauty: Aesthetics, the Human Spirit and the Church*, Cleveland: United Church Press, p. 53.
79 Eusden and Westerhoff, *Sensing*, p. 55.
80 Westerhoff, *Children*, p. 25.
81 Westerhoff, *Children*, p. 29.
82 Westerhoff, *Children*, pp. 45–6.
83 Westerhoff, *Children*, p. 74.
84 Westerhoff, *Children*, p. 89.
85 Westerhoff, *Children*, p. 96.
86 Westerhoff, *Children*, pp. 100–3.
87 Westerhoff, *Children*, p. 91.
88 Westerhoff, *Children*, p. 90.
89 Westerhoff, *Children*, p. 93.
90 Westerhoff, *Children*, pp. 93–4.
91 Westerhoff, *Children*, p. 88.
92 Westerhoff and Eusden, *The Spiritual Life*, pp. 125–6.
93 Westerhoff, *Children*, p. 95.
94 Maidment, Pete, Mapledoram, Susie, with Lake, Stephen, 2011, *Reconnecting with Confirmation*, London: Church House Publishing, pp. 58–63.
95 Westerhoff, *Children*, p. 95.
96 Westerhoff, *Children*, p. 101.
97 Westerhoff, *Children*, p. 102.
98 Westerhoff, *Living*, p. 30.
99 Slee, Nicola, 1999, 'The Patterns and Processes of Women's Faith Development: A Qualitative Study', unpublished thesis, University of Birmingham.
100 Slee, Nicola, 2000, 'Some Patterns and Processes of Women's Faith Development', *Journal of Beliefs and Values*, Vol. 21, No. 1, pp. 5–16.
101 Slee, *Women's*.
102 Slee, Nicola, Porter, Fran and Phillips, Anne, eds, 2013, *The Faith Lives of Women and Girls: Qualitative Research Perspectives*, London: Routledge; Slee, Nicola, Porter, Fran and Phillips, Anne, eds, 2018, *Researching Female Faith*,

London: Routledge; Slee, Nicola, Llewellyn, Dawn, Wasey, Kim, Taylor-Guthartz, Lindsey, 2024, *Female Faith Practices: Qualitative Research Perspectives*, London: Routledge.

103 Slee, *Women's*, pp. 8–9, 28–32.
104 Slee, *Women's*, p. 9.
105 Slee, *Women's*, p. 9.
106 Slee, *Women's*, p. 5.
107 Slee, *Women's*, pp. 9–10.
108 Slee, *Women's*, p. 16, citing Kegan, Robert, 1994, *In Over Our Heads: The Mental Demands of Modern Life*, Cambridge: Harvard University Press, p. 229.
109 Slee, *Women's*, p. 29.
110 Slee, *Women's*, p. 9.
111 Slee, *Women's*, pp. 17–19.
112 Slee, *Women's*, pp. 19–22.
113 Slee, *Women's*, pp. 22–4.
114 Slee, *Women's*, pp. 25–7.
115 Slee, *Women's*, pp. 164, 168.
116 Slee, *Women's*, p. 166.
117 Slee, *Women's*, pp. 163–4.
118 Slee, *Women's*, p. 107.
119 Slee, *Women's*, p. 139.
120 Slee, *Women's*, p. 166.
121 Slee, 'Some Patterns', p. 8.
122 Slee, 'Some Patterns', pp. 62–79.
123 Slee, 'Some Patterns', p. 10.
124 Slee, *Women's*, p. 84.
125 Christ, Carol, 1986, *Diving Deep and Surfacing: Women Writers on Spiritual Quest*, Boston: Beacon Press; Monk Kidd, Sue, 1996, *The Dance of the Dissident Daughter: A Woman's Journey From Christian Tradition to the Sacred Feminine*, New York: Harper; Ostriker, Alicia Suskin, 1987, *Stealing the Language: The Emergence of Women's Poetry in America*, London: Women's Press; Heibrun, Carol, 1989, *Writing a Woman's Life*, London: Women's Press; Belenky, Mary, 1986, *Women's Ways of Knowing: The Discovery of Self, Voice, and Mind*, New York: Basic Books; Rubin, L. B., 1979, *Women of a Certain Age*, New York: Harper and Row; Estes, Clarissa Pinkola, 1992, *Women Who Run with the Wolves: Contacting the Power of the Wild Woman*, London: Rider; Brown, L. M and Gilligan, C., 1992, *Meeting at the Crossroads: Women's Psychology and Girl's Development*, New York: Ballantine Books; Hess, Carol Lakey, 1997, *Caretakers of Our Common House: Women's Development in Communities of Faith*, Nashville: Abingdon Press; Osiek, Carolyn, 1986, *Beyond Anger: On Being a Feminist in the Church*, Dublin: Gill and Macmillan; Fitzgerald, Constance, 1986, 'Impasse and Dark Night', in Conn, J. W., ed., *Women's Spirituality: Resources for Christian Development*, New York: Paulist Press.
126 Slee, *Women's*, p. 85.
127 Slee, *Women's*, p. 106.
128 Slee, *Women's*, p. 110, pp. 176ff.
129 Slee, *Women's*, pp. 114–21.
130 Slee, *Women's*, pp. 125–9.

131 Slee, *Women's*, pp. 129–33.
132 Slee, *Women's*, pp. 140–5.
133 Slee, *Women's*, p. 146–9.
134 Slee, *Women's*, p. 149–54.
135 Slee, *Women's*, pp. 154–9.
136 Slee, *Women's*, p. 167.
137 Slee, *Women's*, pp. 168–70.
138 Slee, *Women's*, p. 170.
139 Slee, *Women's*, pp. 173–4.
140 Slee, *Women's*, pp. 178–80.
141 Slee, *Women's*, pp. 175–7.
142 http://www.janethagberg.com/uploads/3/9/3/4/39346357/spiritual_life_inventory_120910.pdf, accessed 09.05.2025.
143 Hagberg, Janet O. and Guelich, Robert A., 2005, *The Critical Journey: Stages in the Life of Faith*, Salem: Sheffield Publishing Company, original edn, 1989, pp. vii–xix, 20–30.
144 Hagberg, and Guelich, *Critical*, pp. viii, 22, http://www.janethagberg.com/background.html, accessed 09.05.2025.
145 Hagberg and Guelich, *Critical*, p. 25, https://www.harpercollinschristian.com/author/2366/robert-a-guelich/, accessed 09.05.2025; https://www.latimes.com/archives/la-xpm-1991-07-13-mn-1669-story.html, accessed 09.05.2025.
146 Hagberg, and Guelich, *Critical*, p. viii.
147 https://www.latimes.com/archives/la-xpm-1991-07-13-mn-1669-story.html, accessed 09.05.2025.
148 Hagberg, and Guelich, *Critical*, pp. 6–7.
149 Hagberg, and Guelich, *Critical*, p. 33.
150 Hagberg, and Guelich, *Critical*, p. 40.
151 Hagberg, and Guelich, *Critical*, p. 5.
152 Hagberg, and Guelich, *Critical*, pp. 189–214.
153 Hagberg, Janet O., 2013, *Who Are You, God? Suffering and Intimacy with God*, CreateSpace Independent Publishing Platform.
154 Hagberg, Janet O., 1984, *Real Power: Stages of Personal Power in Organisations*, Salem: Sheffield Publishing Company.
155 May, Rollo, 1972, *Power and Innocence: A Search for the Sources of Violence*, London: Souvenir Press.
156 Hagberg and Guelich, *Critical*, p. 3.
157 Hagberg and Guelich, *Critical*, p. 4.
158 Hagberg and Guelich, *Critical*, pp. 164, 167, 169, 172, 175, 179, 182.
159 Hagberg and Guelich, *Critical*, p. 14.
160 Hagberg and Guelich, *Critical*, pp. 11–12.
161 Hagberg and Guelich, *Critical*, p. 8.
162 Hagberg and Guelich, *Critical*, p. 7.
163 Hagberg and Guelich, *Critical*, p. 9.
164 Hagberg and Guelich, *Critical*, p. 13.
165 Hagberg and Guelich, *Critical*, pp. 8–9.
166 Hagberg and Guelich, *Critical*, p. 9.
167 Hagberg and Guelich, *Critical*, p. 11.
168 Hagberg and Guelich, *Critical*, p. 15.

169 Hagberg and Guelich, *Critical*, pp. 34–7.
170 Hagberg and Guelich, *Critical*, pp. 37–9.
171 Hagberg and Guelich, *Critical*, p. 39.
172 I Hagber and Guelich, *Critical*, p. 43.
173 Hagberg and Guelich, *Critical*, pp. 46–7.
174 Hagberg and Guelich, *Critical*, pp. 53–5.
175 Hagberg and Guelich, *Critical*, pp. 57–8.
176 Hagberg and Guelich, *Critical*, pp. 59.
177 Hagberg and Guelich, *Critical*, p. 62.
178 Hagberg and Guelich, *Critical*, pp. 63–6.
179 Hagberg and Guelich, *Critical*, pp. 74–6.
180 Hagberg and Guelich, *Critical*, pp. 77–9.
181 Hagberg and Guelich, *Critical*, pp. 81–5.
182 Hagberg and Guelich, *Critical*, pp. 94–6.
183 Hagberg and Guelich, *Critical*, pp. 97–8.
184 Hagberg and Guelich, *Critical*, pp. 99–101.
185 Hagberg and Guelich, *Critical*, pp. 105–6.
186 Hagberg and Guelich, *Critical*, pp. 106–9.
187 Hagberg and Guelich, *Critical*, pp. 116–18.
188 Hagberg and Guelich, *Critical*, pp. 120–3.
189 Hagberg and Guelich, *Critical*, pp. 136–40.
190 Hagberg and Guelich, *Critical*, pp. 144–7.
191 Hagberg and Guelich, *Critical*, pp. 153–8.
192 https://cac.org/about/what-we-do/, accessed 09.05.2026.
193 Rohr, Richard, 1992, *Experiencing the Enneagram*, New York: Crossroad; Rohr, Richard, 1994, *Enneagram II: Advancing Spiritual Discernment*, New York: Crossroad; Rohr, Richard and Ebert, Andreas, 2002, *The Enneagram: A Christian Perspective*, New York: Crossroad.
194 Rohr, Richard, 2002, *Hope Against Darkness: The Transforming Vision of Saint Francis in an Age of Anxiety*, Cincinnati: Franciscan Media; Rohr, Richard, 2014, *Eager to Love: The Alternative Way of Francis of Assisi*, London: Hodder and Stoughton.
195 Rohr, Richard, 2003, *Everything Belongs: The Gift of Contemplative Prayer*, New York: Crossroad; Rohr, Richard, 2014, *Silent Compassion: Finding God in Contemplation*, Cincinnati: Franciscan Media.
196 Rohr, Richard, 2019, *The Universal Christ: How a Forgotten Reality Can Change Everything We See, Hope For and Believe* New York: Convergent Books.
197 https://soulforce.org/, accessed 09.05.2025.
198 Rohr, Richard, with Morrell, Mike, 2016, *The Divine Dance: The Trinity and Your Transformation*, London: SPCK.
199 Rohr, Richard and Martos, Joseph, 1991, *The Wild Man's Journey: Reflections on Male Spirituality*, Cincinnati: Franciscan Media; Rohr, Richard, 2010, *On the Threshold of Transformation: Daily Meditations for Men*, Chicago: Loyola Press.
200 https://store.cac.org/collections/the-divine-feminine/products/god-as-us-the-sacred-feminine-the-sacred-masculine-mp3, accessed 09.05.2025.
201 Rohr, Richard, 2012, *Falling Upward: A Spirituality for the Two Halves of Life*, London: SPCK, p. 100.

202 Rohr, *Falling*, p. 111.
203 Rohr, *Falling*, p. 103.
204 Rohr, *Falling*, p. 65.
205 Rohr, *Falling*, pp. xix–xx.
206 Rohr, *Falling*, p. 8.
207 Rohr, Richard, 2013, *Immortal Diamond: The Search for Our True Self*, London: SPCK.
208 Rohr, *Falling*, p. xxi.
209 Rohr, Richard, 2009, *The Naked Now: Learning to See as the Mystics See*, New York: Crossroad Publishing Company, pp. 164–6.
210 Rohr, Richard, 2020, *The Wisdom Pattern: Order, Disorder, Reorder*, Cincinnati: Franciscan Media.
211 Rohr, *Falling*, pp. 1–4.
212 Rohr, *Falling*, pp. 9, 18–19.
213 Rohr, *Falling*, p. 65.
214 Rohr, *Falling*, p. 71.
215 Rohr, *The Naked Now*; Rohr, Richard, 2010, *The Art of Letting Go: Living the Wisdom of St. Francis*, Louisville: Sounds True Inc.
216 Rohr, *The Art*, chapter headings.

4

Cycles

There are two groups of models that use the word season. I use the term 'cycle' in order to clarify that the models I am looking at here are those that use the full model of the seasons as they turn in an ongoing cycle. These models of Faith Development identify particular styles of faith that do not progress forwards, with or without regression, but simply cycle through over and over again. Some other texts also use the term season to mean four phases in a single cycle throughout a person's lifecycle. I cover this second group also in this section (though they might more rightly feature in the stage section) because they each focus strongly on seasonality and share some of the characteristics of seasons described in other models that are more genuinely cyclical. Daniel Levinson, Anita Spencer and Paul Tournier have written about the seasons of a person's life, not specifically with reference to faith but in ways that speak of the kind of lived experience that Faith Development models explore. We will reflect on each of these before looking at the model offered by Dick Hall, which does come from a theological perspective and also talks about seasons identifying spring with early life and winter with the end of life.

Having explored these texts which look at a single cycle of the seasons, we will move on to look at the truly cyclical models. These are those that identify our experience of faith throughout life not as an onward progression from one stage to the next but as something that is experienced through a number of distinct and connected repeating phases which follow each other invariably in a particular order. Brian McLaren and Richard Blackaby both present such cyclical models of Faith Development using the term seasons.[1] When we explored the models of Westerhoff earlier, I mentioned a cyclical model that he proposed, so, in addition to these models from new voices in our conversation, in this section we will also explore Westerhoff's cyclical model.

The first of our non-theological seasonal models is the research conducted by Daniel Levinson into the lives of men.[2] He used seasons as a way of exploring the ageing process of men and the attendant life changes. This is reminiscent of Shakespeare's idea of the seven 'ages of man':

> All the world's a stage,
> And all the men and women merely players;
> They have their exits and their entrances;
> And one man in his time plays many parts,
> His acts being seven ages. At *first the infant*,
> Mewling and puking in the nurse's arms;
> And then *the whining school-boy*, with his satchel
> And shining morning face, creeping like snail
> Unwillingly to school. And then *the lover*,
> Sighing like furnace, with a woeful ballad
> Made to his mistress' eyebrow. Then *a soldier*,
> Full of strange oaths, and bearded like the pard,
> Jealous in honour, sudden and quick in quarrel,
> Seeking the bubble reputation
> Even in the cannon's mouth. And then *the justice*,
> In fair round belly with good capon lin'd,
> With eyes severe and beard of formal cut,
> Full of wise saws and modern instances;
> And so he plays his part. The *sixth age* shifts
> Into the lean and slipper'd pantaloon,
> With spectacles on nose and pouch on side;
> His youthful hose, well sav'd, a world too wide
> For his shrunk shank; and his big manly voice,
> Turning again toward childish treble, pipes
> And whistles in his sound. Last scene of all,
> That ends this strange eventful history,
> Is *second childishness* and mere oblivion;
> Sans teeth, sans eyes, sans taste, sans everything.[3]

Levinson interviewed 40 men about their lived experience and then identified what he called *The Seasons of a Man's Life*. He essentially divided the lifeline of the male lived experience into a series of seasons, each with a distinct character. The 11 seasons he identified were Early Adult Transition (17–22), Entering the First Structure (22–28), Age Thirty Transition (28–33), Settling Down into Second Structure (33–40), Mid Transition (40–45), Entering the Mid-Structure (45–50), Age Fifty Transition (50–55), Building a Second Mid-Structure (55–60), Late Transition (60–65), Late Adulthood (65–80) and Late, Late Adulthood (80+).

From the very start of her work, it is clear that Anita Spencer is responding to Levinson's *The Seasons of a Man's Life*. She quotes from his text early in her introduction and sets out her own response to his work:

> I found both the Levinson and Vaillant studies to be of significant interest. But as I reviewed their work I kept wondering if the woman's life-cycle development would follow the same pattern as the man's. I thought about this issue at great length and talked to many women friends about this and related matters. As I pondered over my own life, I saw many discrepancies between my experience and those of the men reported on in these studies. As a result, I concluded that the seasons of a woman's life would be significantly different from those of a man's life.[4]

She clearly adopts Levinson's lifecycle in terms of ages, and in exploring each in turn she refers to Levinson.[5] However, she doesn't adopt Levinson's method of interviewing to conduct her own interviews, but instead turns to a variety of writers on female development such as Washbourn and Hoffman, or other research projects that gained similar qualitative data to that of Levinson from interviews with women.[6] Spencer's perspective as a sociologist and psychologist is focused not explicitly on faith but explores the quest for ego-autonomy, which she summarizes as three perspectives: the woman's sociocultural world, the woman's self (whether lived out, inhibited or neglected), and the woman's participation in the world.[7] Her socio-psychological approach is coupled with an element of autoethnography as she seeks to understand her own lived experience. She explores seasons both as an ongoing cycle and as a series of periods of life.[8]

Swiss psychiatrist and physician Paul Tournier has written of the seasons of life in a similar fashion to Levinson and Spencer. He incorporates psychological insights from the likes of Jung, Freud and Buber as well as scriptural examples. His model maps the whole of a person's life across the seasons, with childhood represented by spring as a time of passive consumption,[9] summer equated with adulthood and the season of productivity and action, and autumn as the declining years of retirement when action gives way to being.[10] He identifies Winter as that season beyond death when a person shall truly become themselves in the fullness of God.[11] For Tournier, therefore, there are what he calls 'two great turning-points in life: the passage from childhood to adulthood and that from adulthood to old age'.[12]

There are some theological writers who talk about seasons in Faith Development without going as far as presenting formal models. Ross

Thompson explored faith through the Christian year.[13] Thompson was a parish priest in Bristol for 20 years and taught systematics and spirituality at St Michael's College, Llandaff, and Cardiff University.[14] He roots his work in the field of spirituality rather than in Faith Development and, though he makes mention of Fowler, notably alongside Jung and Erikson, he admits to a lack of rigorous engagement with reference to Faith Development and tends towards summarizing faith stages from a more sociological and less theological stance:

> In terms of the classic spiritual stages – and generalising wildly – our early years are generally spent on illumination; it is the time when we are educated … This gives way in early adulthood to an active time of work, family-building and achievement … In middle age, this can lead to a 'mid-life crisis' – a time of doubt when the temporal finitude of life begins to bear down on us, requiring the purgation of much that was once held dear. Finally the weakening of our faculties marks the onset of old age, which can lead to bitterness and regret or to deepening union with God.[15]

Similarly, Canadian writer Mark Buchanan writes about seasons and rhythms to help people understand their spiritual lives. Buchanan is a Canadian academic who works in the field of Pastoral Theology and, although he doesn't present a model of Faith Development as such, he describes the seasonality of our spiritual experiences in terms of winter, spring, summer and autumn. He talks about the tasks of each season and within those tasks he uses various metaphors regarding trees, such as pruning and planting.[16] He draws mostly on scripture and his own life experiences to give encouragement to people to live with and respond appropriately to the four spiritual seasons. He then goes on to present what he calls 'a collection of musings, eight in all, about spiritual rhythm'.[17] He goes on to echo Westerhoff's model and explore his own spiritual life as made up of tree rings, and reflect upon those years where growth was more substantial and those where it was weaker. Though both Thompson and Buchanan might be interesting conversation partners with Westerhoff's work, neither quite qualify in their own right to offer a seasonal model. They offer some metaphors that are echoed in part in my own model at the end of this book, though my model has more in common in structural terms with the two genuinely cyclical models that follow.

Dick Hall

Dick Hall's work on seasons emphasizes the natural rhythms present in the Bible and in life.[18] Hall was a British United Reformed Church (URC) pastor and theological educator. Born in 1911 he trained at New College, London and served in local churches in Haywards Heath, Potters Barr and Brookmans Park, and Cambridge. He was Youth Secretary of the Congregational Union of England and Wales and tutor at Cheshunt College, Cambridge. He served as moderator of the URC for a total of 13 years and was elected to the highest office in the URC, the Moderatorship of Assembly from 1976 to 1977. He retired in 1978 and died after a short illness in October 1990. He was described in his obituary as 'completely unspoiled by high office and countless ministers and church members always found in him a sympathetic listener and staunch friend'.[19] His extensive pastoral experience evidently underpins his work, with a close engagement with scripture.

Hall was not setting out to write a book delineating stages of faith, and therefore does not give a definition of faith, nor indeed speak about faith specifically very much except in his third chapter on 'Seasons of Faith'. Even here he talks rather more about the seasons of the church, though he does say this:

> Other seasons come upon us in our Christian life. There are times of doubt and of assured faith. Sometimes they really do seem to be seasonal and we should all beware of criticising those who feel differently. Some of those who feel deep certainty about their faith, who often boast that they never have doubts, look scornfully, pityingly, on others who confess to doubts, almost suggesting that something is morally wrong with them. And many a doubter says that belief comes too easily to the people of the assured faith, as though they had not even asked questions.[20]

His text is focused on seasonality within the life of Christians and so it is seasons that he defines. He links the seasons he explores firmly to scripture from the very start:

> They are as fixed as Ecclesiastes suggests. Spring, Summer, Autumn, Winter – we cannot create them. Day and night – they move on regardless of anything we can do. There are seasons of faith and of experience that come to us as given from outside. Yet in fact they are not always rigidly separated.[21]

This is a somewhat confusing statement as, at first, Hall emphasizes the rigidity of the seasons but then suggests they are not rigid. He also describes not only these external seasons which fall outside an individual's control but also talks about certain personal rhythms of life, 'which we create or encourage, times of hard work, of study, of faith and of worship'.[22] Hall makes clear that, although he describes the seasons individually, they are inseparable and make up between them something that is whole. This echoes Oser and Gmünder's concept of models needing to be coherent.[23] He links the seasons to God's promise to Noah and his family in Genesis 8.22, that after the flood the seasons will turn as usual. He also explores our relationship with the seasons as exemplified in W. B. Yeats's poem 'The Wheel':

Through winter-time we call on spring,
And through the spring on summer call,[24]

Yeats's image is, characteristically, that of a human fighting against these imposed forces of nature. Hall, however, goes on to describe the seasons in turn in a more positive light as differing times to be embraced for their unique purposes.

Spring, says Hall, is a time of expectance and awakening, followed by summer as a season of activity, work and play alike.[25] Autumn he calls a season of completion and fruitfulness, and winter as a time of catching up and preparing, of drawing in.[26] He goes on to trace these four seasons on to a single day: morning with spring, midday with summer, evening with autumn and winter with night.[27] Although Hall does not explicitly set out his work as a model of Faith Development, he is clearly encouraging people to think in terms of these seasons for their spiritual and working lives. In addition to the external seasons, he explores the internal seasons of faith and doubt and the potential link between the two: 'The season of faith may well follow the time of doubt. So much depends upon our willingness to face both honestly.'[28] Hall seems therefore to antithesize faith and doubt. I would suggest, as other models have hinted, that doubt is part of faith not its opposite. Hall also looks at seasons that come only once, especially the seasons of a person's life: childhood, youth, maturity and old age.[29] Through these, he explores a patterned season of giving and receiving, with receiving during childhood and old age, and giving in midlife.[30]

There is another set of seasons that Hall explores more clearly in terms of an ongoing cycle. He notes how the people of Israel's life with God was also ordered by certain seasons[31] and how, similarly, those of us in modern Christian churches follow a pattern of seasons to a lesser or greater extent through Advent, Christmas, Epiphany, Lent, Passiontide, Holy Week and Easter, Pentecost, Trinity and the season after Trinity.[32] Yet Hall does not go into great depth as to how these seasons relate to an individual's or indeed a community's faith. Westerhoff has, however, done this work. Drawing strongly on Ecclesiastes 3 and Genesis 8.22 for the foundation of his model, Richard Blackaby claims to reject the association of the seasons with the ageing and maturing process as a single iteration of each season and suggests that what he offers is a cyclical model.[33]

Richard Blackaby

Richard Blackaby is a pastor born in Saskatoon, Saskatchewan, Canada and currently serves in Atlanta, Georgia. His academic origins are in history, with a BA from the University of Saskatchewan and an MDiv and PhD in church history from Southwestern Baptist Theological Seminary. He also has an honorary doctorate from Dallas Baptist University.[34] He has written dozens of books on Christian living, including topics such as leadership, faith at home, parenting, prayer and biblical reflection. Rather than using empirical data or engagement with any other Faith Development models, Blackaby's work is drawn from some autoethnographic reflection, such as his reflection on a series of new beginnings or spring seasons in his life.[35] Through his text, we get a sense of the person behind the model.

Blackaby draws more widely, and arguably more consistently, on scripture for each of his explorations of the seasons than other models we have considered. This results in his model being less well defined as a Faith Development model though much more richly resourced theologically. For each season, he explores one of four facets through a variety of sources, many of them, though not all, biblical passages. For example, in exploring the spring of self, Blackaby uses the lenses of 'newness of life' (Rom. 6.4), 'new self' (Col. 3.10), 'newness of the Spirit' (Rom. 7.6), Christ 'making all things new' (2 Cor. 5.17) and the concept of being 'transformed by the renewing of your mind' (Rom. 12). He goes on to engage with the stories of Noah, then Isaac and Rebekah and finally Joseph in Genesis.[36] This is followed by some reflective questions for the reader in relation to the preceding text and their own experience of the season. This text is clearly intended more for the Christian in the pew than an academic model for assessing and exploring Faith Development.

Blackaby identifies four distinct seasons, which he declares to follow in a definite order of spring, summer, autumn and winter.[37] Based on his reading of Ecclesiastes, he suggests that 'every aspect of our lives is governed by the ebb and flow of seasons'.[38] The characteristics for these seasons are spring as a time of new beginnings, summer as a time of growth through labour, autumn as a time of reaping, and winter as a time of rest.[39] He suggests that there are certain seasons that some individuals are keen to bypass: those who seek results from new beginnings without labour and those who resist the pause that winter offers. Seasons, he suggests, can nonetheless vary in length, intensity and their positive/negative impact on us.[40] He goes on to argue that how we engage with or respond to one season has an impact on the nature of the subsequent season.[41] This somewhat echoes Yeats's poem.

In each season, he focuses on four facets that need to be considered, namely our identity, our relationships, our roles and our faith. I would suggest that though he separates out faith as a category of its own, arguably the other three aspects would also constitute aspects of our lived experience of faith. Yet Blackaby is clear that he considers these are separate: 'The reality is that we can be in one particular season in regard to the stage of our family's development yet be in a very different season in terms of our career.'[42] He gives a variety of hypothetical examples of people experiencing growth in one aspect of their life while simultaneously experiencing pause or labour in another. What then is Blackaby's definition of faith, if these other aspects are not part of it? He says that this fourth facet of faith is simply about knowledge of God. He is not particularly explicit about this in his introduction but elucidates it slightly more in each season. In his section on faith in autumn he elaborates on how growth in faith works:

> This spiritual development comes through reading, believing, and obeying the Bible. It also results from prayer, being actively involved in a local church and participating in Bible studies, worship and mission endeavors ... Spiritual development occurs like physical growth – by regularly practising good habits.[43]

In terms of faith in spring, Blackaby essentially talks about new vocation. With examples from scripture, such as Abraham, Jacob or the fishermen Peter, Andrew, James and John, as well as reflections on his own father's vocation at various stages, he talks about the experience of a new call and an individual's response to it.[44] In this section, it is not entirely clear how this is distinct from his other category of role, or indeed how this really relates to 'knowledge of God', which was his opening definition for this facet. Yet in his description of summer and faith, he makes this clearer: 'While spring is when God invites us to enter into a deeper, more vibrant walk with Him [sic], summer is when we put in the time it takes to get there.'[45] His description of faith in autumn uses various stories of people who had experienced a spring and then laboured in summer to reap results. However, he does not really talk about the characteristics of autumn except in contrast to the season that is to follow. Essentially, he seems to present autumn as a time of maturity; the time of healthy and successful productive faith in terms of works that are now due, in some way, to decline in the following season of winter.[46] Yet when he goes on to describe winter and faith, he speaks of it in terms of celebration, blessing and rest. Despite his earlier insistence that these seasons rotate in a cycle throughout life, Blackaby seems to associate winter quite strongly with maturity and old age, using stories where those of mature years have blessed younger people walking the path that they have previously trodden themselves. For his third aspect of winter faith, Blackaby references the concept of sabbath in Genesis.[47] Yet again, however, despite some mention of preparing for the next season, he does seem to associate winter with finitude rather than rest before regrowth and has not explored, therefore, any sense of the hiatus present in other models.

John Westerhoff

John Westerhoff is much better known for the progressive/regressive model that we explored in an earlier chapter but he was particularly interested in the role of the community in the formation of faith: 'We become a people, a community, as we acquire a story. And we remain a community so long as we retell that story.'[48] He maps not the story of an individual faith but of 'a liturgical people on a pilgrimage through seasons of profane time made holy by the eternal cycle of sacred time'.[49] Westerhoff presents a version of this in two ways. First, he takes the reader on a journey, week by week, engaging with the story of Christ, starting unusually with Holy Week and Eastertide. Second, he re-presents this in a clearer overview of the whole. He maps familiar Faith Development motifs on to seasons of the liturgical Christian year, beginning with Maundy Thursday, through to the darkness of Tenebrae on the Wednesday of Holy Week, with the cycle beginning again with Maundy Thursday. Easter then is the 'new beginning for all human life' with the naive 'honeymoon season' of Eastertide. This period of naivety is followed by a more active missionary period of Pentecost and a focus on community on Trinity Sunday. Westerhoff locates Ordinary Time as 'the story of the struggle to discover what it means to live our baptism', followed by a season when we 'become weary in well-doing'.[50] This is reminiscent of the hiatus that others have described. Westerhoff connects this to Advent, as a time when 'our wells run dry and we are discouraged by the darkness of the world and our own souls', with Advent being able to offer a chance to recapture 'lost dreams' ahead of preparation for Christ's second coming and the new hope of Christmas. Westerhoff then pairs the second naivety with Epiphany and a time of reconciliation with Lent and a readiness once more for rebirth.[51] Essentially in this model Westerhoff is presenting something of a continuing cycle of seasons of faith. This is echoed in a more recent model for catechism introduced to the Diocese of Oxford by Bishop Steven Croft, which links the nurture of new believers to the Christian year, encouraging a regular cycle of engaging with those seeking faith with deliberate catechesis during Lent and ongoing deepening of engagement. This is a model that the Diocese of Oxford has explored to some extent by engaging in a cycle of evangelism and discipleship aligned with the cycle of the Christian year.[52] In this Westerhoff model, there is an assumption that, for the most part, these seasons are an extension of his previous models. The seasons are experienced by those who have already travelled through the earlier stages of faith, which he describes in his other models either as Experienced, Affiliative, Searching or Owned faith, via the Experiential, reflective or Integrative ways of exploring faith together.

Brian McLaren

Brian McLaren graduated from Maryland University with Bachelor's and Master's degrees in English literature, and went on to be a college lecturer in English literature with particular interest in medieval drama as well as the Romantic poets. He also focused on modern philosophical literature and the novels of Dr Walker Percy. While teaching, he helped found Cedar Ridge Community Church, a non-denominational church, and left teaching to become its founding pastor. As well as his own church leadership, he has supported others in networks of leadership and church founding. His other written works focus on engaging with postmodernism,[53] spiritual friendship,[54] interfaith relations,[55] and his ecclesiological work *A Generous Orthodoxy* has become a key text for the emerging church movement.[56] He has also written fiction,[57] an illustrated book for children,[58] an eco-spiritual travel memoir[59] and refers to his own composition of songs.[60] He describes himself as an author, speaker and activist. He has recently joined the Center for Contemplative Action and hosts their podcast 'Learning to See', as well as appearing at multiple conferences and on US mainstream television. McLaren has offered two books that explore to a greater and lesser extent the concept of Faith Development: *Naked Spirituality* and *Faith After Doubt*.[61] The first presents a model and the second focuses mostly on the issue of doubt while also representing the model in a slightly revised form. His latest Faith Development work, *Do I Stay Christian?*, is a further extension of *Faith after Doubt*.[62] He has also since published a book about living through a climate crisis.[63]

McLaren talks more in *Faith after Doubt* about the foundations for his Faith Development model presented in *Naked Spirituality*. He credits his training as a college lecturer for introducing him to the work of William Perry on adolescent stages of development which led him to explore further and engage with a wide range of works on learning and development, including those of Fowler, Ricoeur, Rohr and Peck.[64] He humbly admits to having been challenged by a friend that his reading list was predominantly male and therefore added Slee, Belenky and others to his explorations. Taking this further he also explored racial identity theorists such as Bailey Jackson, Rita Hardiman and others.[65] I can see that these models of identity revelation could be especially useful to those who have been brought up in households of faith and are seeking to discover for themselves what it means to own that identity. Though he mentions these and many other authors as sources of inspiration, because McLaren is writing for a more universal (non-academic) audience, he doesn't often identify precisely where he has been influenced by particular authors. Instead, much of his exploration of his model is in fact founded upon the experience of journeying alongside others in their evolving lives of faith and indeed in his own faith journey.

What intrigues me, given his background in the study of literature, is that McLaren does not mention Northrup Frye as a voice that has spoken into his concepts. We will explore the work of this literary scholar a little further in the styles chapter as they are picked up by James Hopewell in his model. Frye's concepts are somewhat noticeable in McLaren's work in the way he characterizes the seasons. His Simplicity stage echoes the Comic-Gnostic, the Complexity stage the Romantic-Charismatic, the Perplexity the Ironic-Empiric and, to a lesser extent, Harmony echoes Tragic-Canonic. A further nuance that McLaren also talks about at greater length in *Faith After Doubt* is the difference between these genuine stages of Faith Development and momentary 'states' of faith which might reflect regression or a foretaste of a future stage.[66]

McLaren does not offer a single definition of faith though he does credit influence from twentieth-century philosopher of Eastern Religions Alan Watts, with a working definition of faith that seeks to differentiate faith from belief as something that is not about accepting credal statements but being open to an exploration of truth without such preconceptions.[67] More than this, in his summary of the various stages in his model, McLaren writes a brief definition for faith in each stage, suggesting therefore that faith itself is no one particular thing but that the definition of faith is something that develops. So, to McLaren, faith, depending on your stage of development, is either, 'Trust in my caregivers (or in my own ability to get what I need by any means necessary)', 'Assent to required beliefs', 'Means to desired ends', 'An obstacle to critical thinking', or 'A humble, reverent openness to mystery that expresses itself in non-discriminatory love'.[68]

Given the similarity with the definition of faith in the pinnacle stage of his model and the definition he offered from Watts, you could question whether McLaren considers only one of these a 'true' definition of faith and the others as lesser understandings on the path to enlightenment. This is further supported as McLaren suggests that the impetus for development from one stage of the cycle to the next is, in every instance, doubt in whatever authority has been governing the previous stage.[69] You could argue that McLaren presents a model of Doubt Development as much as a model of Faith Development. There are likely strong influences of Peck's description of doubt here.[70]

As described above, McLaren's model is not based on empirical research but based on his observations of his own and others' lived experience of faith. His original model has four stages; his updated version adds a preliminary stage and goes on to say something more about how the cycle works. He proposes that people move between stages sequentially in a cycle of what he calls seasons from Simplicity to Complexity, Perplexity and Harmony back to Simplicity, and so on. For each of these four seasons, in *Naked Spirituality*, McLaren offers three words to live by. The first season of his model, *Simplicity*, is subtitled 'The Season of Spiritual Awakening'. This is a 'spiritual springtime' of faith when loyalty to an in-group is made clear.[71] He talks in *Faith after Doubt* about this being a stage when we begin to make sense of the world in essentially dualistic ways. There is good and evil; joy and sorrow.[72] McLaren's three words for this first stage are: 'Here', 'Thanks' and 'O!' These three words encapsulate what is needed for someone to embrace this stage, namely a sense of being present with God, of being grateful to God and to others, and of experiencing awe and wonder. His second stage, *Complexity*, is 'The Season of Spiritual Strengthening'. The transition to this stage echoes something of what Fowler's model identifies as the motivating force for transitions. This new stage initiates when individuals doubt the value of simplicity, and change from seeing things simply to engaging with complexity. This is evident in Fowler's description of, for example, the transition from Synthetic-Conventional to Individuative-Reflective.[73] Yet there is also an echo of Westerhoff's model as McLaren makes clear that the transition to Stage 2 has Stage 1 still embedded within. It is not replaced but built upon.[74] He describes this as the summer of faith, 'a time of hard work and getting things done during long sunny days'.[75] Those in Stage 2 have come to realize that the authorities on which our understanding of the world in Stage 1 depended are not 'always absolute and appropriate', and the lines that held us in the in-group of a particular faith group begin to blur. This stage is characterized by 'pragmatism and independence'.[76] In McLaren's model, this second stage has three more challenging words to live by: 'Sorry!' 'Help!' 'Please!' Thriving in Stage 2 is about growing self-awareness about our own failings, our own need for something from others, and an empathy for others.

His third season is *Perplexity*: '"The Season of Spiritual Surviving" [when] the autumn winds of perplexity blow in a biting cold rain ... [yet also] there's beauty in perplexity, the autumn blaze of colour between green and gone.'[77] This echoes Fowler's Stage 4 with two of the words to live by being interrogatives: 'Why?' 'When?' And the other being a term of rejection: 'No'. This stage is characterized by relativity, which is an extension of that embracing of complexity. Not only is it more complicated than a simple good/bad paradigm, but it is also possible that what we thought good could in fact be bad some, if not all, of the time. In many ways, I think this stage is the one that interests McLaren most as he sees it as the stage at which people struggle to stay with faith. In fact, he rather presents Stage 4 as the solution to the problem that is Stage 3. This is a difficult stage because the inherent distrust of authority figures means it is unlikely for there to be a church specifically for those in this stage, and churches made up of people of Stages 1 and 2 struggle to cope with those in Stage 3.[78] That is not to say that McLaren's first two stages are not to be valued. Indeed, he suggests in *Faith After Doubt* that they provide essential underpinnings of faith to those navigating the stage of

Perplexity. McLaren suggests that some who get towards Stage 3 but have not done the work of Stage 2 fully 'might have good ideas and lots of talent but they lack the stage two qualities of self-discipline, flexibility, cleverness, resilience and persistence'.[79] Some, therefore, reaching the end of Stage 2, might prefer to regress to Stage 1 rather than do the difficult work of moving to Stage 3 and then go back to Stage 2 to do the work that that stage needs.[80]

The final season he offers is *Harmony*, 'The Season of Spiritual Deepening'. This stage echoes Fowler's Conjunctive faith.[81] It is characterized by humility and an awareness of our own lack of knowledge of the deeper meanings of life and their essential unknowability.[82] Unsurprisingly, then, the three words to live by for this stage are in fact only two words: 'Behold' and 'Yes', followed by an ellipsis. This is a stage at which contemplation, acceptance and an openness to the unknown typify the experience of faith. McLaren connects this Harmony stage with his original Stage 1 as a new kind of Simplicity. He links this to the concept of the second naivety which makes the cyclical nature of his model more apparent.[83] He extends this model further and links these four seasons to a model not unlike John H. Westerhoff's (though without direct acknowledgement of that model), suggesting that each of these seasons of faith is like the ring of a tree built up one upon the other. McLaren in fact attributes inspiration for this to the integral philosopher Ken Wilber.[84] He suggests that the seasons fall in two phases; two stages of growth and two stages of dormancy.[85] He goes on to add further that these seasons continue in their cycle, building layer upon layer as rings in the tree, with this overlapping Harmony and Simplicity as the join of the cycle. He also goes on to reference the work of Fr Thomas Keating, who has written on John of the Cross, to describe these rings as the addition of new dimensions.[86] What McLaren doesn't seem to do is map what happens beyond this second simplicity in terms of second complexity and second perplexity, and whether these stages have a repetition and if so how they are different in their repetition.

His updated model appears to be based on a wider reading of Faith Development models and has charted his model against various others.[87] In this updated model, McLaren has also added a stage for faith in early childhood which he styles as either Before Simplicity, Infancy or Egocentricity.[88] There are two problems with this addition. First, it does not seem to fit with his new overlapping Harmony/Simplicity concept. Second, the tone of the description of this stage in the model might not sit easily with some of the models of children's spirituality that we explore in this text as it focuses on immaturity of faith, much as Fowler did in his model. His use of the terms narcissistic and self-centred with regard to a child's outlook on life is also somewhat unfortunate.[89] McLaren adds some detail about the fact he sees, in general, no link between a particular age and these stages, though at the same time hopes for a time when people will enter the higher stages at a younger age.[90] More than this, he has also explicated 17 facets of each stage. These are evidently more akin to outworkings of each stage rather than the categories for determining stage as used by Fowler. These 17 include the faith definitions we explored earlier as well as what I would categorize as ways of understanding the world (perception, focus, motive, key values, assumption, life is), how individuals relate to others (authority figures, us/them, belonging), ways of understanding the ultimate (God is ..., core question, good news), understandings of the spiritual (faith is, attitude towards doubt) and understandings of the self (mistakes, strengths, weaknesses).[91]

McLaren's model is arguably focused tightly on those who are of a particular faith, and, in general, those who are Christian. He links maturity in faith to those who have a churched faith because he suggests that it is only in such communities of faith that doubt can lead to transformation rather than a dead end.[92] Nevertheless, he also links an increasing maturity of faith with a greater openness to the teaching of and engagement with people of other faiths so this angle might be more related to the intended audience of his work, rather than to his idea of faith in general.[93]

Having explored a number of models that claim to delineate faith in a cyclical movement, it is evident that these types of model often struggle to clarify what further iterations of the cycle have in common with previous iterations and what, if any, differences they have. It is also not clear how frequently these cycles of faith turn through a full cycle. For local worshipping communities, such models might seem a sensible place to seek wisdom in relation to people with longstanding relationships with and within the worshipping community. Ministers could either use this model in reflection of Westerhoff's concept of thinking in terms of a community as a whole or use it to reflect on individuals making a change of season at different times to other individuals and what that might mean for collaborative ministry and mission.

Notes

1 McLaren, Brian D., 2011, *Naked Spirituality: A Life with God in Twelve Simple Words*, London: Hodder and Stoughton; Blackaby, Richard, 2012, *The Seasons of God*, New York: Waterbrook Multnomah.
2 See Levinson, D., 1978, *The Seasons of a Man's Life*, New York: Knopf.
3 Shakespeare, William, *As You Like it*, Act 2, Scene 7, lines 139–66.
4 Spencer, A., 1982, *Seasons, A Woman's Search for Self through Life Stages*, New York: Paulist, p. 3.
5 Spencer, *Seasons*, p. 7.
6 Spencer, *Seasons*, pp. 12–14, 20–1.
7 Spencer, *Seasons*, pp. 5–6.
8 Spencer, *Seasons*, p. 5.
9 Tournier, Paul, 1963, *The Seasons of Life*, trans. Gilmour, John S., Eugene: Wipf and Stock, p. 36.
10 Tournier, *Seasons*, pp. 37, 54.
11 Tournier, *Seasons*, p. 63.
12 Tournier, Paul, 1971, *Learning to Grow Old*, trans. Hudson, Edwin, London: SCM Press, p. 9.
13 Thompson, Ross, 2008, *Spirituality in Season: Growing through the Christian Year*, London: SCM Press.
14 https://scmpress.hymnsam.co.uk/books/9780334040934/scm-studyguide-christian-spirituality, accessed 09.05.2025.
15 Thompson, *Spirituality*, p. 8.
16 Buchanan, M., 2010, *Spiritual Rhythm: Being with Jesus Every Season of Your Soul*, Grand Rapids: Zondervan, pp. 47, 100.
17 Buchanan, *Spiritual*, p. 195.
18 Hall, Richard, 1986, *For Everything a Season*, London: United Reformed Church.
19 United Reformed Church, 1990, *URC Yearbook*, United Reformed Church, p. 228, kindly provided by Michael Hopkins.
20 Hall, *For Everything*, p. 28.
21 Hall, *For Everything*, p. 5.
22 Hall, *For Everything*, p. 5.
23 Oser, Fritz and Gmünder, Paul, 1991, *Religious Judgement: A Developmental Approach*, Birmingham: Religious Education Press, p. 63.
24 Yeats, W. B., 1928, 'The Wheel', in *The Tower*, London: Macmillan and Co.
25 Hall, *For Everything*, p. 11.
26 Hall, *For Everything*, p. 12.
27 Hall, *For Everything*, pp. 19–20.
28 Hall, *For Everything*, p. 29.
29 Hall, *For Everything*, pp. 33–7.
30 Hall, *For Everything*, pp. 43–9.
31 Hall, *For Everything*, p. 9.
32 Hall, *For Everything*, pp. 22–7.
33 Blackaby, Richard, 2012, *The Seasons of God*, New York: Waterbrook Multnomah, p. 24.

34 https://www.richardblackaby.com/about/, accessed 09.05.2025.
35 Blackaby, *Seasons*, pp. 16–22.
36 Blackaby, *Seasons*, pp. 68–76.
37 Blackaby, *Seasons*, p. 27.
38 Blackaby, *Seasons*, p. 14.
39 Blackaby, *Seasons*, p. 24.
40 Blackaby, *Seasons*, pp. 27–8.
41 Blackaby, *Seasons*, p. 32.
42 Blackaby, *Seasons*, p. 37.
43 Blackaby, *Seasons*, p. 176.
44 Blackaby, *Seasons*, p. 100–5.
45 Blackaby, *Seasons*, p. 142.
46 Blackaby, *Seasons*, pp. 176–81.
47 Blackaby, *Seasons*, p. 211.
48 Westerhoff, John H., 2004, *A Pilgrim People: Learning through the Church Year*, New York: Church Publishing Inc., p. 1.
49 Westerhoff, *Pilgrim*, p. 95.
50 Westerhoff, John H., 1985, *Living the Faith Community: The Church that Makes a Difference*, rev. and expanded edn, Minneapolis: Winston Press, pp. 30–1.
51 Westerhoff, *Living*, p. 32.
52 See also Croft, Steven, ed., 2019, *Rooted and Grounded*, Norwich: Canterbury Press.
53 McLaren, Brian D., 2000, *The Church on the Other Side: Doing Ministry in the Postmodern Matrix*, Grand Rapids: Zondervan, rev. edn; Campolo, Anthony and McLaren, Brian D., 2003, *Adventures in Missing the Point*, Grand Rapids: Zondervan.
54 McLaren, Brian D., 2002, *More Ready than You Realize*, Grand Rapids: Zondervan.
55 McLaren, Brian D., 2012, *Why Did Jesus, Moses, the Buddha, and Mohammed Cross the Road?*, London: Hodder and Stoughton.
56 McLaren, Brian D., 2004, *A Generous Orthodoxy*, Grand Rapids: Zondervan.
57 McLaren, Brian D., 2001, *A New Kind of Christian*, Hoboken: Jossey-Bass; McLaren, Brian D., 2003, *The Story We Find Ourselves In*, Hoboken: Jossey-Bass; McLaren, Brian D., 2005, *The Last Word and the Word After That*, Hoboken: Jossey-Bass;
58 McLaren, Brian D. and Higgins, Gareth, *Cory and the Seventh Story*, New York: Random House.
59 McLaren, Brian D., 2019, *The Galapagos Islands: A Spiritual Journey*, Minneapolis: Fortress Press. Released in the UK as *God Unbound: Theology in the Wild*, Norwich: Canterbury Press.
60 McLaren, Brian D., 2021, *Faith After Doubt: Why Your Beliefs Stopped Working and What to Do About It*, London: Hodder and Stoughton, pp. 111–13.
61 McLaren, *Naked Spirituality*; McLaren, *After Doubt*.
62 McLaren, Brian, 2022, *Do I Stay Christian? A Guide for the Doubters, the Disappointed and the Disillusioned*, London: Hodder and Stoughton.
63 McLaren, Brian D., 2024, *Life After Doom: Wisdom and Courage for a World Falling Apart*, London: Hachette.

64 McLaren, *After Doubt*, pp. 64 and 131.
65 McLaren, *After Doubt*, p. 65.
66 McLaren, *After Doubt*, p. 138.
67 McLaren, *After Doubt*, pp. 160–1.
68 McLaren, *After Doubt*, pp. 299, 303.
69 McLaren, *After Doubt*, p. 125.
70 Epstein, Robert, 2002, 'Interview of M. Scott Peck', *Psychology Today*, November December, p. 70.
71 McLaren, *Naked Spirituality*, p. 38.
72 McLaren, *After Doubt*, pp. 67–9.
73 Fowler, James W., 1995, *Stages of Faith: The Psychology of Human Development and the Quest for Meaning*, San Francisco: Harper, p. 161.
74 McLaren, *Naked Spirituality*, p. 105.
75 McLaren, *Naked Spirituality*, p. 107.
76 McLaren, *After Doubt*, pp. 70–1.
77 McLaren, *Naked Spirituality*, pp. 176–7.
78 McLaren, *After Doubt*, pp. 92–5.
79 McLaren, *After Doubt*, p. 107.
80 McLaren, *After Doubt*, p. 87.
81 https://www.slideshare.net/brianmclaren/stages-of-faith-1920055, McLaren's own PPT, accessed 09.05.2025.
82 McLaren, *Naked Spirituality*, p. 233.
83 McLaren, *After Doubt*, p. 131.
84 McLaren, *After Doubt*, pp. 65–6.
85 McLaren, *After Doubt*, p. 65.
86 McLaren, *After Doubt*, p. 143, https://www.contemplativeoutreach.org/wp-content/uploads/2020/04/dec2019newsletter.pdf, accessed 09.05.2026.
87 McLaren, *After Doubt*, pp. 305–6.
88 McLaren, *After Doubt*, pp. 301–2.
89 McLaren, *After Doubt*, p. 302.
90 McLaren, *After Doubt*, p. 132.
91 McLaren, *After Doubt*, pp. 297–302.
92 McLaren, *After Doubt*, p. 156.
93 McLaren, *After Doubt*, p. 131.

5

Styles

The third group of Faith Development models are style based. There is some irony in a book about how faith develops in including a section on models which do not readily suggest that faith has a growth cycle or trajectory but instead is identified by varying types. These models offer such a different perspective that, in a previous (much shorter) study, I mostly excluded them from consideration.[1] However, as this section progresses, it should become obvious that most of the models we explore speak of faith developing via various types rather than suggest that a person has one faith type which is set for life. Yet the most significant trend in the study of Faith Development in recent years has been the postmodern critique of the very concept of Faith Development. The most substantial current research in this field has been conducted by Heinz Streib's team. This project concluded a longitudinal study based on the fact that faith-stage models have never been empirically established as models that describe a series of stages in particular individuals but that there are a number of faith styles that different people prefer or demonstrate. Style-based models suggest that these experiences identified in individual lives through research such as that of Fowler have shown distinction and perhaps change, but had not been demonstrated categorically as progression towards or from anything.

We will explore Streib's work along with the work of James Hopewell who looked at personalities of whole congregations rather than individuals.[2] In more recent years, the work of David Csinos, in the field of children's spirituality, has also identified some faith styles that would sit firmly within this set. Finally, we will consider the beautiful model developed by Maria Harris, which arguably defies categorization according to my criteria; it is not specifically a styles model, though it is certainly not a progressive or cyclical model either, but arguably has elements of each of these. Opening up the field of Faith Development to include styles of faith is facilitated by bringing in the works of Howard Gardner and Friedrich Von Hügel as constructive conversation partners. Alongside these you could also add those studies that suggest that our faith lives are governed more by our personality.

There is, of course, a field of study (and a substantially lucrative trade) connected with personality types in both secular and church publishing. Though most of these personality type models do not specifically talk about growth, there have been some explorations of how growth might be explored by those of particular types, which we will briefly explore as a preamble to the models to be examined in greater depth. If we disregard the concept of faith being something that changes or grows over time, reflecting on the faith lives of individuals could instead be seen as an extension of the study of personality and character. There are a number of modern models for exploring personalities, some of them founded on very little research data but which nonetheless have become popular. The enneagram, for example, has a substantial popularity despite its lack of empirical foundation. Books such as Bruce Duncan's *Pray your Way*, or Julia McGuiness's *Growing Spiritually with the Myers-Briggs Model*, could be considered as taking a closer step towards integrating personality type and Faith Development. I don't intend to explore these models here. Instead, I will begin with a brief survey of some of the more evidentially based theories of the difference of persons.

Gardner argued for there being eight different intelligences that people could develop, namely linguistic, logical-mathematical, interpersonal, intrapersonal, spatial, bodily-kinesthetic, musical and naturalistic.[3] Exploring people's faith in terms of developing these eight intelligences echoes some of Fowler's work in terms of the exploration of logical thinking and interpersonal knowledge and the understanding of symbols.

Table 1: Gardner's Intelligences mapped against Fowler's seven lenses for assessing faith stage.

Gardner's Intelligences	Fowler's lenses
Linguistic	The ways of unifying meanings (Erikson) The understanding of symbols (Kegan)
Logical-mathematical	The development of logical thinking (Piaget)
Interpersonal	The understanding of social reference points The interpretation of what legitimates commitments (Erikson)
Intrapersonal	The construction of social perspective (Selman) The development of moral judgements (Kohlberg)
Spatial	*Not evident*
Bodily-kinesthetic	*Not evident*
Musical	*Not evident*
Naturalistic	*Not evident*

This map of Gardner's intelligences against Fowler's seven lenses demonstrates aspects of personhood that Fowler's work may have left unexplored. There could be some argument that Fowler's assessment of the importance of ritual could be reflected in the last four intelligences listed in the table. What this table does demonstrate is the intellectual bias of Fowler's outlook, which focused more on the hard intelligences than those that are less tangible and often valued less by society. Fowler acknowledged that one of the seven aspects of Faith Development, 'Symbolic Functioning', is an area of research where 'much work remains to be done' to explore the relationship between thought and imagination.[4] This echoes some of Nicola Slee's critique that the data she collected from women and girls demonstrated the significance of metaphors and symbols and particularly of images drawn from the natural world and art.[5] These critiques could equally be made of other models, though Bickford has affirmed Westerhoff's model as evidencing an awareness of Gardner's ideas,[6] and McLaren and Jamieson clearly use metaphors within their models.

Similarly, Von Hügel's style model suggests that there are three modes of spiritual development, namely Institutional, Critical/Intellectual and Mystical. These have each alternatively been associated with three apostles. They are styled '"traditional, historical" of the Petrine, the "speculative-internal" of the Pauline, and the "mystical-internal" of the Johannine',[7] or more simply Tradition, Philosophy and Prayer.[8] Von Hügel is clear that these three modes, however, are not options but integrally linked and equally necessary, much like the Trinity.[9] Arguably, some of the modern models we have explored have focused on the Critical more than the Mystical, and indeed Institutional, in terms of exploring credal beliefs. The models proposed by Willow Creek and, to some extent, Brian McLaren have also explored the Institutional in terms of relationship to a church community.

Heinz Streib

Heinz Streib studied first at Tübingen, Württemberg, and then Yale before going on to study for his PhD under Fowler at Emory. In Faith Development, he is in many ways the successor to Fowler academically though he has not gained the same kind of recognition more widely in church circles. The focus of his PhD dissertation was on Faith Development in terms of metaphor, symbol and narrative with a particular focus on Fowler and Ricoeur. He went on to work at the University of Frankfurt, then Bayreuth, before moving to Bielefeld where he is now Senior Professor of Practical Theology and Religious Education. He has continued his interest in how people experience faith.[10] Though a student of Fowler, Streib moved away from the staged-theory model of Fowler, despite something that Fowler himself wrote about Streib: 'My hope for his work is that he will not exchange the stage theory for a theory of types but, rather, expand the theory by crosscutting it with an empirically tested typology.'[11] Arguably he has partly followed Fowler's guidance. He was behind a substantial longitudinal study into faith styles to test the accuracy of Fowler's original assertion that people transition through a developmental scale (rather than Streib's assertion that what Fowler's research discovered was a number of non-progressing styles). However, Streib's main research interests have now moved away from strictly studying faith styles or stages to using his model to help explore the way that faith styles, as he identifies them, influence other aspects of life. Currently he focuses on the faith of young people and whether the faith styles he has identified relate to (and can therefore predict) the experiences of deconversion and the adoption of fundamentalism and the converse of fundamentalism, which he describes in the concept of xenosophia – being open to the wisdom of the other.[12] His significant contribution to Faith Development is in methodologies. He collaborated with Fowler and later with Barbara Keller in producing the *Manual for the Assessment of Religious Styles in Faith Development Interviews*, encouraging and enabling other scholars to use Fowler's model interview and assessment methods.[13] He has recently published the text of various interviews and his significant longitudinal study.[14]

Streib's work is in response to the existing Faith Development models, notably Fowler and Oser and Gmünder. However, he questions the validity of the construction of Faith Development along the model of Lawrence Kohlberg's cognitive structural theory. In 2013, before he began his longitudinal study, he suggested:

> in religious development research, we hardly have any longitudinal study … So it is safe to claim that there is no empirical evidence so far for religious development at all … all of research, including our own, is designed as a comparison of synchronic data against a model or models of religious development.[15]

He argues that the influence of Kohlberg on Faith Development models has included the insistence that such models should demonstrate certain characteristics. One such characteristic is the concept of 'structural wholeness'. Streib's research suggests that the movement in faith is far more complex than a simple staged development and his analysis has given evidence of elements of various religious styles in people of different types. Kohlberg's structural rules, Streib suggests, 'rule out both the simultaneous existence of several styles and the possibility of regression or revival which we see e.g. in fundamentalist orientation'.[16] Streib's work is founded on substantial empirical research involving Fowler-style interviews of 677 individuals for approximately one to two hours from three distinct research projects.[17] As most of Streib's research seems to focus on adolescents and adults, there is not much evidence with regard to the earliest stages in Fowler's model. The interview involves a life review, discussion of relationships, values and commitments as well as religion and worldview. In assigning faith styles, Streib and his team assess 'not so much the "what" of content, but the "how" and the "why" that indicates structure and style'.[18] They measure how the patterns of responses to a series of questions about their faith fall between five particular styles.

Streib does not speak generally about faith but about religiosity. In one article he speaks of spirituality as 'individualized experience-orientated religiosity'.[19] He also points out that there is still no consensus about the definition of spirituality or religion and that facets such as spiritual well-being and day-to-day spiritual experience are being studied independently from some scales on religiosity. In his final longitudinal study report, he talks about 'differences and life span developmental changes (intraindividual differences) in religious, spiritual, or nonreligious faith' and goes on to quote Fowler's definition:

> People's evolved and evolving ways of experiencing self, others and world (as they construct them), as related to and affected by the ultimate conditions of existence (as they construct them), and shaping their lives' purposes and meanings, trusts and loyalties, in the light of the character of being, value and power determining the ultimate conditions of existence (as grasped in their operative images – conscious and unconscious – of them).[20]

Streib clearly distances himself from cognitive development, critiquing models from both Fowler and from Oser and Gmünder for their focus on assessing faith in too narrow terms[21] preferring to 'hold fast to the irreducibility of religion to cognitive operations' and suggesting that a model of religious styles rather than stages 'helps to emphasize the relevance of experiences, contents, and functions'.[22] He argues:

'faith development' should not be confused with the accumulation of religious knowledge or an increase in strength of religious conviction; faith development does not mean an increase in frequency of private or public religious praxis, nor an increase in observing religious prescriptions and leading a moral–religious life; and finally, faith development does not mean an increase in religious experience.[23]

This definition would perhaps challenge Willow Creek's model most of all.

He argues that the faith examined as 'developing' by Fowler and others falls short of the fullness of faith as it does not take into account the dimensions of the relationships of someone to their own self, the relationship between the self and others, the relationship between the self and the tradition, and the relationship with self and the world.[24] He suggests that the work of Erik Erikson and Ana-Maria Rizzuto should be factored more into Faith Development models.[25] Streib, however, commends Fowler for the multiple perspectives that his model incorporates:

> Fowler's heptagonal model illustrates the view that (A) the 'form of logic' according to Piaget, (B) 'perspective taking' according to Selman, and (C) the 'forms of moral judgment' according to Kohlberg, together with the aspects added by Fowler: (D) the 'bounds of social awareness,' (E) the 'locus of authority,' (F) the 'forms of world coherence,' and (G) the 'symbolic function,' all develop simultaneously in a correlative network, and that the perspectives presented by these theories all taken together describe one style of 'faith' respectively, in a multi-perspectival and correlative manner.[26]

Streib regrets that this great multiplicity of perspectives is then measured by Fowler in purely cognitive terms, thus losing strength. He therefore suggests a total reconsideration of the means for measuring faith and advocates instead the primacy not of cognitive development but of 'biography and the lifeworld', reflecting his preference for the term 'religious styles', by which he means 'the biographically generated modi of accessing and dealing with religion', with an emphasis particularly on two factors, 'self-other dynamics and the world of stories', or, as he puts it: '"styles of religion" are modes of accessing and dealing with religion in its narrative, symbolic, and ritual forms of expression, forms that are generated by a multiplicity of factors – namely by both lifeworld and biography.'[27]

Streib's research has great weight for being the result of a longitudinal study supported by substantial grant money from the John Templeton Fund. As part of his study, he and his team reinterviewed initially 90 participants of previous studies[28] and ultimately 75 individuals participated in all three stages of the study.[29] He admits that 75 is not a particularly large sample and that the diversity from nationality is not strong as there were relatively few participants from the US as compared to Germany. He also admits that the sample were much more educated than the average population, with 72% of the group being educated to tertiary level. This rather repeats one of the weaknesses of Fowler's original selection of participants. He did have a greater gender balance among participants, though discerned no statistical significance in age or gender for the movement of styles. But he doesn't account for race as this is not something he has noted for his participants.[30] Nor does this study assess the faith of anyone under the age of 18. Furthermore, it is possible that someone's faith might not change in the ten-year period of the study but might have changed just before or just after that period.

In his earliest research, Streib tended towards arguing that faith did not come in stages but had different styles. His assessment was rooted in his view that faith is not something that is a 'monodirectional, stagewise, and irreversible development',[31] as other models such as Fowler's had suggested. Streib therefore moved from describing faith as not having stages to suggest that faith has styles. Indeed he suggests that individuals do not simply have one style but have a 'profile of religious styles which concerns, among other things, the sources where they derive validity and stability, when confronted with religious and existential questions or inter-religious challenges'.[32] This profile of styles is assessed by Streib and his team to be reflected in four particular combinations of these styles to make four types of religiosity. Although much of Streib's writing speaks about styles and types, he did not completely abandon the concept of progression. He suggests a significance for the past lived experiences in the formation of current faith styles, saying: 'Present-day styles do not come into being isolated in the here and now. Instead, for all their cognitive and emotional transformations, these styles have biographical roots.'[33] More than this, he acknowledges that change happens but suggests that 'abandoning the terminology of stages intends to free the description of religiosity from the confinement to a model of a stagewise, monodirectional, and invariantly sequential line of development'.[34] Indeed, his longitudinal study has demonstrated that some of the people changed type. In the initial two-wave study, the team found that of the 14 individuals who had previously tested for Style 2, only two continued to demonstrate that style but two others who had tested for Style 3 later tested for Style 2. Aside from these two, of the 39 who had tested for Style 3, 25 continued to demonstrate that style while ten later demonstrated Style 4 and two demonstrated Style 5. Of the 24 who had previously been assessed as Style 4, 13 continued in that style, seven later tested as Style 3, and four later tested as Style 5. Of the 13 who tested originally as Style 5, only one tested again as this style while seven tested instead as Style 4 and five as Style 3.

In the conclusion of the three-wave study, the team were able to prove that faith is something that progresses and regresses, showing that of the 75 interviewed three times in the first 20 years in this century, only 25 tested as the same religious type either across all three times of interview or moved up or down midway but ultimately tested as the same again between Wave 1 and Wave 3 of the study. Supporting the idea that faith does develop, 34 moved upwards at some point, sometimes moving upwards twice (though some moving down again but not usually to their original religious type). The minority group were those who generally moved down in type. All of these ended on a lower religious type than they originally started. Streib's research sought to determine whether faith does develop and succeeded in doing so:

> Our data generally confirm assumptions of change and development in religious type, including the results presented by Fowler (1981, pp. 317–319), but they indicate a higher portion of movers in a longitudinal sample of adults with a mean age of 45.8 at Wave 1 and a mean age of 57.0 at Wave 3, and with a time lag of almost 10 years between the first and the last interviews.[35]

To me, this not only confirms the concept of Faith Development but it also suggests that we should be focusing more of our efforts on those in this mid-point of life, as movement in faith, according to Streib, can go up or down. We cannot assume that people, once they have reached adulthood, have plateaued in their faith lives or will inevitably progress, and, as some were shown to regress, this makes the impetus to support the Faith Development of individuals and the need to understand how faith develops much more pressing.

Streib's longitudinal study also sought to explore some of the instigators of change in faith. They have evidenced that one of the so-called 'big five' of psychological type theory, 'openness', is one of the key indicators to movement between styles. Those with greater openness at the start of their ten-year study were more likely to have moved to a style further on in the hierarchy of styles than those with a low score for openness.[36] Streib and his team also identified a correlation between two other factors on their religious schemata which could be linked to movement between styles. These were xenosophia (or openness to the wisdom of the other) and what they term the 'truth of texts and teachings'. This is a subscale assessing 'an exclusivist and authoritative understanding of one's own sacred texts'.[37]

He describes how he has used an adapted form of the Faith Development interview devised by Fowler and assigned the responses of participants to each of the 25 questions to one of his five styles. Assignation to a spiritual type is then done according to the percentages of a participant's answers that conform to the various types according to particular formulae.[38]

Streib has created both a styles model (based on Fowler) and a Religious Schema Scale.[39] We will look briefly at his Religious Schema Scale before moving on to his model as, although Streib constructed this scale and has continued to use it in his research, he does so in combination with the Faith Development interview devised by Fowler. Thus Streib clearly does not view it as an alternative to the full assessment, even if that is what he might have intended it to become. The schema has three subscales: truth of texts and teachings (TTT), fairness, tolerance and rational choice (FTR) and xenosophia/inter-religious dialogue (xenos). Streib designed these subscales to reflect three particular stages in Fowler's model. The TTT scale relates to Fowler's Stage 2 (mythic-literal faith) as well as to his own instrumental-reciprocal religious style. The FTR subscale relates to Fowler's Stage 4 (individuative-reflective) and to his own individuative-systemic. The third subscale, xenos, relates to Fowler's Stage 5 and Streib's own dialogical religious style.[40]

Streib's construction of a model of religious styles and types evolved over a substantial period. He assessed participants on five styles and from the distribution of those styles then assigned each participant a type. It is key to distinguish in this description between Streib's use of styles and types. A type is a category of participant demonstrating certain styles. His religious styles model equates to Fowler's stages (and to a lesser extent the work of Oser and Gmünder) but Streib originally described them as five non-progressive styles, namely, subjective (echoing Intuitive-Projective), instrumental-reciprocal (also called *do-ut-des* and reflecting mythic-literal), mutual (corresponding to the Synthetic-Conventional), individuative (Individuative-Reflexive) and dialogical (linked to Conjunctive and not Universalizing as Streib rejects Fowler's weak accounting for the existence of his final stage).[41] More recently the assessment of participants in his research has progressed to consolidate the expression of these five styles as suggesting four types. In other words, these four types reflect a combination of the five styles numbered one to five (to echo in part Fowler's model). His final schema of types includes: One: Subjective Religious Style; Two: Instrumental-reciprocal Religious Style; Three: Mutual Religious style; Four: Individuative-systemic style; Five: Dialogical Religious Style.[42] When he talks about style, Streib says that it

> refers to habitus such as ways of interpreting texts and teachings of a religious tradition (hermeneutical structures), ways of explaining what happens to one and why (structures of world coherence), or ways of meeting the challenge of inter-religious difference (structures of communicative action; structures of in-group-out-group relations).[43]

Ultimately, Streib decided to drop *Style 1* because it is so rarely found in adults. His focus was on adult religiosity, so this is understandable in terms of his research aims, though unfortunate in terms of the model being applicable to children and those with reduced mental capacity as well as to normally developing adults considering their journey. Though Streib suggests in his earlier writings that these are styles not developments, he suggests that there is a hierarchy of styles and acknowledges the presence of elements of other styles within the data for those who were assessed at a particular style.

He describes *Style 2* as a substantially ethnocentric style characterized by a mono-religious claim to the exclusive truth of the faith of the group to which they belong and a mythic-literal understanding of religious texts, life and the rules of morality and justice, with attendant focus on punishment and reward. Streib describes *Style 3* as predominantly conventional, reflecting an inclination to consent to the beliefs of the faith group or immediate culture because of a desire for mutual harmony. This is accompanied by an avoidance of critical questioning. *Style 4* is described as predominantly individuative-reflective and involves a practice of critical and autonomous reflection and an openness to religious plurality. When faced with conflicting claims to validity, those of this style tend towards models of tolerance. Finally, Streib's *Style 5* is described as an emerging dialogical-xenosophic style. This is a development of the previous style and is not only open to plurality in terms of religion but also to inter-religious dialogue which can involve being willing to be changed by an encounter with a faith or worldview other than one's own.

In each style, individuals tended to evidence more of the previous style than any other but some still had indications of the styles that were higher in the hierarchy, although these were noticeably much lower in number. Streib's work has suggested that there are four religious types indicated by their reflection of five religious styles. From his data, those demonstrating predominantly Style 2 also had substantial scores in Style 3 but those with the strongest score in Style 3 exhibited very low numbers of indicators for Style 2 and some indicators for Style 4. Those in Style 4 included some indicators for Style 2 but very low indicators for Style 1 and almost equally low indicators for Style 5. Of those demonstrating Style 5 the picture is slightly different. They demonstrated a substantial number of data points for Style 4, often more than for Style 5 but their indicators for Style 2 were incredibly low and for Style 3 much lower than for those in any other style.[44] In summary elsewhere he says:

> Each of the four religious styles (instrumental-reciprocal, mutual, individuative-systemic, dialogical) can and should be the primary characteristic of one type, while other styles have lower frequency. Thus, we conceptualize four types: substantially ethnocentric (Type 1), predominantly conventional (Type 2), predominantly individuative-reflective (Type 3), and emerging dialogical-xenosophic (Type 4).[45]

Streib does not simply research faith styles in order to understand them but to understand how people function and what we might be able to learn about those who exhibit different styles. His findings include that those with what he himself calls 'higher scores' in Faith Development show considerable correlation to 'deconversion or disaffiliation from religious traditions', lower scores on 'Religious Fundamentalism' and 'Right-Wing Authoritarianism', as well as scoring more highly for 'openness to experience', and predicting a greater likelihood that people identify as 'spiritual rather than religious'.[46] This may explain some of the affiliation between Bible Belt Christianity and political fundamentalism in the US. Streib's subsequent work has, in fact, moved into the field of religious extremism and fundamentalism. His work has established that faith does grow and change over time and this is useful for those wishing to support the faith lives of others. However, in terms of using his model with a worshipping community, I think it would need considerable explanation. His concept of identifying a number of styles and, from the pattern of an individual's styles, attributing a type could be a useful kind of model within a local setting though I am not certain that the model as it is represents something easily transferable to a worshipping community; it may be more suited to exploring wider trends in society.

Rebecca Nye

Rebecca Nye has worked in the fields of adult and child psychology with a particular focus on children's spirituality and ministry. She gained a PhD in psychology from the University of Nottingham and currently teaches with the Open University and the Cambridge Theological Federation. She is associated with the international Godly Play initiative and is one of their trainers. She does not suggest that she has developed a Faith Development model. However, her work on children's spirituality is fundamental to understanding the way that faith develops in children and serves as an important challenge to some of the descriptions of child faith in Faith Development models that include childhood stages. She writes about the spirituality of children in her PhD dissertation,[47] in a co-authored academic text,[48] and in a more accessible text for the non-academic market.[49]

Rather than defining faith, Nye carefully defines spirituality. She devotes a considerable section of her first book to the relationship between and distinctive characteristics of spirituality and religion, suggesting that it can be useful to see them as those in her workshops have sometimes compared them, 'referring to spirituality as a journey and to religion as the mode of transport'.[50] Her second book describes the relationship between faith and spirituality with the analogy of a car, in which faith is the full tank of fuel but spirituality is the oil.[51] Having highlighted the lack of connection between education research and psychology,[52] Nye draws on a number of thinkers from psychology, education and theology, and comes ultimately to her own definition of what we might call children's faith: 'God's ways of being with children and children's ways of being with God'.[53]

Nye refers not to staged growth but to 'a stronger sense of continuity and gradual unfolding'.[54] She talks about the changeability of spiritual experience, noting the ways children can present sometimes as being deeply faithful then at other times seem not so spiritually connected. The erratic nature of children's spirituality identified by Nye and by other research that she incorporated emphasizes the inability of developmental models to properly account for children's spiritual experiences.[55] Her recognition of these patterns here echoes the stalling and regression recognized by some other adult models such as Slee's. Nye reflects on the way that children's faith grows: 'Despite all the efforts leaders put in, a lot of children seem to grow out of faith rather than into it.'[56] She attributes this to the fact that 'children can all too easily tread water spiritually' through the provision of children's ministry in some of its traditional forms and that children's ministry needs to engage children in the Christian faith at a much deeper level. Nye also notes that John Hull had suggested a tentative developmental model for children's spiritual development which saw children's beliefs about the world being turned into belief-informed action. She elaborates about the model as one

> in which such individual features (including experiences of significant spiritual moments) are simply precursors to 'real' spirituality expressed broadly as social action (and not inner reflection). He defines the education of spirituality (and by implication spirituality itself) as involving being inspired to live for others.[57]

Nye makes connections to developmental ideas when she explores the way that children think: 'Child psychology has demonstrated that children's minds are not just like adults' minds but with "less inside"! Children's *ways* of thinking are different.'[58] Nye makes connections between cognitive developments and the spiritual development of children. She highlights the cognitive changes in 4–5-year-olds which includes 'a new ability and desire to organise and sort information',[59] while for adolescents she attributes 'increasing powers of reflective thinking'.[60]

This suggests that any adult model of faith development which has sought to offer a lifespan model without adjusting their research methods when involving children may not have adequately taken account of this difference. She suggests something based on Piaget's model, that children in infancy

> draw first on bodily experience ('sensori-motor thought'), then from about the age of two on feelings and images. By about the age of six thinking is often most easily collected in story and literal patterns. Finally, from about 11 years, abstract, conceptual ways of putting ideas together become more natural and efficient.[61]

This is not so different from what Fowler ultimately describes in his earlier stages, but an important factor for me in including studies of children's spirituality is, as Nye has suggested:

> taking children's spirituality seriously can significantly influence our view ... to embrace the reality that children are made in God's image,

that they are already spiritually switched on, and also to challenge the view that children come in a kind of 'kit version' that we must make into a 'God compatible' model.[62]

Nye found that children demonstrated what she terms 'relational consciousness', in that 'children's spirituality was recognized by a distinctive property of mental activity, profound and intricate enough to be termed "consciousness", and remarkable for its confinement to a broadly relational, inter- and intra-personal domain'.[63] Nye notes some studies that have considered childhood experiences of faith as

> at least a significant period for religion. Rizzuto's (1979) study of how adults form and process their representations of God, and Meissner's (1984) model of how adults experience the religious, have both traced these crucial constituents of personal religious constructions to childhood influences.[64]

She laments the academic secular bias that has restricted research into spirituality. 'Their stress on the development of intellectual and moral reasoning in children means that they downplay the spiritual dimension.'[65] She asserts that the focus of models on assessing spirituality through the medium of language is inherently prejudiced against children and indeed against any adults with diminished mental capacity either congenital or acquired.[66]

Nye distances her research from that of Fowler. She says that there are commonalities in the way she has incorporated 'autobiographical language as one of the important conditions in which children expressed their spirituality', yet within her research this is only one facet by which children's spirituality was assessed, alongside languages of play and of fiction, whereas for Fowler it was his only source.[67] Picking up on the ideas of Karl Rahner, Nye refers to childhood as part of spiritual growth but not as something to be abandoned, rather that 'we are called not so much to grow out of our childhood as to grow *into* it'.[68]

Like many of the studies that she surveys, Nye's own research into the spirituality of children was founded upon qualitative data gained from interviews with children.[69] The group from the West Midlands involved 38 children of whom 37 were white and one black Caribbean. There were 18 children aged between six and seven and 20 children aged between ten and eleven. Most of the children (28) had no particular religious affiliations, while four identified as Muslim, two as Roman Catholic and four as Church of England.[70] David Csinos has pointed out that the research does not pay much attention to the cultural aspect of the children's experiences when assessing their responses.[71]

Rather than proposing a model, Nye has suggested facets of children's spirituality. She has picked up on models such as that proposed by Clive and Jane Erricker, which suggested four genres of child spirituality: '"My Little Pony" – a Disneyesque approach concentrating on the welfare of animals; "All American kid" – theme parks, McDonald's and consumerism; "Family Centred" – relational; and "The Hard Man" – tough, street-wise, into football'.[72] Instead of a model, she presents 'a flexible exploratory guide' to help people understand children's spirituality,[73] proposing three categories of spiritual sensitivity: Awareness-sensing, Mystery-sensing and Value-sensing.[74] First, *Awareness-sensing* is about being able to locate oneself in the present, 'here and now', as well as 'tuning in' to something like music or a piece of liturgy.[75] This kind of tuning in is extended further with the idea of 'flow', echoing the work of Isabella Csikszentmihalyi on that experience of peak engagement within a creative or physical activity.[76] Isabella Csikszentmihalyi links this sensation to the work of Ignatius of Loyola and also to the notion of vocation in general. Finally, this first category of spirituality encompasses 'focusing' on bodily feelings, which comes far more naturally to children than to those who have intellectualized their engagement with the world.[77] Nye's second category of *Mystery-sensing* encompasses two facets of mystery, one that journeys from the external to the internal and one that originates internally. First, there is the sense of awe and wonder, at creation or at something new or exciting. Second, the work of a child's imagination can be a rich source of spiritual engagement and something that Ignatius of Loyola also prized in his Spiritual Exercises. Drawing on the work of Margaret Donaldson and John Macmurray, Nye's final category is that of *Value-sensing*, which places importance on the sense of feeling about something often dismissed in the search of supposed 'objectivity'. This category is best understood through an exploration of the sub-categories of 'delight and despair', 'ultimate goodness' and 'meaning'. Delight and despair might each be experienced in response to a lived experience but equally in response to a spiritual one such as, Nye suggests, John of the Cross's descriptions of spiritual ecstasy and the Dark Night. Ultimate goodness, she describes as that sense often invested by young children in the parent or carer who can 'make things better', which, for children, can also be applied to an understanding and experience of the divine. The final sub-category of 'meaning' encompasses that sense of searching and discovery that leads to a developing sense of self in relation to the world.[78]

Nye resists some of the traditional shapes of development models for their linear and hierarchical qualities: 'That kind of model does not fit spirituality, which does *not* necessarily go from less to more, from simpler to complex ... [L]inear thinking can make it hard to value "earlier" stages in spiritual development as highly as later stages.'[79] In an endeavour to move away from hierarchical models, Nye offers a model that focuses on capacities of children rather than seeing immaturity as a kind of handicap. She makes suggestions for those in a variety of age ranges: the youngest children (0–3), the small child (approximately 3–6), the older child (approximately 7+).[80] To the youngest children she attributes 'embodied kinds of knowing', sensitivity to the here-and-now and attitudes of trust and hope. In this listing by age bracket it might be inferred that Nye does, at least in some ways, see her model of Awareness-sensing, Mystery-sensing and Value-sensing as staged across these three age ranges, though she resists this inference. There also seems to be a correlation between her model here and that of Ronald Goldman which she previously critiqued.[81] Elsewhere, the age divisions vary as she, Watts and Savage write about just two age groups, pre-school children and school children.[82] Yet her model of Awareness-sensing, Mystery-sensing and Value-sensing is not strictly delineated. Nye is very clear that there is overlap, movement between, and overlaying of these modes of spirituality, echoing Streib's overlapping of styles to indicate types. The 'childhood' that individuals grow through, out of and into is the embodied spirituality of these three modes. Nye acknowledges the possibility that children might experience something like a hiatus: 'As children experience some quite dramatic shifts in their thinking, there will be times when what used to hold together stops doing that, leaving them, hopefully temporarily, with "nothing".'[83] She also attributes to children capabilities such as using 'transitional space', which adults find more challenging and which might generally be located, for adults, in what might be termed a much 'higher' faith stage.[84]

Though resistant to the inevitable corollary between her model and a sense of development of faith to suggesting that earlier stages are in any way 'lesser', Nye sees spirituality as something that does develop. She also sees the potential for external factors to help or hinder that: 'Spirituality is not constant, nor something that will develop and grow regardless of what we do.' She encourages the concept of an immediate-term view in combination with a long-term view, where there is focus on 'How is this experience, right now a positive, that is, developing experience of God for this child or these children?', combined with attention to what may be 'much more slowly, shaping the child's lifelong spiritual attitude'.[85]

Although most of her work is on the spirituality of children, in her book with Watts and Savage, we see Nye's thought turn to adolescents. She picks up from Fowler the 'shift in adolescence from the "story mode" to a "master story mode."'[86] It is possible therefore to extrapolate a fourth mode to Nye's model of Awareness-sensing, Mystery-sensing and Value-sensing to include Ideology-sensing. As this model is not a staged one, while adolescents may bring in the new aspect of ideology, there is important work to be done in adolescence in terms of the other modes. For example, Awareness-sensing is key as teenagers grapple with identity. An increased awareness of the politics of church in adolescence might also mean young people need work in terms of mystery-sensing, seeking spirituality more than religion.[87] Within this collaborative book, there is also a summary of Fowler's model. The summary has clearly been informed by Nye's work and denotes each stage according to 'the different ways in which coherence for faith is sought (Stage 1: in emotion-laden images; 2: in narratives; 3: in the interpersonal; 4: in argument; 5: in paradox)',[88] with the notable absence of Fowler's mostly untested Stage 6.

Nye's most recent book explicitly suggests how her research can be used within the pastoral context. She suggests that in order to support the spiritual lives of children, those parenting them or in ministry with them should offer the SPIRIT model (an acronym of six factors, namely: Space, Process, Imagination, Relationship, Intimacy and Trust).[89] This suggests the importance of *Space* both in terms of a physically warm and welcoming location but also metaphorically in terms of emotional space and a space where they can be heard. The second strand is about *Process*. This is in terms of allowing children enough time and freedom to go through the process of spiritual development (rather than expecting quick successes), valuing the process of spirituality (not just the result) and encouraging an open process to the way that children's work is conducted. The third strand is about the importance of *Imagination* for children in their spiritual lives, not simply as those who receive imaginatively presented stories from scripture but as creative and imaginative beings themselves who are encouraged to tell their own stories. Nye's fourth strand is *Relationship*, suggesting the importance of focusing on the way each member of a church community of any age is respected and included. The penultimate strand is about *Intimacy*, not simply in terms of between children and those who care for them but in enabling intimacy with the divine by helping children to feel safe. Finally, Nye stresses the importance of *Trust* not only in terms of children being able to trust adults and adults honouring children's value by trusting them but also in the validity of knowing and not knowing about spiritual things and being able to hand some things over to God. Nye also reflects on these six strands in connection to prayer.[90] This is a really important model for work in local ministry and, like many ideas drawn from work with children and young people, is equally applicable to work with multiple generations within a worshipping community.

David Csinos

David Csinos is a Canadian practical theologian currently serving at Atlantic School of Theology in Halifax, Nova Scotia as Associate Professor of Practical Theology.[91] He studied at Wilfrid Laurier University, McMaster University and Union Presbyterian Seminary. Some of his work is in collaboration with others such as Ivy Beckwith. He focuses on children and those who support them through ministry; he has also written on the culture of children and youth ministry,[92] and preaching.[93] He founded the organization Faith Forward, which promotes 'innovation in ministry with children, youth, and families',[94] and has edited three volumes of texts on children's and youth ministry by a variety of international authors. In his book on preaching for all ages, he comments on the concept of Faith Development as one of the causes of division between generations that has made up what he terms the 'disembody of Christ', so it is not surprising that his model of children's spirituality falls in the category of style rather than progressive model. He first proposed this model (based on a small qualitative research study as part of his MA thesis[95]) in an article in 2009.[96] He also co-produced a test to help others assess children according to the model.[97] It is later explored more substantially in his books.[98] Csinos has more recently conducted some more qualitative research with children as a doctoral thesis[99] that was later published.[100]

Like Nye, Csinos does not talk about Faith Development but primarily about spirituality, specifically Christian spirituality. He defined spirituality initially as 'an inherent and biological human condition ... a relational connection, whether realized or ignored, to a being or power that transcends beyond the limits of ordinary, material existence',[101] and later as 'a sense of felt connection' whereby 'the human spirit is an agent of communication, potentially in communicative engagement with the self, other people, Nature and God'.[102] He picks up on Nye's use of the term 'relational consciousness' in describing how he came to his definition. As his definitions imply, Csinos's focus in assessment of his data was on communication. He suggests that development happens when people 'try to improve a situation'. In designing the assessment for styles, 'meaning' is taken into consideration as the questions he used were designed to 'clarify what people focus on as they try to make meaning of life experiences or carry out daily tasks'.[103] In explaining what he intended to cover in his research into spirituality, Csinos comments on the attention of other research into children's spirituality as being focused on 'generating insight into the content of children's theological ideas' rather than 'the processes by which they come to make such theological meaning' to which he instead attends.[104]

Although Csinos's focus might be on spirituality, he also explores the concept of faith, defining it distinctively from theology, spirituality and belief as something that:

> can involve beliefs, but speaks of something broader and more abstract. As I conceive of it, faith is a gift from God, freely given to all people. It is a sense of and trust in God or a higher power, *and it can grow, change, and be nurtured over time*. Faith can include beliefs, but it does not consist solely in statements that one holds to be true. Rather, it is at some level that unnameable, indefinable conviction in something greater than ourselves, one that people can respond to with acts of faithfulness that extend from one's experiences of faith. (my italics)[105]

This definition implies that, although Csinos presents a style model, he sees in faith the inherent characteristic of development. Indeed, he references both Westerhoff's and Fowler's development models in his latest work when interpreting the qualitative data from the children he spoke with at four churches.[106] He does not apply his own spiritual styles model to this data, though this may be because he is speaking instead about their theological processes rather than their spiritual styles.

Csinos references the work of the Willow Creek model and in doing so acknowledges that his model is not to be used in isolation: 'While I affirm ... that people at different stages of spiritual trans/formation and growth require different approaches to ministry, I take it further by adding that people of different spiritual styles also have different needs.'[107] This suggests that Csinos may consider spiritual styles as not something comparable to Faith Development models but something that should be used alongside them, or that Faith Development models should take style as well as stage into account.

Although Csinos offers a style-based model, he refers to humans as 'transforming creatures' who while they may 'possess one dominant spiritual type, characteristics of others often overlap'. He gives examples of where some of the styles overlap in terms of what activities those of different types might appreciate. A symbol-focused or action-focused individual might enjoy both 'planting trees or picking up litter at a conservation area' but for different reasons. For the first, it ensures the natural beauty of the world and, for the latter, it cares for the planet and combats ecological damage.[108] He also suggests that people 'are able to change their dominant personalities throughout their lives'.[109] Later, Csinos suggests that 'most people have *one or two styles* that tend to dominate their spiritual experiences' (my italics).[110] Indeed, he identifies in his own experience times when he has preferred each of the four styles. He cites Urban T. Holmes as suggesting that a balance between all four styles might be the clearest indicator of a healthy spiritual individual. Like Streib, Csinos's work could be extended to explore combinations of styles into types.

Csinos also acknowledges another form of development in these spiritual styles, that is the distortion of a style to the point of problems. For each style, he describes the healthy aspects and what happens when the style is 'extreme' or 'distorted'.[111] The logic underpinning his model suggests that individuals do not follow a linear or cyclical model in terms of the way their faith changes over time but that there are four essential modes which he calls spiritual styles, between which individuals can move. Csinos also gives some guidance for how each stage can be encouraged to grow.[112] He seems to suggest that the styles he identifies are essentially a toolkit that all people can draw from in their communication with others and with God and in their learning. For children, to learn all four styles improves the way they can relate to others, the world and to God. Yet, confusingly, the assessment tool is designed to identify someone's spiritual style, singular, which implies the model is more definitive.[113]

Csinos rooted his styles model in a small research study with 13 children from two Baptist churches and a Presbyterian church in Canada.[114] Though he does acknowledge that his sample group is far from representative of all children,[115] he later pays more attention to culture.[116] In his initial work he did not specify the ethnic diversity of the group, though he did describe each child and indicated ages and genders. The group was made up of five girls and eight boys, of whom two were 7-year-old boys, two were 8-year-old boys and one was an 8-year-old girl, two were 9-year-old girls and two were 9-year-old boys, and finally three were 10-year-old boys and one a 10-year-old girl. As a sample of childhood years, this features only one age group from the groupings

Nye identified.[117] Csinos met with the children in focus groups of varying sizes on five occasions and in some of these groups the children drew pictures as well as described their experience of spirituality in words.[118]

In addition to his own qualitative research, Csinos also acknowledges the influence of the spiritual styles work of Joyce Bellous and Corinne Ware on the formation of his four styles. They proposed 'head, heart, mystic, and kingdom' which he has reinterpreted, in collaboration with Bellous and through engagement with Urban Holmes' work categorizing historical spirituality (using two axes of apophatic/kataphatic and speculative/affective)[119] to become four styles (in the matching order to Ware's model) centred on a particular concept: word, emotion, symbol or action.[120] In developing his thesis into a book, Csinos added another concept as a founding principle of his model, namely 'object relations theory', which he describes as 'essential for understanding how children, and all human beings, make meaning and come to understand God, faith communities and the world'.[121]

Although Csinos's initial research was with just 13 churchgoing Christian children and Ware's model was based on Judaeo-Christian belief, in developing the Spiritual Styles Assessment, he and Bellous suggest that their model is applicable across all faiths and none.[122] My reservation with the spiritual styles model is twofold. First, on the basis of the foundations of the model. Although Csinos goes on to much more in-depth and nuanced work, the initial model for spiritual styles is not established on substantial empirical evidence, merely on a small-scale observation, backed up with the reading of two particular books on spirituality. Even though an assessment for style was developed and used with nearly 200 adults before the initial article was published, this does not seem to have been used as any kind of formal validation of the model. To give a more specific example of the tenuous nature of the model, one style is based on the evidence of just one of the 13 children involved in the research.[123] Csinos includes the stories of some of the 13 children involved in his previous research project to exemplify each of the styles, though this is not comparable to the way in which such data is used in the studies of Fowler, Slee or Streib, or indeed in Csinos's much more impressive later work *Little Theologians*. Second, the model is rather too simplistic to be ultimately useful. With only four styles, if an individual can have two dominant styles and have characteristics of others that overlap, I'm not entirely certain how useful categorizing individuals according to these four styles really is, especially without anything within Csinos's model to suggest why the person may have changed style (merely that they might do so at different times in their life). Aligned with this, it seems to have echoes of learning styles that have generally been questioned by those in education circles and suggestion made that far from being helpful these concepts are somewhat unfounded and do much less to promote good learning than other strategies.[124] Csinos urges readers not to confuse his action-centred style with kinaesthetic learning, which might suggest that others have noticed the commonality.[125]

For each of the styles he describes, Csinos identifies not only the characteristics of the stage but also a transformative goal of each style. This indicates both the nature of the style and the relationship it has to the next style. Csinos describes the *word-centred approach* as a kataphatic mode, with an emphasis on the clarity of positive definition in which concrete and clear understanding through the correct use of the right words is prized. To those who prefer this style, 'there is a focus on telling, instructing, preaching and proclaiming'.[126] Therefore in worship, the spoken and written word are both significant, be it in scripture readings, sermons or responses, because 'their ability to engage in logical and rational thinking is their primary means for connecting with God and understanding the world'.[127] This style inclines towards Bible study groups, especially those led by 'individuals who are knowledgeable of the Scriptures'.[128] This is the style of those who produce scholarly, including theological, texts and also those who can shape arguments to win others to faith through logic. Yet this style is more than simply about the words themselves. The focus on order also means that someone who prefers this style also 'prizes what can be seen, touched, conceived'. This is also taken into the moral framework for individuals so that they also emphasize 'right living that relies on ethical imperatives'.[129] The distorted version of this style involves an over-rational approach whereby 'all that matters is having the right idea, word or interpretation and practising in the right way by carrying out rituals with precision' to the point of oppressive moralizing and the prioritizing of thinking over feeling, or even doing, because individuals 'underanalyse the impact of emotion on their own thinking'. The impact of this style on relations with others is that 'while worthy people are seen as having the right words with the right definitions, those who cannot properly express themselves are devalued'.[130] Unlike the following styles, Csinos does not identify a transformative goal for the word-centred style. I suspect this is because the style is focused more on the rightness of what already is rather than seeking change.

In contrast to those who are word-centred, for those who are *emotion-centred*, while 'concrete expressions of God are highly prized', they are sceptical of intellectualism, preferring 'flashes of insight', hunches, gut instinct and, in religious contexts, words of knowledge. For this group, God is experienced as 'here, now, immanent, relational',[131] so the transformative goal is 'personal renewal of the heart'.[132] Those who prefer this style 'place a high value on music, dance and personal testimonies pointing to God's interventions in one's life' and to stories as a means of expressing values.[133] Individuals can be inclined to follow hunches over reasoned logic and are able to support others emotionally and inspire others to live well, as 'they're likely to emphasize evangelism through sharing personal experiences and direct communication with God'.[134] In leadership, this style can be inspiring if the individual practices sufficient self-reflection. However, without this, leadership can be manipulative due to the tendency towards a need for affirmation leading to 'unchecked and chaotic leadership that disenchants followers through causes that are laden with emotion yet worthless in the long run'.[135] An extreme or distorted form of the emotion-centred style can manifest as pietism, or emotionalism where 'all that matters is feeling good in the moment'.[136] For some, problems might arise due to a lack of awareness of the unresolved issues that might be driving them, such as pain or loss.

The *symbol-centred* style is the mystic, apophatic style in Csinos's model. Those favouring it 'put significant worth on the power of quiet and silence, listening and hearing' for connection with God.[137] They find mystery elusive and reject the idea that such things can be expressed in words. Individuals can favour solitude and have 'a strong experience of transcendence'. For them, engagement with God is often through the beauty of creation or silence and stillness. Though it is almost impossible to capture spiritual experience in words, as Csinos asserts, 'if one tries, any attempt to fully explain God is believed to lose that which is precious about God'. The transformative goal of this style is 'trans/formation that enables union with God ... ultimately unattainable [though] mystics are satisfied with the journey to discover this union'.[138] Csinos suggests that people who are symbol-centred 'struggle to fit in with organized religion', though I wonder if that depends on the style of religion as more symbolically expressive forms might satisfy them. Nonetheless, Csinos assigns to this style those who offer devotional texts to the church. In its extreme form, a person preferring this style might withdraw to a solitary or ascetic and eremitic life. Csinos appears to consider this a negative outcome because of the loss to the church of the wisdom they could bring rather than honouring the work of those who follow in the steps of the desert fathers and mothers today for their prayerful presence in the world. Doctrinally, the extreme form of this style is Gnosticism and, for some, the attendant rejection of all things physical and therefore an unhealthy rejection of the body through extreme asceticism or through rejection of family and socializing.

As the name implies, those with an *action-centred* style are focused on what is to be done. Meaning is found in deeds not words. Individuals who prefer this style will be drawn to the third, fourth and fifth marks of mission over the first two as they seek to change the world. This is their defining transformational goal: 'to change the oppressive, harmful, and destructive features of society while stressing the presence and justice of God'. In order to achieve this goal, those who prefer this style are therefore observant and very driven. This can sometimes extend to single-mindedness and even impatience. One extreme of this style is 'single-minded "tunnel-vision"' about a particular cause,[139] which can alienate them from society. Csinos links this with an early Christian sect called Encratism, which practised extreme abstinence from meat, wine and marriage.[140] In order to be adopted healthily, this style needs compassion and humility. Without this, in extreme forms, this style can lack the ability to communicate the cause that they so passionately wish to champion or even become overly judgemental of those less committed to action as 'encratists see little use for words and are often inarticulate about their goals and theological assumptions'.[141]

I have certainly used the spiritual styles model in helping people understand that a church community of all generations is not homogenous. It has been an excellent tool in helping people understand different ways of planning worship and activities. However, as a tool about Faith Development, I have reservations. It may simply be that Csinos is not seeking to present something comparable with other models we have explored. Indeed, in his latest work, he talks about Faith Development, referencing Fowler's work when discussing the experiences of the children he interviewed and about the potential for research in a longitudinal study of 'how children's theological meaning-making changes as they grow older'.[142] This text brings Fowler's model into conversation with the data Csinos's own research discovered and compares some of the children's constructions of theology to both Mythic-Literal and Intuitive-Projective stages, as well as to the Synthetic-Conventional stage.[143] A strength of this model is its simplicity. It can be explained to and understood by a broad community and, as a tool for understanding diversity of a cohort (rather than the nature of an individual), it has merit. Csinos suggests that children should be taught all of the styles and that adults should be aware of all styles. As a tool for reflecting on the provision of ministry to a whole church, I can see that it offers a simple framework that is understandable to a broad audience and yet enlightening about difference. Csinos acknowledges the partial nature of his model, asserting that he is not seeking an ultimate and perfect model that will fit everyone and define them, but rather 'partial, imperfect glimpses into people's spiritual lives'.[144]

James Hopewell

James Hopewell was born in Cincinnati, Ohio. He studied at the University of Cincinnati before attending Episcopal Theological School in Cambridge, Massachusetts. He later gained a doctorate in the history of religions from Columbia University. He spent part of his ministry in West Africa, where he was ordained and worked at the Cuttington College and Divinity School in Suacoco, Liberia, as Professor of Bible and Comparative Religion, then later as Dean of the Divinity School and Vice President. He became the Director of the Theological Education Fund Committee of the World Council of Churches in 1964 and visited various theological institutes worldwide, including Asia and Latin America. He was involved in the establishment of colleges in a number of countries, including Indonesia and Nigeria. He was Professor of Religion in Contemporary Sub-Saharan African Society at the Hartford Seminary Foundation in Connecticut before moving to Emory as Professor of World Religions. Later he was appointed as Director of the Institute for Church Ministries. His work combined ministry and academia as he also established the Episcopal Church of the Holy Spirit in Cumming, Georgia, in 1974 and served as its first vicar. He became Professor of Religion and the Church, and Director of the Rollins Center for Church Ministries at the Candler School of Theology, Emory University.[145] Hopewell's work was published posthumously through the editing of Barbara G. Wheeler who, coincidentally, lodged with James Fowler while compiling the book.[146]

As his study is focused not simply on the individual but the corporate faith of the church, Hopewell does not work with a definition of faith in individual terms but explores instead the 'idiomatic code by which a congregation communicates itself, enabling it to identify and integrate itself, to express its faith and love, to govern and sometimes to change its corporate behavior'.[147]

A major critique of Faith Development is that it panders to an individualistic view of faith when so much of scripture is focused on whole peoples – the people of Israel and the Body of Christ. Hopewell's work, though not a model of Faith Development, could be viewed as a Faith-Community Development model. Hopewell's academic work and time spent around the world brought him into contact with those of other faiths and he acknowledges the influence of this experience on his theological thinking.[148] Writing on world religions, he assessed faith in more of a community-focused rather than individual-focused mode: 'The study of other religions gives me fresh access to the nature of congregations, enabling me to glimpse better how local churches particularize their religious behavior and concretely express the faith.'[149]

Taking this kind of focus has similarities to Fowler's emphasis on meaning-making and to the stories and biographical element of Streib. Hopewell suggested that his approach 'considers the congregation less a texture or machine or organism than a discourse, an exchange of symbols that express the views, values, and motivations of the parish'.[150] He focused on worldview as the definitive aspect distinguishing one congregation from another. This was no doubt rooted in his experience of working alongside many different religious groups, but he was prompted to develop the model during his experience of terminal illness and the different responses that those visiting him in hospital exhibited in the face of his diagnosis.[151] Based on this experience, he developed a model for congregational stories reflecting the literary analysis of Northrup Frye.[152] He endeavoured to support his model by two methods – 'participant observation and guided interviews'[153] – spending a year focused on two particular churches (one Baptist, one Methodist).[154] He used a semi-structured interview, beginning with a question relating to death as that seemed to prompt open and honest responses from the outset.[155] Later he devised a questionnaire designed to establish the worldview of an individual and, if completed by a whole congregation, the worldview of the congregation.[156]

He asserts that 'the congregation's self-perception is primarily narrative in form. The congregation's communication among its members is primarily by story.'[157] Hopewell suggests that any congregation holds one cultural story out of a possible four. He reflected on the stories told to him about his terminal cancer and further explored these modes by inviting people to talk about their own stories of difficulty. So, like the Willow Creek model, Hopewell's work is prompted by an engagement with challenge. In categorizing people's stories, Hopewell expected to find a single continuum of story from conservative to liberal but found instead that a modified form of Frye's Comic/Romantic/Tragic/Ironic model seemed to fit better. Hopewell explores the idea of studying the culture of a church, citing Eaton and James Whitehead as well as

Westerhoff.[158] These calls upon texts from the field of Faith Development further validate the inclusion of his model here.

The four categories Hopewell identified, as mapped against Frye's original narrative model, were Tragic-Canonic, Comic-Gnostic, Romantic-Charismatic and Ironic-Empiric. He identified elements to the story of each mode, assigning a motif (a guiding theme) as well as the overall sense of movement. For individual scenarios within the story, either on a personal, social or cosmic level, he suggested three aspects. Each scenario could be defined by a situation, a response and a resolution. He also assessed what he called cognitive features of how the story held together in terms of sources of authority, focus of integrity and valued behaviour. Finally, he offered distinctive perceptions of a particular set of Christian concepts, namely: God, Jesus, evil, time, Bible, minister, Eucharist, church and gospel.

The first of the four categories he identified was a *Comic-Gnostic* story. This does not mean it is all about jokes and comedy but, more in the vein of a Shakespearean comedy, that the central characteristic of the story is a happy ending in which problems are resolved. The motif of this story is integration and the movement within it is towards union. For individuals, the situation is viewed as ignorance, the response to that is enlightenment and the resolution therefore is peace. In social terms, the scenario is one in which there is discord, which through wisdom can be brought to harmony and, on a cosmic level, the scenario is one of illusion in which union can be brought about through process. Authority in this worldview is found in intuition, the esoteric and wisdom. The focus of integrity is a trustworthy cosmos and inner awareness is a valued behaviour. This worldview is one that 'ultimately integrates its seemingly antithetical elements'.[159] There may be a crisis but a congregation living a Comic-Gnostic story is convinced it 'will all work out in the end'. Within Christian communities, the prospect of heaven can serve as the ultimate happy ending. For this congregation, God is seen as a Ground or Force, with Jesus a living symbol of that force. Evil is to be found in ignorance, the Bible is allegorical and the gospel is consciousness. Clergy and other ministers act as guides to the church as if it is a pilgrimage, and the Eucharist is a sacrament. Time is viewed as cyclical; what has happened before can happen again.

The second mode of story is the *Romantic-Charismatic*. Within this worldview, the motif is a spirit of adventure that views challenges as opportunities. The movement of the story is to be found in uniformity moving towards variation. The personal scenario in this story is one of weakness and the response to that is tarrying, which leads to empowerment. In social terms the situation is conventionality, which, through charism, leads to transformation. For a Christian community, a confidence in what Frye called 'prodigies of courage and endurance unnatural to us' are expected in terms of the miraculous.[160] On a cosmic level, the scenario is one of perpetuity which, through certain signs, will lead to the day of the Lord. Authority is to be found in the personally manifested evidence of God's immanence. The focus of integrity is the providence of God, and recognition of God's blessings is a valued behaviour. God is seen as Spirit and Jesus as Lord. Evil is personified in demons and time is viewed as premillennial (a time before the end). The Bible is a programme, and any minister of the church is seen as an exemplar to the church, which is viewed as the harvest. The Eucharist is presence and the gospel represents power.

The third story is that of the *Tragic-Canonic*. A worldview lived through the tragic lens sees difficulty as 'necessary sacrifice'.[161] The main motif of the story is of sacrifice and the movement of the story lies in union towards subordination. There is no expectation of a miraculous work of wonder to resolve everything. Rather, resolution is found within the difficulty. The situation is one of hubris, the response to which is surrender, which leads to a resolution of justification. On a social level, the situation is one of vice that, through righteousness, leads to judgement. On a cosmic level, the story is one of principalities and powers that, through the Passion, leads to the kingdom. This mode always reminds me of the song of Jonah in the belly of the whale:

'The waters closed in over me;
    the deep surrounded me;
weeds were wrapped around my head
    at the roots of the mountains.
I went down to the land
    whose bars closed upon me for ever;
yet you brought up my life from the Pit,
    O LORD my God.
As my life was ebbing away,
    I remembered the LORD;
and my prayer came to you,
    into your holy temple.'
(Jonah 2.5–7)

Authority is viewed as God's revealed word and will, and the focus for integrity is scripture. A valued behaviour is obedience. God is viewed as the Father, Jesus as Saviour and evil as the devil. Time is understood as linear. The Bible is the word and any minister a messenger of that word. The Eucharist is viewed as a memorial. The church is understood as a covenant and the gospel is all about salvation.

The final mode of story that Hopewell presents is the *Ironic-Empiric*. This mode of viewing the world might claim to be 'realistic'. There are no heroes and the difficulties that we face are part of life and we should expect them. As challenges are to be expected, they can be a source of unity among those experiencing them, which might be characterised by ironic humour. The main motif of this worldview is testing, and movement takes place from variation towards uniformity. The situation on a personal level is viewed as bondage that can be resolved into love through honesty. On a social level, the current situation is oppression which, through justice, can resolve into community, and on a cosmic level the situation is characterized by absurdity and through science can be resolved into regularity. Authority therefore is to be found objectively and verified by one's own five senses. Integrity is to be found in one's own self and a valued behaviour is realism. God in this worldview is seen as the Ultimate Concern and Jesus as a teacher. Evil is seen as demonic and time is amillenial (not concerned with, or believing in, Christ's return). The Bible is viewed as history. The minister is viewed as an enabler of the church, which is viewed as a fellowship. The Eucharist is an agape and the gospel is about freedom.

To understand how these stories might operate in practice, the example I have used with ordinands is the diversity of portrayals of a modern Christmas on film. The *Ironic-Empiric* story might best be personified in the pre-Epiphany Ebenezer Scrooge in conversation with his clerk Bob Cratchit in the *Muppet Christmas Carol* version, where, when Scrooge indicates there will be eviction notices to send the next day, Cratchit exclaims that this would be on Christmas Day. In reply, Scrooge suggests he may giftwrap them.

Meanwhile the *Romantic-Charismatic* mode is best exemplified by the ever-redoubtable Mr Maddens in *Nativity!* battling to get through Christmas and the production of a nativity play without losing all hope. The Comic-Gnostic mode is personified in Buddy from the movie *Elf*, for whom everything is always perfect (despite much evidence to the contrary!). Finally, the Tragic-Canonic mode for me was captured in a short film, *Just Another Day*, made for Age UK, which pictures a lone, elderly man on his daily trudge to the shop as Christmas approaches and the sad emptiness of his life when faced with the closed doors of the shops on Christmas Day itself and his weary steps home, without supplies, to an empty house.[162]

Though he talks of them as separate, Hopewell also suggests that these four stories interrelate in two ways. He argues that they are not simply styles but sit in a cycle. A community or individual, like a story, can combine two neighbouring stories, such as a comic-irony or a romantic-tragedy. He even identifies the possibility of a congregation reflecting two or three stories. This does weaken his case as it suggests that Hopewell's model might encompass not simply four but eight or even 12 stories. In fact, he suggests that his model certainly doesn't account for the stories of all congregations: 'I devised the categories as a more adequate way to acknowledge variables of belief than a two-point liberal-conservative categorization permits. But even a four-fold typology does not delineate the full picture of self and world that the congregation sees.'[163] Communities can also move and change their story, but Hopewell is insistent that they cannot simply jump from one to another; rather, they must move clockwise or anticlockwise around a circle of these stories, as shown in Figure 1. Jumping from comedy to tragedy or romance to irony is not possible. The story must travel through an intervening story first.[164] Although the stories are in a cycle, Hopewell does not necessarily suggest that the story of a community shifts regularly through the cycle. Rather, he notes that within each of these storied understandings of the world or cultural plots, the plots link, unfold, thicken and twist.[165] So he identified movement within each style more than movement between them.

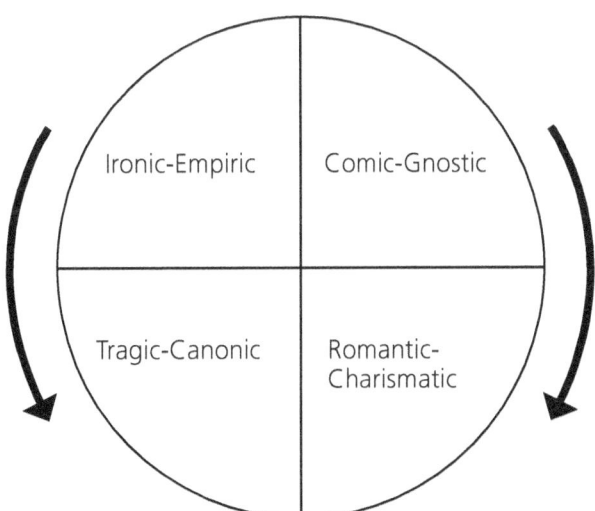

Figure 1: The cyclical movement of communities

Hopewell created a tool for helping individuals and congregations to discern their determining narrative.[166] This is something that a church could use to explore where they are as a community in terms of their Faith Development. Fowler's discussion of his Stage 3 Synthetic-Conventional faith reflects the way in which a whole church can be at one stage, and in some ways Hopewell's model is a more nuanced exploration of this phenomenon. His work has been taken up more recently by Vaughan S. Roberts and David Sims in their excellent book *Leading by Story*, which would be a more accessible way to explore the role of Hopewell's model within a pastoral context.[167] Hopewell's model might be particularly useful for ministers beginning in a new context or considering combining communities into a new larger benefice.

Maria Harris

Maria Harris was a Catholic theologian and educator who, while studying at St John's University, left her studies and joined the Sisters of St Joseph, an order predominantly focused on teaching.[168] She began her ministry with the Sisters teaching music in a number of schools while also studying music herself at Alverno College, Milwaukee. She later completed a degree in English literature, returning to St John's University. Somewhat restricted by her duties with the order, she turned down a scholarship from another university and instead completed her Master's degree in 1967 at Manhattan College before moving on to study for an EdD (a joint doctorate in education and religious studies) via Columbia Teacher's College and Union Theological Seminary.[169] She directed the adult education programmes for a diocese via the Rockville Centre Diocesan Office of Religious Education and also taught at a Roman Catholic seminary. She co-wrote her first book with Gabriel Moran, a man who would go on to become her husband.[170] Five years after this book, she left the Sisters of St Joseph and became the principal of a middle school for a year, before taking up a teaching role at Andover Newton Theological School, Massachusetts. There she published four more books.[171] Marrying Moran, she moved to join him in New York, becoming Professor of Religious Education at the Graduate School of Religion and Religious Education at Fordham University. There she published again, becoming a popular lecturer worldwide.[172] She went on to write further texts focused on feminism, spirituality, justice and education,[173] before writing the work that is the focus of our concern. This was her first book for a popular rather than academic audience.[174] She went on to write two further texts, first an expansion on the Levitical idea of Jubilee[175] and then, in collaboration with her husband, on the subject of religious education.[176] Harris died in 2005, in a nursing home on the grounds of the Motherhouse of the Sisters of St Joseph, after being diagnosed four years previously with Parkinson's and dementia.

As I said in the introduction to this section, in some ways Harris's model defies classification as stage, cycle or style. It inspired my own model, which also defies these categorizations. Instead of being a sequence, cycle or simply a choice of styles, Harris's dance model has more scope to reflect real life experience of faith, suggesting that different movements of faith are not necessarily experienced sequentially or ordered in any hierarchy of progression.[177] Yet she, as other styles-based models' creators, negates the validity of there being some sense of seasonal or progressive development in faith despite describing her model in terms that speak in some ways of a natural progression from one stage to another. She says the steps may be taken in any order (and yet her own descriptions imply a clear progression between most of the stages).

Harris is not writing about Faith Development as her text is intended to be a personal workbook and echoes more the medieval models with a focus more on spirituality than on faith. She talks around the subject of spirituality in her Prologue, describing the tasks of spirituality as taking seriously 'the major issues in women's lives and the major elements in women's daily experience: issues such as brokenness, connection, and power; elements such as love, work, and death'.[178] She also describes spirituality as 'the undersong of our lives – the innerness of our lives' – which works 'according to a form and framework that allows us to live the questions, love the questions, dance the questions'.[179] In later work, Harris describes spirituality as something that

> can be understood as our way of being in the world in the light of the Mystery of God or the Sacred ... [W]omen's spirituality is characterized as rooted in our bodies, attentive to ritual, inclusive of the nonhuman universe, reliant on women's experience (not only on men's), and insistent that the political cannot be separated from the personal.[180]

Her definition of spirituality echoes definitions of faith, incorporating as it does the interaction with God and with fellow creatures.

Harris suggests that the movement in her model is not upward and onward in a straight line, nor cyclical: 'The next "stage" is not a movement upward to a superior vantage point but a step toward an integration of previous stages.'[181] This echoes Westerhoff's notion of stages growing outwards from each other, with early stages embedded within later stages. She offers the model of a dance where steps whirl and interchange:

> Women's spirituality is a rhythmic series of movements, which unlike the steps of a ladder or a staircase, do not go up and down. Instead the steps of our lives are much better imagined as steps in a dance, where there is movement backward and forward, turn and return, bending and bowing, circling and spiraling; and no need to finish or move on to the next step, except in our own good time, and God's.[182]

She expands this in a later work describing the movement as involving others and not simply ourselves, whereby 'we move backward *and* forward; we are alone *and* partnered; we are slow *and* swift; we are solitary *and* we are celebratory'.[183] The Holy Spirit has a key role in Harris's model, saying that all Faith Development is 'the Dance of the Spirit'.[184]

Harris acknowledges the voices of many women worldwide in the foundation of her model. These voices were not gathered as part of formal research but stem from Harris's extensive academic study and involvement in the education of women over many years. To explicate each stage, she uses these voices alongside texts from mystical writers, ancient and contemporary. Walter Brueggeman described the unique way that she was able to engage with ideas, saying, 'Harris has refused to leave things in the conventional categories and so can bring matters into new relationships that quietly resketch our usual segmentations of the world.'[185] One of the ways she does this is through her reflection on the whole idea of development.

Harris's understanding of development is focused on more than merely the individual. Her focus on justice drew her to look instead to the development of society on a macro level. She and her co-author acknowledge the work on Faith Development but consider it more important to focus on a wider community.

> When I was beginning my professional life as a religious educator, I assumed that the term 'development' referred to personal human life. Like many of my colleagues and peers, I equated development with psychosocial/ cognitive/ moral/faith issues as these gave insight into human being and human life.[186]

She describes how this understanding changed through reading the work of her co-author (and husband) Gabriel Moran:

> By the time his *Religious Education Development* was published in 1983, I had begun to suspect that the major aspect of development calling out to religious educators and pastoral ministers was not only or even fundamentally in the realm of psychology. It was in the arena of economics.[187]

She links this notion to the 'divine economy'; God holding creation and the concept of community or *oikonomia*, with individual households on a micro level and ecology on a macro level. Harris uses the idea of 'home' as the place where humans are truly themselves, seeing significance in the way we keep our homes as reflecting the way we share with the rest of humanity and creation.[188]

Harris's model is distinctive in its use of the metaphor of dance. She suggests assorted 'steps' in Faith Development, which may be taken in various orders, though she orders them to some extent and suggests that each of the steps leads in some way to the next, at least in the first experience of that step. For example, when describing the movement from the second step to the third, she says, 'And out of Dis-covering then comes the impulse to take what we have found and gently mold our findings into a shape fitting for us in our time and in our world, bringing us into the step of Creation.'[189] So there is a sense of a clear order at first but scope for what might be termed improvisation with what steps are taken next. Harris sees these steps as interchangeable in the way they might be experienced throughout life. She suggests five initial steps, namely awakening, discovering, creating, dwelling, nourishing, with two subsequent ones, traditioning and transforming. For each of the seven steps she also offers at the conclusion of each chapter seven practices to help women identify and engage with that step.

Harris identifies *Awakening* with Meister Eckhart's description of the awakening of spirituality,[190] as well as to the experience of artists and poets.[191] This step can occur at any time though Harris associates it particularly with what she calls 'crucial times', which might in psychological terms be called crises, whether tragic or in relation to change, bad or good. It is an embodied experience that involves 'sensual attentiveness', being a new awareness of existing possibilities and abilities.[192] This is not an external force acting upon a person but a woman's understanding of her own potential, particularly looking at her own body and seeing it as good, to echo God in creation. This new understanding, Harris says, leads naturally to the next step in the dance.

The second step, *Dis-covering*, is intentionally hyphenated. Harris says it is about re-finding the self.[193] Unlike the first step, this can involve another person as a source of that dis-covery. There is some form of catalyst, which is either a person or a text, experience or image, that prompts the woman to see something in a new way. It is an epiphanic step. Harris gives this step its own four-stage cycle. It is only in a person *responding* to the dis-covery with a willingness to engage that she begins *searching* and therefore *finding*. This *finding* results in a *re-membering*; a putting back together that can then lead back to *responding*.[194] What the woman might dis-cover can vary: power, community, brokenness or divinity. In this latter category, Harris makes links to the works of Julian of Norwich.[195] She suggests that discovery leads logically to the impetus to do something with the dis-covery.

Once something has been discovered, Harris says a woman therefore feels the need to make something of it, to create something: 'Having awakened to our spirituality and Dis-Covered its main features, we take upon ourselves the vision of the creative artist.'[196] This *Creating* can be in the form of making something outside oneself or creating something within. Again, Harris breaks this step down into four areas or, in this case, 'laws' of creating. She says the first law of creating is that we become what we create. This is a facet of inhabiting and waiting for creation to be possible. Her second law is that creating is not instant but 'a continuing process' that does not have a clear ending. Her third law is about the importance of the Holy Spirit; you do not create alone. Creation is a collaborative act: 'The brooding hovering presence we have already met holds us gently and tenderly in its everlasting arms, at times making us lie down in green pastures, at others leading us beside still waters.'[197] Her fourth law is that a woman must give up preconceived ideas about what spirituality is and what will be created. It is a birthing process. Somewhat confusingly, she also offers five 'moves' for this step, namely 'Contemplation, Engagement, Formgiving, Emergence and Release'.[198] Aptly, for a step about creation, and uniquely for our models, Harris offers the reader a song including music, words and dance actions as a final practice of this step.[199] After the final move, the release, Harris identifies the logical transition to the next step.

The fourth step of *Dwelling* grows naturally out of the first three: 'Having Awakened to our spirituality, Dis-Covered its features, and undertaken Creating its form in our lives, we now reach the centre-point of spirituality; the place and time of Dwelling.'[200] Harris identifies the commonality in the way we inhabit physical spaces and spiritual places. She suggests that those who inhabit this step of dwelling in their spiritual place or 'soulroom or spiritroom'[201] also find a new relationship with the physical spaces they inhabit. Harris describes this step in the spiritual dance as one in which being truly present and resting play a key part. It is about spending time in both the challenging places or 'deserts' and the places of flourishing, the 'gardens'.[202] Alongside this axis of opposites, she places another pair of places. The 'city' represents an individual's relationship with the cosmos and Harris contrasts this with a space in which many women have found themselves for large parts of their lives, 'home'.[203] She also brings a relational element to this step in which the individual reflects on the way that they dwell with themselves, with other people, with other creatures and with God.[204]

The fifth step of *Nourishing* is in many ways the culmination of what has gone before and, arguably, if her model functioned as the other models we've explored, Harris could end her model here. The step of nourishing can be somewhat surprising after those that precede it in that it doesn't necessarily grow out of the one before it as others have done. Instead, it grows from all that has gone before and brings them together. Harris offers a model of three interlocking circles of disciplines (grouped as personal, communal and integrating). These three interlock on a central circle called 'adoration'. This echoes the universalizing stages at the summit of other models. It is where it all comes together in the adoration of God; with the focus not on the individual but on the integration of everything. Uniquely to Harris, this universalizing phase of personal integration is not the pinnacle and the ultimate goal. There is further to go.

Harris proposes that a natural outworking of the first five steps of the dance of spirituality, the result of a woman coming to a sense of universalizing wholeness is *Traditioning*; to look to the passing on of the good that she has found. This supports the critique of other models which tend towards a more male construction of maturity in faith. As Slee has argued, women with mature faith exhibit caring responsibilities for others, though in models such as Fowler's this can be perceived as a lack of independence that limits the assessment of their faith to a lower stage.[205] Unlike the previous steps, the dance at Step 6 'shifts to movement executed in partnership'.[206] Traditioning involves loving, teaching, mentoring and modelling, either as part of a formal role for which someone is trained or as a natural outworking of the prior experience or role.

Harris offers her final step of *Transforming* as one in which 'we dance now into the great discovery that in giving birth to our Spirituality, we are giving birth to ourselves'. This rebirth or 'finale', as Harris calls it, affects the individual and also brings about a wider renewal: 'Renewal in our own lives has the ripple effect of renewing the face of the earth.'[207] This finale of a step has within it its own four movements of listening (drawing on the previous steps of Dis-Covering and Creating), which leads to questioning. These two then lead not to action but to a pause to acknowledge what has been that has not been good, a movement of mourning. This mourning leads to an essential part of women's spirituality, that of bonding, which in turn gives way to birthing, the culmination of the transforming.

Harris added a further factor a decade after her original model. This emphasizes women whom she terms Jubilarians, those who have passed their jubilee year of 50. It links well to her ideas of Traditioning and Transforming.[208] These women, her research found, have particular foci on attaining wisdom and wholeness, especially in interdependence and mature moral agency, as well as the important task of divesting and letting go of things in preparation for death.

Harris's model is not in the same style as any other model we have encountered. She was more focused on the tasks of each step than the characteristic of the person. Yet her model indicates that the move away from an upward trajectory model is possible. Her model is, of course, written particularly in reflection on the lives of women. Can it be adapted to apply also to men? Should it? Much of what she says is not uniquely characteristic of women and is clearly more than merely a corrective to other models. What might it look like in the church if we saw the maturation of faith for our members as a process that is both individual and corporate? This echoes again Westerhoff's later model for the Faith Development of a whole community and Hopewell's notion of whole-community stories. Harris's model clearly offers a number of exercises for each stage, so these could certainly be used in a local worshipping community either at regular groups or at dedicated quiet days.

Notes

1 Brush, S. 2014, 'Imaging Faith: Faith Development and Responses to Art', unpublished MA dissertation.

2 Hopewell, James, 1988, *Congregation: Stories and Structures*, London: SCM Press.

3 Gardner, Howard, 1999, *Intelligence Reframed: Multiple Intelligences*, New York: Basic Books.

4 Fowler, James W., 1986, 'Faith and the Structuring of Meaning', reprinted in

Dykstra, Craig and Parks, Sharon, eds, *Faith Development and Fowler*, Birmingham: Religious Education Press, pp. 15–42, p. 37.

5 Slee, Nicola, 2004, *Women's Faith Development: Patterns and Processes* London: Routledge, pp. 65–8.

6 Bickford, Michael S., 2011, 'John H. Westerhoff III: A Humanistic and Historical Analysis of His Impact on Religious Education', unpublished dissertation, p. 84.

7 Adair-Toteff, Christopher, 2021, 'Friedrich Von Hügel's philosophy', *History of European Ideas*, Vol. 47, No. 7, pp. 1079–93, p. 1080.

8 Biallas, Leonard J., 1979, 'Von Hügel's Contribution to Religious Studies and to Religion', *Horizons*, Vol. 6, No. 1, pp. 59–80, p. 68.

9 Adair-Toteff, 'Friedrich Von Hügel', p. 1081.

10 Streib, Heinz, 2005, 'Faith Development Research Revisited: Accounting for diversity in structure, content, and narrativity of faith', *The International Journal for the Psychology of Religion*, Vol. 15, No. 2, pp. 99–121.

11 Fowler, J. W. 2001, 'Faith Development Theory and the Postmodern Challenges', *The International Journal for the Psychology of Religion*, Vol. 11, No. 3, p. 164.

12 Klein, Constantin, and Streib, Heinz, eds, 2018, *Xenosophia and Religion: Biographical and Statistical Paths for a Culture of Welcome*, Cham: Springer International Publishing.

13 Fowler, J. W., Streib, H. and Keller, B., 2004, *Manual for Faith Development Research*, Bielefeld: Universität Bielefeld/Research Centre for Biographical Studies in Contemporary Religion; Streib, H. and Keller, B., 2018, *Manual for the Assessment of Religious Styles in Faith Development*, interviews, Bielefeld: Universität Bielefeld/Research Centre for Biographical Studies in Contemporary Religion.

14 Streib, Heinz and Hood Jr., Ralph W., eds, 2024, *Faith in Development: Mixed-Method Studies on Worldviews and Religious Styles*, Bielefeld: Universität Bielefeld / Research Centre for Biographical Studies in Contemporary Religion.

15 Streib, Heinz, 2013, 'The Hierarchy of Religious Styles', Contribution to the Discussion Forum on 'Religious, Faith, and Spiritual Development: Future Perspectives' at the Conference of the International Association for the Psychology of Religion in Lausanne, 27–31 August.

16 Streib, 'Question', p. 20.

17 Fowler et al., *Manual*.

18 Streib, H. and Keller, B., *Manual*, p. 19.

19 Streib, Heinz, Klein, Constantin and Keller, Barbara, 2021, 'The Mysticism Scale as Measure for Subjective Spirituality: New Results with Hood's M-Scale and the Development of a Short Form', in Ai, A. L., Wink, P. and Harris, K. A., eds, *Assessing Spirituality in a Diversified World*, New York: Springer.

20 Streib et al., 'Faith Development', p. 1, citing Fowler, *Stages*, pp. 92–3.

21 Streib, 'Question', p. 5.

22 Streib, 'Question', p. 7.

23 Streib et al., 'Faith Development', pp. 1–2.

24 Streib et al., 'Faith Development', p. 8.

25 Streib et al., 'Faith Development', p. 15.

26 Streib et al., 'Faith Development', p. 11.

27 Streib et al., 'Faith Development', pp. 14–20.
28 See Streib et al., 'Faith Development'; Streib, Heinz, 2019, 'How Religious Styles Develop: Typology and Longitudinal Perspectives', presented at the Conference of the Society for the Study of Human Development (SSHD), Portland, USA; Streib, Heinz, and Klein, Constantin, 2015, 'Do Religious Styles and Schemata Change over Time: Results with the Religious Schema Scale', presented at the Annual Meeting of the Society for the Scientific Study of Religion, Newport Beach.
29 Streib et al., 'Faith Development', p. 9.
30 Streib et al., 'Faith Development', p. 5.
31 Streib et al., 'Faith Development', p. 1.
32 Streib, Heinz, Chen, Zhuo Job and Hood, Ralph W., 2020, 'Categorizing People by Their Preference for Religious Styles: Four Types Derived from Evaluation of Faith Development Interviews of Faith Development Interviews', *The International Journal for the Psychology of Religion*, Vol. 30, No. 2, pp. 112–27, p. 2.
33 Streib, 'Question', pp. 14–15.
34 Streib et al., 'Faith Development', p. 2.
35 Streib et al., 'Faith Development', p. 7.
36 Streib et al., 'Categorizing', pp. 123–4.
37 Streib et al., 'Categorizing', p. 118.
38 Streib et al., 'Faith Development', p. 2.
39 Streib, Heinz, Hood, Ralph W. and Klein, Constantin, 2010, 'The Religious Schema Scale: Construction and Initial Validation of a Quantitative Measure for Religious Styles', *The International Journal for the Psychology of Religion*, Vol. 20, No. 3, pp. 151–72.
40 Streib et al., 'The Religious Schema Scale', p. 158.
41 Streib, Heinz, 2001, 'Faith Development Theory Revisited: The Religious Styles Perspective', *International Journal for the Psychology of Religion*, Vol. 11, No. 3, pp. 150–2. On universalizing, see Streib et al., 'Categorizing', p. 114.
42 Streib, 'Revisited', pp. 143–58.
43 Streib et al., 'Categorizing', p. 115.
44 See Figure 1 in Streib et al., 'Categorizing', p. 120.
45 Streib et al., 'Categorizing', p. 115.
46 Streib, 'The Hierarchy'.
47 Nye, Rebecca, 1998, 'Psychological Perspectives on Children's Spirituality', unpublished thesis, Nottingham University.
48 Hay, David and Nye, Rebecca, 2006, *The Spirit of the Child*, London: Jessica Kingsley.
49 Nye, Rebecca, 2009, *Children's Spirituality: What it is and Why it Matters*, London: Church House Publishing, p. 5; Watts, Fraser, Nye, Rebecca and Savage, Sara, 2002, *Psychology for Ministry* London: Routledge.
50 Hay and Nye, *Spirit*, p. 20.
51 Nye, *Children's Spirituality*, p. 18.
52 Nye, *Psychological Perspectives*, pp. 28–9.
53 Nye, *Children's Spirituality*, p. 5.
54 Watts et al., *Psychology*, p. 112.
55 Nye, *Psychological Perspectives*, pp. 35–6.
56 Nye, *Children's Spirituality*, p. 13.

57 Nye, *Psychological Perspectives*, p. 43.
58 Nye, *Children's Spirituality*, p. 84.
59 Watts et al., *Psychology*, p. 92.
60 Watts et al., *Psychology*, p. 94.
61 Nye, *Children's Spirituality*, p. 84.
62 Nye, *Children's Spirituality*, p. xii.
63 Nye, *Children's Spirituality*, p. 109.
64 Nye, *Psychological Perspectives*, p. 75, referencing Rizzuto, A. M., 1979, *The Birth of the Living God*, Chicago: University of Chicago Press; Meissner, W. W., 1984, *Psychoanalysis and Religious Experience*, New Haven and London: Yale University Press.
65 Hay and Nye, *Spirit*, p. 50.
66 Hay and Nye, *Spirit*, p. 59.
67 Nye, *Psychological Perspectives*, p. 256.
68 Nye, *Children's Spirituality*, p. 81.
69 Nye, *Psychological Perspectives*, pp. 171–82.
70 Hay and Nye, *Spirit*, pp. 86–7.
71 Csinos, David M., 2017, 'An Exploration of Children and Culture in the United Church of Canada', unpublished PhD thesis submitted to the Faculty of Emmanuel College and the Pastoral Department of the Toronto School of Theology, p. 215.
72 Hay and Nye, *Spirit*, p. 62, referencing Erricker, C. and Erricker, J., 1996, 'Where Angels Fear to Tread: Discovering children's spirituality', in Best, R., ed., *Education, Spirituality and the Whole Child*, London: Cassell, pp. 184–95.
73 Nye, *Psychological Perspectives*, p. 128.
74 Hay and Nye, *Spirit*, pp. 65–77.
75 Hay and Nye, *Spirit*, pp. 66–7.
76 Csikszentmihalyi, M. and Csikszentmihalyi, I., eds, 1988, *Optimal Experience: Psychological Studies of Flow in Consciousness*, Cambridge: Cambridge University Press.
77 Hay and Nye, *Spirit*, pp. 70–1,
78 Hay and Nye, *Spirit*, pp. 71–7. See also Donaldson, M., 1992, *Human Minds*, London: Allen Lane/Penguin Press, and Macmurray, J., 1957, *The Self as Agent*, London: Faber and Faber, reissued with an Introduction by Stanley M. Harrison in 1995.
79 Nye, *Children's Spirituality*, p. 85.
80 Nye, *Children's Spirituality*, pp. 86–7.
81 Nye, *Psychological Perspectives*, pp. 83–5; Watts et al., *Psychology*, pp. 102–5. See also Goldman, R., 1964, *Religious Thinking from Childhood to Adolescence*, London: Routledge and Kegan Paul; Goldman, R., 1965, *Readiness for Religion*, London: Routledge and Kegan Paul.
82 Watts et al., *Psychology*, pp. 89–93.
83 Nye, *Children's Spirituality*, p. 93.
84 Watts et al., *Psychology*, p. 93.
85 Nye, *Children's Spirituality*, p. 85.
86 Watts et al., *Psychology*, p. 97.
87 Watts et al., *Psychology*, p. 98.
88 Watts et al., *Psychology*, p. 113.

89 Nye, *Children's Spirituality*, pp. 41–56.
90 Nye, *Children's Spirituality*, pp. 57–64.
91 Csinos, *Exploration*, p. 21.
92 Csinos, David M., 2020, *Little Theologians: Children, Culture, and the Making of Theological Meaning*, Montreal: McGill-Queen's University Press.
93 Csinos, David M., 2022, *A Gospel for All Ages: Teaching and Preaching with the Whole Church*, Minneapolis: Fortress Press.
94 https://www.davecsinos.com/about, accessed 09.05.2025.
95 Csinos, David M., 2008, 'Including All Children: A Qualitative Exploration of Spiritual Personalities and Children's Experiences with God and Church', unpublished thesis submitted to the Faculty of McMaster Divinity College.
96 Bellous, Joyce E. and Csinos, David M., 2009, 'Spiritual styles: Creating an environment to nurture spiritual wholeness', *International Journal of Children's Spirituality*, Vol. 14, No. 3, August, pp. 213–24.
97 Bellous, Joyce E., Csinos, David M., Peltomaki, Denise A., Bellous, Karen L., 2009, *Spiritual Styles Assessment – Children*, Warsaw: Tall Pine Press.
98 Csinos, David M., 2011, *Children's Ministry that Fits: Beyond One-Size-Fits-All Approaches to Nurturing Children's Spirituality*, London: Wipf and Stock; Csinos, David M. and Beckwith, Ivy, 2013, *Children's Ministry in the Way of Jesus*, Madison: Intervarsity Press.
99 Csinos, *Exploration*.
100 Csinos, *Little Theologians*.
101 Csinos, *Including*, p. 12.
102 Bellous, and Csinos, 'Spiritual styles', p. 213.
103 Bellous, and Csinos, 'Spiritual styles', pp. 214–15.
104 Csinos, *Exploration*, p. 30.
105 Csinos, *Exploration*, p. 20.
106 Csinos, *Exploration*, pp. 95, 111.
107 Csinos, *Children's Ministry*, p. 71.
108 Csinos, *Children's Ministry*, pp. 67–8.
109 Csinos, *Including*, p. 46.
110 Csinos, *Children's Ministry*, p. 49.
111 Bellous and Csinos, 'Spiritual styles', p. 216.
112 Csinos, *Children's Ministry*, pp. 73–84.
113 Bellous and Csinos, 'Spiritual styles', p. 215.
114 Csinos, *Children's Ministry*, pp. 32–5.
115 Csinos, *Children's Ministry*, p. 36.
116 Csinos, *Exploration*, pp. 20–5.
117 For her three age-groups, see Nye, *Children's Spirituality*, pp. 86–7; or for the two age-group model, see Watts et al., *Psychology*, pp. 89–93.
118 Csinos, *Children's Ministry*, pp. 37, 42–5.
119 Ware, C., 2000, *Discover your Spiritual Type: A Guide to Individual and Congregational Growth*, Bethesda: Alban Institute; Holmes, U. T., 1980, *A History of Christian Spirituality: An Analytical Introduction*, New York: Seabury. Csinos references Holmes' newer text in later works: Holmes, Urban T., III., 2002, *A History of Christian Spirituality: An Analytical Introduction*, Harrisburg: Morehouse Publishing.
120 Csinos, *Including*, p. 46.

121 Csinos, *Children's Ministry*, p. 20.
122 Csinos, *Children's Ministry*, p. 49.
123 Csinos, *Children's Ministry*, p. 51 (see table).
124 Pashler, Harold, McDaniel, Mark, Rohrer, Doug, Bjork, Robert, 2008, 'Learning Styles: Concepts and Evidence', *Psychological Science in the Public Interest*, Vol. 9, No. 3, December, pp. 105–19.
125 Csinos, *Children's Ministry*, p. 65.
126 Bellous and Csinos, 'Spiritual styles', p. 216.
127 Csinos, *Children's Ministry*, p. 51.
128 Csinos, *Children's Ministry*, p. 53.
129 Bellous and Csinos, 'Spiritual styles', p. 216.
130 Bellous and Csinos, 'Spiritual styles', p. 216.
131 Bellous and Csinos, 'Spiritual styles', p. 216.
132 Bellous and Csinos, 'Spiritual styles', pp. 216–17.
133 Csinos, *Children's Ministry*, p. 56.
134 Csinos, *Children's Ministry*, p. 56.
135 Csinos, *Children's Ministry*, p. 57.
136 Csinos, *Children's Ministry*, p. 57.
137 Csinos, *Children's Ministry*, p. 60.
138 Csinos, *Children's Ministry*, p. 61.
139 Csinos, *Children's Ministry*, p. 65.
140 Bellous and Csinos, 'Spiritual styles', p. 218.
141 Csinos, *Children's Ministry*, p. 65.
142 Csinos, *Little Theologians*, p. 104 n19, p. 209.
143 Csinos, *Little Theologians*, pp. 107–8, 133, 145, 155–6.
144 Csinos, *Little Theologians*, p. 50.
145 https://findingaids.library.emory.edu/documents/P-MSS080/, accessed 09.05.2025.
146 See editor's Foreword in Hopewell, *Congregation*.
147 Hopewell, *Congregation*, p. 7.
148 Hopewell, *Congregation*, p. 17.
149 Hopewell, *Congregation*, p. 3.
150 Hopewell, *Congregation*, p. 28.
151 Hopewell, *Congregation*, p. 55.
152 Hopewell, *Congregation*, pp. 46–51.
153 Hopewell, *Congregation*, p. 88.
154 Hopewell, *Congregation*, pp. 95–9.
155 Hopewell, *Congregation*, pp. 90–1.
156 Hopewell, *Congregation*, see Appendix.
157 Hopewell, *Congregation*, p. 46.
158 Hopewell, *Congregation*, pp. 27, 29, 37 n54, 38 n68. See also Whitehead, E. and Whitehead J., 1982, *Community of Faith: Model and Strategies for Developing Christian Communities*, New York: Seabury Press.
159 Hopewell, *Congregation*, p. 58.
160 Hopewell, *Congregation*, p. 59.
161 Hopewell, *Congregation*, p. 60.
162 https://www.youtube.com/watch?v=1a-vyaXSf2U, accessed 17.06.2025.
163 Hopewell, *Congregation*, p. 87.

164 Hopewell, *Congregation*, p. 61.
165 Hopewell, *Congregation*, pp. 153–9.
166 Hopewell, *Congregation*, pp. 203–11.
167 Roberts, Vaughan S. and Sims, David, 2017, *Leading By Story: Rethinking Church Leadership*, London: SCM Press.
168 Smith, Joanmarie, 2005, 'Memorial: Maria Harris 1932–2005', *Religious Education*, Vol. 100, No. 3, Summer, pp. 235–8.
169 Harris, Maria, 1971, 'The Aesthetic Dimension in Redefining Religious Education', unpublished dissertation submitted to Columbia University.
170 Harris, Maria and Moran, Gabriel, 1968, *Experiences in Community*, New York: Herder and Herder.
171 Harris, Maria, 1976, *The D.R.E. Book*, New York: Paulist Press; Harris, Maria, ed., 1978, *Parish Religious Education*, New York: Paulist Press; Harris, Maria, ed., 1978, *The D.R.E. Reader*, Winona: St. Mary's Press; Harris, Maria, 1980, *Portrait of Youth Ministry*, New York: Paulist Press.
172 Harris, Maria, 1987, *Teaching and Religious Imagination*, San Francisco: Harper and Row.
173 Harris, Maria, 1988, *Women and Teaching: Themes for a Spirituality of Pedagogy*, New Jersey: Paulist Press; Harris, Maria, 1989, *Fashion Me a People: Curriculum and the Church*, Philadelphia: Westminster Press.
174 Harris, Maria, 1989, *Dance of the Spirit: The Seven Steps of Women's Spirituality*, New York: Bantam Books.
175 Harris, Maria, 1996, *Proclaim Jubilee: A Spirituality for the 21st Century*, Louisville: Westminster John Knox Press.
176 Harris, Maria, and Moran, Gabriel, 1998, *Reshaping Religious Education: Conversations on Contemporary Practice*, Louisville: Westminster John Knox Press.
177 Slee, Nicola, 2004, *Women's Faith Development: Patterns and Processes* London: Routledge, p. 39, referring to Harris, *Dance*.
178 Harris, *Dance*, p. xi.
179 Harris, *Dance*, p. xi.
180 Harris and Moran, *Reshaping*, p. 77.
181 Harris and Moran, *Reshaping*, p. 65.
182 Harris, *Dance*, p. xii.
183 Harris and Moran, *Reshaping*, p. 77.
184 Harris, *Dance*, p. xiii.
185 Harris, *Jubilee*, p. xi.
186 Harris and Moran, *Reshaping*, p. 65.
187 Harris and Moran, *Reshaping*, p. 66.
188 Harris and Moran, *Reshaping*, pp. 68–70.
189 Harris, *Dance*, p. xii.
190 Harris and Moran, *Reshaping*, p. 77.
191 Harris, *Dance*, p. 3.
192 Harris, *Dance*, p. 4.
193 Harris, *Dance*, p. 31.
194 Harris, *Dance*, p. 32.
195 Harris, *Dance*, p. 44.
196 Harris, *Dance*, p. 60.

197 Harris, *Dance*, p. 63.
198 Harris, *Dance*, pp. 64–75.
199 Harris, *Dance*, pp. 84–5.
200 Harris, *Dance*, p. 87.
201 Harris, *Dance*, p. 89.
202 Harris, *Dance*, pp. 94–7.
203 Harris, *Dance*, pp. 97–102.
204 Harris, *Dance*, pp. 102–5.
205 Slee, *Women's*, pp. 9, 35, 165.
206 Harris, *Dance*, p. 146.
207 Harris, *Dance*, p. 181.
208 Harris and Moran, *Reshaping*, pp. 79–81.

6

The Way Through the Trees

The Landscape

Before moving to my own model, I think a survey of the landscape we have already explored is needed. As our exploration of these models of Faith Development shows, some common themes are evident. The most significant of these is the relationship between stages. Several models hint towards the concentric nature of stages, whereby previous stages can be discerned within later stages (Westerhoff, Hagberg and Guelich, Harris, and Jamieson), while at the same time other models assert the need for structural clarity (Oser and Gmünder), for them to be distinct from each other. However, others occasionally blur the transition between stages (Csinos, and Hagberg and Guelich). There are similarities between stages from various models, which can be mapped to some extent. There are also some models that seem to indicate a twin movement, alternating between a movement inwards, reflecting on self, and a movement outwards, reflecting on the connection with others, as stages progress (McLaren, Hagberg and Guelich, and Oser and Gmünder). Some models map Faith Development to the point of what might be called full discipleship (e.g. Willow Creek, Peck), while others offer further stages of maturation as a disciple (e.g. Harris, Rohr). In addition to commonalities in movement, there are also commonalities of destination. The pinnacle of many models is something akin to self-actualization and for others something like oneness with God. For some this is during a human lifetime while for others (like Tournier, Porete, Eckhart and *The Cloud of Unknowing*) it is only after union with God after death. Harris and Hagberg and Guelich suggest stages after what we might call personal fulfilment, which turn the individual to the service and society of others. Although this kind of selflessness is evident in the description of the universalizing guru in Fowler, serving others is not the main characteristic he emphasizes.

Even though these models fall into three rough groupings of movement, a common feature of transition is discernible across those groupings, namely the concept of hiatus as both a cause of transition generally between stages and more significantly as a necessity in the transition towards some kind of deeper personal growth in faith at one (or sometimes more than one) point in the model. This important hiatus in most of the models we've explored centres on doubt, loss, inertia, questioning, and has been described as a dark night (John of the Cross), a chrysalis (Jamieson), a wall (Hagberg and Guelich), a shipwreck (Parks) and a pit (Hagberg and Guelich).

An important consideration of Faith Development models for use in local ministry is in helping us reflect on when we think faith starts. For some models, faith begins at a moment of conversion, perhaps specifically conversion as an adult. For others, Faith Development runs concurrent with development as an individual and is not necessarily tied to the espousal of a particular creed. Loder suggests:

> The question of the relationship between conversion and a faith stage generates six possibilities: a change in faith stage precipitates a conversional change, a conversional change precipitates a faith stage change, each may change independently of the other, they may co-exist or block each other.[1]

The concept of whole-life Faith Development encompasses the possibility and, dare I say, the reality of Faith Development among children and young people more naturally: 'Children are spiritual beings first and then are acculturated (or not) in a religious tradition that channels intuitive spirituality into particular expressions (rituals, creeds, etc.) that have been passed through the faith tradition.'[2] The implication of these two perspectives on Faith Development will influence the way worshipping communities engage with children and young people and also how they engage with those encountered in the community without a pre-existing relationship with the church. How might mission and evangelism that honours the existing faith lives of those outside the church differ from that which assumes a person's faith-life begins on conversion to Christianity? In the model that follows, I hope to draw from the wisdom across the models we have explored and to suggest a model that will help individuals, church communities and their leaders to reflect on how faith develops.

I think it is only fair to give an introduction to the person behind this final model. I am an ordained priest and deacon in the Church of England with a background in medieval history and youth work. I am a cradle Christian who has experienced faith as something that has developed over time from early childhood and without any sense of a dramatic conversion experience though with significant moments in my life when I have experienced a strong sense of God's presence and a clear sense of vocation felt within me (and confirmed by the encouragement of others) as well as times of doubt in myself, in the church and, though rarely, in God. Working alongside young people in a church that is demonstrably older than the wider UK society, I have been attentive to the lived experiences of those younger than me and older than me, and have been viewed simultaneously as both old and young by those around me. Most of my adult work has included the encouragement and training of others, through university lecturing, youth work, training or formation for ministry, and most recently as a theological educator in a college that trains ordinands, Readers and other lay people for ministry in the Church of England in residential, context-based and part-time pathways. I enjoy puzzles, murder mysteries and creativity, especially lino-cut printing, acrylic painting, needle-felting and singing in choirs, and have found some of my most profound connections with God in the process of creativity and in time spent in nature, especially in the presence of trees and the sea.

While researching the connection between Faith Development and appreciation of art, I explored a thought experiment: a narrative model of Faith Development using the metaphor of trees. I was using images of trees for my initial research, so this model naturally grew from the two strands of my research. A tree for me is something that is recognizable even in relatively immature form. A tree as a seedling looks somehow distinct from a small plant. My proposed metaphor of understanding Faith Development as a growing tree that also endures various seasons accounts for those dark times or winters in young faith and those blossoming times in long-lived faith.

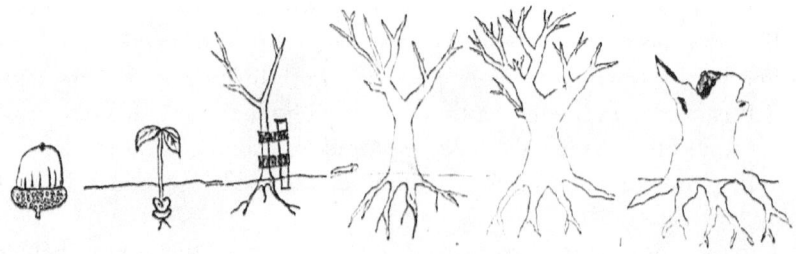

As I said at the start of this book, I have found a richness in the various modes of engaging with Faith Development. There is much to be learned from the theopoetic engagement with Faith Development by the medieval mystics, while the rigour of modern Faith Development models offers a stronger evidential base of lived experience, even if I have found myself dissatisfied with some of them for various reasons. Partly, this is because they feel clinical and rigidly fixed as either progressive or cyclical. More than this, they are generally descriptive of a faith that is constantly getting better, which may sound like no bad thing until you realize the implications of that notion for the 'lower' stages of faith; the stages that children and young people naturally inhabit.

Several key factors underpin my own metaphor. It is founded on a wide reading of empirical models as well as being rooted in the Christian tradition, including scripture and the writings of the church. It encompasses a focus on whole-life faith, inclusive of children and young people, and is intended to counter some of the white, male, western bias present in this field by offering something with a cross-cultural appeal. It is structured in such a way that it accounts for complex modes of change and does so not by the logic of its construction but by captivating the imagination through narrative. My creative side has played a significant part in the creation of this model both in the weaving of words to form the metaphor itself and also in the creation of images to accompany the model and delineate its stages and seasons. This has taken the form of a diagram, a series of line drawings of an oak tree, a Matryoshka doll (in which each of the stages was depicted nested within the one that followed it, and the outside doll depicting the four seasons) and, ultimately, the lino-cut images that illustrate this section. In addition to these, I created other pieces of art (including the cover image) which have simply helped me shape the model in the light of various ideas associated with the texts I encountered. The ultimate addition of a seventh stage grew partly from engaging with the work of Maria Harris, partly through ongoing conversations in theology about the concept of compost[3] and partly through the sense that the artwork was not yet finished without it.

Although my model owes a great deal to Fowler in terms of the stages, there are also influences from Harris's later stages and it is Westerhoff's imagery of tree rings that probably prompted me to explore the model that I eventually shaped. Despite my reservations about it, the model developed by Fowler, with all its thoroughly critiqued flaws, remains the most solidly established whole-life model (though the adaptation of his adult stages by his collaborator Heinz Streib has more substantiation now). Nonetheless, it remains unsatisfactory on several counts. Its clinical and ever progressive nature does not fully account for the faith lives I have observed, and flaws such as the fundamental research premises led to a bias towards assuming western, academic liberalism as the pinnacle of Faith Development. I acknowledge the likelihood that I remain warm towards Fowler's model because of my own academic background and liberal, middle-class, western attitudes that attune to the participants in Fowler's original research and his own perspective. Aware of this bias, my narrative is loosely based on Fowler but echoes rather more the medieval and patristic writings on Faith Development in that it is less reliant on modern psychological profiling and based more on story. It is intended not as a diagnostic tool but as a reflective one. Slee's participants frequently appealed to images from nature when describing their faith and Nye attests to the powerful nature of narrative within explorations of Faith Development. Some modern models like those by Jamieson and Harris evidently use metaphor. Even Fowler highlighted the importance of story in nurturing spiritual imagination.[4] He acknowledged the need for more research in this area[5] but also indicates the power of images:

> The image, at any age in our lives, involves a *gestalt* of meanings that hold together both a knowing and an encompassing emotion ... [O]ur images – like the symbols that ground our faith – retain and carry what Paul Ricoeur calls a 'surplus of meaning.' True symbols have depths and breadth of meaning that spill over our interpretative categories and abilities. They grow in depth and richness as our abilities to interpret them develop.[6]

The field of Faith Development offers a good grounding in what we might mean by faith through the life cycle, yet, for Christians, a primary source on the nature of faith, alongside our reason and experience, is the tradition of the church, and first among that tradition is scripture. In our Introduction we explored the various understandings of faith as described in scripture and these passages were key in helping me understand what we might mean by faith and how scripture describes faith growing and changing; however, for my model, scripture had a second strand of influence in the description of trees in scripture.

Trees feature from the very start of the Bible and right up towards the end. The Bible is arguably framed by two great trees: the tree of the knowledge of good and evil in Genesis 2.17 and 'the tree for the healing of the nations' in Revelation 22.2. Some might argue that a tree also stands at the centre of the Bible in the form of the cross. The translation of ξύλον (xylon) in 1 Peter 2.24 (ἐπὶ τὸ ξύλον ἵνα ταῖς) as Jesus being hung upon a 'tree' is not always considered a strong translation of the Greek (perhaps meaning pole or wooden thing rather than specifically 'tree'), yet it is also this word that is used in Revelation 2.22 to describe the tree of life (καὶ ἐκεῖθεν ξύλον ζωῆς ποιοῦν). It is also used in the Greek Septuagint version of Genesis 2.17. In the Hebrew scriptures, the word עץ (*ets*), tree, occurs 350 times, and in the New Testament the Greek δένδρον (*dendron*), tree, occurs 25 times. In addition, there are numerous references to specific species of tree such as cedars, oaks and terabinth.[7] Many trees in the Bible are simply part of a description of nature, or sometimes even of nature acting in praise of the Creator.[8] Elsewhere, however, trees are used as a metaphor for human interaction or spiritual growth. Such comparison can be found in Jeremiah 17.8:

> They shall be like a tree planted by water,
>   sending out its roots by the stream.
> It shall not fear when heat comes,
>   and its leaves shall stay green;
> in the year of drought it is not anxious,
>   and it does not cease to bear fruit.

There is a similar image in Psalm 1. As well as elsewhere in the prophets (Jer. 8.13 and 12.2), the prophet Job describes himself as a tree: 'my roots spread out to the waters, with the dew all night on my branches; my glory was fresh with me, and my bow ever new in my hand' (Job 29.19–20). Similarly, righteousness is compared to healthy tree growth: 'the righteous will flourish like green leaves' (Prov. 11.28); 'I am like a green olive tree in the house of God' (Ps. 52.8); 'They will be called oaks of righteousness, the planting of the LORD' (Isa. 61.3).

Even considering their comparative lengths, the New Testament has far fewer references to trees. In the NRSV, the word tree appears 208 times in the Hebrew scriptures, 31 times in the Apocrypha and only 49 times in the New Testament. It is noticeable that the Epistles are particularly low on the use of the word with only five instances. Nonetheless, Jesus certainly drew on nature metaphors. He used the image of the death of a seed restarting the cycle of growth to talk about his own death and resurrection (John 12.24) and compared people and their faith to trees bearing fruit: 'Either make the tree good, and its fruit good; or make the tree bad, and its fruit bad; for the tree is known by its fruit' (Matt. 12.33). There are also passages where people are condemned for lacking in spiritual depth, as unhealthy trees: 'autumn trees without fruit, twice dead, uprooted' (Jude 12). The best-known use of faith developing like a tree is Jesus' story of faith growing like a tiny mustard seed: 'yet when it is sown it grows up and becomes the greatest of all shrubs, and puts forth large branches, so that the birds of the air can make nests in its shade' (Mark 4.32; cf. Luke 13.19).

In addition to these texts from scripture there are numerous places where the church has engaged with the image of trees and the power that they hold for us. Space does not allow for a full exploration of these, so here are a few examples.

In *The Shepherd of Hermas*, the image of trees in winter describes the indistinguishable nature of a healthy and an unhealthy tree in such a season:

> For as in winter trees that have cast their leaves are alike, and it is not seen which are dead and which are living, so in this world neither do the righteous show themselves, nor sinners, but all are alike one to another.[9]

This text also describes a vision of an angel handing out small twigs from a willow tree to people and later collecting them back in various states of decay or growth.[10] Pelagius uses imagery of seasonality, particularly in reference to the way that new life appears each spring.[11] The metaphor of the cross as a tree features in two poems of the early medieval poet Venantius Fortunatus and in the Anglo-Saxon poem *The Dream of the Rood*, which presents the cross of Christ from the perspective of the tree from which it was cut.

We have a number of references to trees in medieval texts. Sara Ritchey records the experience of a young nun from the fourteenth century: 'The chronicle reports that one day, while strolling through the cloister garden, Alheit approached every tree in the garden, threw her arms around their trunks, and proclaimed, "Each tree is our Lord Jesus Christ!"'[12] Similarly, *The Little Flowers of St Francis* records the vision of one of the brothers comparing his community to a tree:

> He saw in a vision a large and beautiful tree, the root of which was of gold, and all the branches were men, and these men were all Friars Minor; and there were as many large branches as there were provinces in the Order, and each branch was composed of as many brethren as there were friars in each province.[13]

Thomas Aquinas reflects on the nature of the Tree of Life in scripture and on passages from Jeremiah about trees:

> Underneath the pictures there lies this thought, that the direction of a man's trust determines the whole cast of his life, because it determines, as it were, the soil in which he grows. We can alter our habitat. The plant is fixed; but 'I saw men as trees – yes! but as "trees walking."' We can walk, and can settle where we shall be rooted and whence we shall draw our inspiration, our confidence, our security.[14]

Catherine of Siena, reflecting on a vision of a tree, describes how the vision taught her that 'the roots were united with the earth of your humanity'.[15] She also presents an image of a tree representing the soul, which might be one of the closest in sense to my own concept:

> Imagine a circle traced on the ground, and in its center a tree sprouting with a shoot grafted into its side. The tree finds its nourishment in the soil within the expanse of the circle, but uprooted from the soil it would die fruitless. So, think of the soul as a tree made for love and living only by love ... the circle in which this tree's root, the soul's love must grow is true knowledge of herself, knowledge that is joined to me, who like the circle having neither beginning nor end ... This knowledge of yourself, and of me within yourself, is grounded in the soil of true humility, which is as great as the expanse of the circle (which is the knowledge of yourself united with me, as I have said). But if your knowledge of yourself were isolated from me there would be no full circle at all. Instead, there would be a beginning in self-knowledge, but apart from me it would end in confusion.[16]

Teresa of Avila describes the one who seeks closeness with God, personifying God as the 'fount of life in which the soul is planted like a tree' (1.2.2).[17] From the seventeenth century, Thomas Traherne wrote about the inspirational nature of trees to open the mind to greater things: 'Objects ... magnify the faculties of the soul beholding them ... A tree apprehended is a tree in your mind; the whole hemisphere and the heavens magnify your soul to the wideness of the heavens.'[18] The eighteenth century gives us various creative pieces reflecting on faith and trees. The poem by John Newton compares individual Christians to those growing alongside each other in a garden, and a poem attributed to Richard Hutchins has been popularized as a carol offering an image of Christ represented by a tree:

> The church a garden is
> In which believers stand,
> Like ornamental trees,

Planted by God's own hand:
His spirit waters all their roots,
And ev'ry branch abounds with fruits.[19]

The tree of life my soul hath seen,
Laden with fruit, and always green;
The trees of nature fruitless be
Compared with Christ the apple tree.[20]

For me, this was a particularly powerful text. I felt that seeing Jesus represented as a tree could help others understand how their faith, modelled on Christ, could also be seen as a tree. It inspired me to create this icon

From the last century, Thomas Merton offers a number of allusions to trees that echo my sense of spiritual connection with trees both as fellow creatures and as teachers:

> One might say I had decided to marry the silence of the forest. The sweet dark warmth of the whole world will have to be my wife. Out

of the heart of that dark warmth comes the secret that is heard only in silence ... I attempt to cultivate this plant without comment in the middle of the night and water it with psalms and prophecies in silence. It becomes the most rare of all the trees in the garden, at once the primordial paradise tree, the axis mundi, the cosmic axle, the Cross. There is only one such tree.[21]

In his great masterpiece *War and Peace* (well known for its Christian themes), Tolstoy describes a tree that influenced my understanding of mature tree growth and the role of seasons:

It was an enormous tree, its girth twice as great as a man could embrace, and evidently long ago some of its branches had been broken off and its bark scarred. With its huge ungainly limbs sprawling unsymmetrically, and its gnarled hands and fingers, it stood an aged, stern, and scornful monster among the smiling birch trees. [*And later*] ... The old oak, quite transfigured, spreading out a canopy of sappy dark-green foliage, stood rapt and slightly trembling in the rays of the evening sun. Neither gnarled fingers nor old scars nor old doubts and sorrows were any of them in evidence now. Through the hard century-old bark, even where there were no twigs, leaves had sprouted such as one could hardly believe the old veteran could have produced.[22]

As I was developing the model, I encountered a poem by J. Moffit (cited in the methodological work of Moustakas) which influenced the seasonality of my model. Moffit's poem *To look at any thing* encourages us to 'look at it long' by looking at a tree not just in the season of green spring but to go deeper by looking into the roots as well as to the spaces between leaves.[23]

This idea echoed for me Martin Buber's exploration of the I–thou relationship with a tree. His reflection on human relationality draws on a poetic reflection on encountering a tree, not purely in scientific or artistic ways but also relationally:

The tree is no impression, no play of my imagination, no value depending on my mood; but it is bodied over against me and has to do with me, as I with it – only in a different way. Let no attempt be made to sap the strength from the meaning of the relation: relation is mutual.[24]

This interconnected relationality with creation extends, for Buber, to our relationship with God. It is through our relationship with the world that we connect with God: 'The extended lines of relations meet in the eternal Thou.'[25]

Many Faith Development thinkers speak about faith as somehow connected to images from nature, most notably Westerhoff with his tree ring model:

> First a tree with one ring is as much a tree as a tree with four rings. A tree in its first year is a complete and whole tree, and a tree with three rings is not a better tree but only an expanded tree ... a tree acquires one ring at a time in a slow and gradual manner.[26]

However, more than this, in talking about the importance of focusing not simply on the big ideas but also in the immediate, Westerhoff suggests:

> Let us use the most ordinary things in talking about beginning, growth and change: rocks and water, trees and clouds ... We need to watch the leaves fall into the brook and talk about this imaginatively and at length, and perhaps after some time a great meaning will come through. We ought not to be afraid of repetition, knowing that there is yet more to be grasped.[27]

Even Fowler compares early faith with the growth of a tree, saying of faith in those of 0–2 months, 'I think of this as the slender trunk of a tree that will continue to grow.'[28] One of Mark Buchanan's musings is focused on trees: 'If our spiritual growth is treelike, seasonal, a cycle of living and dying, then some years, even decades, are bound to be better than others.'[29] Rebecca Nye talks about a tree 'with the roots labelled "spirituality" and the leaves "religion". The roots transmit water to the leaves and support the tree as it grows larger. In turn the leaves manufacture food to nourish the roots.'[30] Csinos includes a story of his father observing the forest driving through Ontario:

> Each of these unique trees sprouted from a common ground. Their roots stretched into the same soil. And they were nourished by the same sun and rain. We human beings are like these trees. We come in many shapes, colors, and sizes. And we express the common spiritual dimension of our humanity in many different ways. Still, we are rooted in the same soil.[31]

Outside the Christian tradition, a key source of illumination for me on trees was engaging with the work of David Hockney.[32] His paintings of trees captivated me. I discovered why at his Royal Academy Exhibition; his work reflected on the trees he saw at various stages of growth and the changes they experienced over days, weeks or seasons. He talks about the similarity between humans and trees: 'The canvases not only summarise the life cycle of the tree in one image, but also hint at our own mortality and connection with the earth.'[33]

We have already established that faith is something that changes not simply from no faith to having faith. It is our mode of engaging with the other; something that grows and changes. It is something that people have at every stage of their life. Yet for many of the models of Faith Development there is a focus on the adult experience of faith, principally because it is difficult to research the faith lives of children empirically. I am glad that people like Sarah Holmes are now working on such research.[34] Of those Faith Development models that are intended to cover whole lifespans, including childhood, some nonetheless treat the Faith Development of children and young people as something that is inherently incomplete and not yet matured into what it is really meant to be. As observed earlier, this can lead to a lack of valuing or inherent contempt of earlier stages rather than celebrating the seasons as they fall. Both Richard Rohr and Scott Peck show some contempt for earlier stages, and Brian McLaren warns that any of his stages will inherently lack tolerance of the previous stage. Miller-McLemore has highlighted for us that Faith Development theories, like Westerhoff's and Fowler's, actually focus on adult development rather than on children's faith, arguing that they reduce childhood to a simple and temporary stage that one must pass through to reach a desired goal: 'It is hard to have a stage theory that does not overvalue the final frame.'[35] As adult models do not account well for the experience of children and young people, we needed to turn to researchers who have proposed models of Faith Development specifically for children or young people, as we did by engaging with the work of Sungwon Kim, Rebecca Nye and David Csinos. These have all contributed to the nuances of the earlier stages of my model.

As I described in the Introduction, almost all those working in this field are white westerners and most of them male. I consciously sought to widen the diversity of voices that could be heard in this book and drew in female voices (some such as Harris and Slee who have already made themselves heard) as well as lesser-known researchers from other parts of the world. Nonetheless, the dominance of white, western, middle-class, academic voices is very strong. I have sought to bring in the mystic voice as part of a counter to this, not that it is not also a western voice of those with educated privilege but because it speaks in a different way from the dominant voice. Other researchers in this field have also endeavoured to broaden their gaze beyond the dominant academic voice. Csinos shifted focus in his later work and critiqued others who have looked at the spiritual lives of children for not paying due attention to culture. He suggests that scholars who do not pay attention to the culture of those interviewed produce results belying a normativity of white, western, often middle-class, culture.[36]

I have shared my model in academic and pastoral settings with those of a range of academic abilities and have also shared it with mixed ethnic groups. When I presented this model to the International Association for the Study of Youth Ministry I found that members (from African nations, Oceania, Northern America and Europe) all found the image of a tree to be one that was recognizable. Participants in the discussion that followed each identified with a different tree specific to their own lived experience, commenting on the uniqueness of the way that trees grow in their region, such as the distinctive lean of the trees in the windy coastal areas of South Africa. Barring the significant minority who live in communities in the extreme deserts of snow or sand or at great altitude (above the treeline), a tree is a near universal image for human beings. As Hockney says:

> Trees are the largest manifestation of the life-force we see. No two trees are the same, like us. We're all a little bit different inside and look a little bit different outside. You notice that more in the winter than in the summer.[37]

Although I may have had a particular tree in mind when I originally described the model and indeed adjusted it from an oak tree to an apple tree in the development of new images to support the model, I believe those from different cultures will be able to hear the description and picture a tree that is familiar to them. Indeed, trees have been associated with the sacred in many cultures across the world, from the Scandinavian Yggdrasil to the Bodhi tree of Buddhist culture, the Palo Santo of South America, the Hindu Banyan tree and the Tane Mahuta of Aotearoa. As such, my metaphor might equally appeal to those of all faiths and none, even though, for me, it has come from a strong root in the Christian tradition.

When considering my own model, there were certain key factors that I thought important and that I found to be lacking in any single one of the other models I have set out so far. Although its stages owe a great deal to Fowler, it is Westerhoff's imagery of tree rings as a diagrammatical representation of how our faith grows that probably sowed the seed of my own model. We've explored the various models in groups according to the description of movement within the models. Most of the models have only one movement of development whether this is cyclical or progressive (some with a combination of regression and progression). Only Harris's model has a sense of movement in multiple directions. Yet, even though Harris made that claim, she didn't give a clear account of how that movement works. A key factor for me was the combination of insights from these cyclical and progressive developments because I am convinced that our faith does not simply grow stronger and mature all the time but has periods of fallowness, even catastrophe and regrowth. As someone who has worked with young people, one of my prime issues with some Faith Development models was the incompleteness of earlier stages of faith. My model attempts to capture that distinctiveness of the earlier stages while maintaining a sense of cohesion with later stages. Equally, as someone who also works with people of older generations, there were failings in the lack of accounting for a lively faith in those of mature years. In some models there is an insufficiency of accounting for the ongoing maturation of faith after the point of personal conversion. This is where the combination of stages and seasons into one model enables a more complex accounting for faith and how it develops.

The notion of seasonality stems from a life lived in the church and surrounded by people who are evidently mature in faith but at times have experienced changeability in their faith lives. Ford-Grabowksy's critique of Fowler, that Mary could be demonstrated to be simultaneously at Stage 3 and Stage 5,[38] and Streib's work on mapping types from various styles,[39] highlight that our faith lives are not simply mapped on one vector but reflect more complex patterns. Blackaby, Buchanan and Hall each talked about the characteristics for each of the seasons.

As any of us who have lived through the last few years of the climate crisis will recognize, the rotation of the seasons is vital. We've seen all too clearly that mild winters, dry springs, followed by very hot summers do not lead to fruitfulness. Seasonality is about variation and gradual change. When those seasons all become indistinguishable or extreme, things cannot grow as they should. In considering seasonality, I was conscious of the critique of cyclical models, which is twofold: the failure to account for any progress and the necessity of particular seasons succeeding in order. Does one season always give way to the next or, like Harris's model, can winter skip to summer? The order of the seasons of our faith may not be as strictly ordered as the seasons of the year and yet there is certainly some logic to the progression from fruitfulness (autumn) to rest (winter) to new beginnings (spring) and then growth (summer) before fruitfulness again. What may vary for us throughout our faith lives will be the length of these seasons, as Buchanan suggested. Sometimes too long a time in one season might lead to a similarly long subsequent season or to a much quicker transition from one to the next. In some instances, one season may naturally lead to another, yet purely seasonal models imply no accumulated progression in each successive season. There is evidence to suggest that both the cyclical and the progressive stages do move naturally to the next, as Ricoeur's deceptively simple concept of naivety suggests; the movement from knowledge to an awareness of lack of knowledge naturally leads to a second naivety.[40] Similarly the hiatus experiences in the Faith Development models from the church tradition and Richard Rohr's idea of 'falling upward' evidence a definite move between stages, precipitated by a negative experience and subsequent reflection. Fowler argued for similar notions in his faith stages through his spiral of progress,[41] the beginning of a needful combined model of progressive and cyclical growth. This acknowledges a double movement of change, namely maturation and recentring or transformation in Christ.[42] Likewise, McLaren, in his seasonal model, describes this experience as part of that which begins the cycle of growth again but in a new and deeper way: 'This new second-simplicity eventually matures into a new season of higher complexity, and so on, in an ascending spiral of growth and discovery that continues as long as life itself.'[43] In my model, the hiatus present in other models is essentially the winter in this cycle of seasons. My combination of two movements was inspired by the feeling that none of the existing models is sufficient because they try to encompass simply something that is complex and individual. Seeking to be definitive rather than expansive, the models tend to categorize and therefore focus mostly on one movement of development, either progressive or cyclical. A more comprehensive model of Faith Development must contain both progressive and cyclical elements (perhaps while also reflecting on style). The challenge in composing the narrative metaphor was how best to interweave these two movements in a way that made them distinctive and yet integrated. This was a challenge both in the narrative and in the creation of images to represent the model. In seeking this kind of unified model, I am cautious of an overambitious reaching for a fully unitive theory (as exemplified by Danah Zohar and Ian Marshall's book on spiritual intelligence, which ultimately falls short of offering something which encompassed all the various models).[44]

To understand how a Faith Development model works, it is important to know what growth the model is seeking to demonstrate. I gave my definition of faith in the Introduction: first, as a generic definition that could apply to any faith group as

> an understanding of the place of self in connection to other people, the world (or universe) and God (which some might call something different, such as a higher power or the universe). This is an evolving system of meaning-making that might include specific credal and doctrinal elements alongside the sense of meaning in terms of oneself and of interpersonal relationships; a sense of connection with God and the other, practices of connection to God and the other and outworkings of those relationships in terms of actions and dispositions.

And then specifically to a Christian faith:

> Christian faith that develops is an understanding of the place of the self in connection to our neighbour, creation and God the Father, Jesus Christ and the Holy Spirit as one Holy Trinity. It is an evolving system of meaning-making including an ongoing exploration of the scriptures, creeds and the teachings of the church through the tradition and in its current expression. It involves meaning-making in terms of oneself as a member of the Body of Christ, through corporate worship and personal practices of contemplation and devotion, as well as enacted works of discipleship through service to others, the church and creation as an individual and as part of the church. It involves the individual in reflective practice of their beliefs in terms of their own character and lifestyle.

These definitions are not overtly reflected in the model itself and should be viewed as the underpinning of how the model was created. There are definite hints towards some aspects of the definition throughout the model but, as it is a narrative metaphor, there is little space for referring back to a definition without interrupting the image that is being explored. Instead we shall explore nuances in the commentary that follows it.

The Model

Imagine a person's faith as a tree grown from a seed.

    Faith develops from seed to seedling
    From seedling to sapling
    From sapling to young tree
    From young tree to mature tree
    From mature tree to totem
    From totem to compost.

Throughout all this another cycle is also happening, the changing of the seasons each year.

Untended, a *seed* (1) can lie underground, unseen and unsprouting, for years. To begin growing and in early growth, it requires nurture and development. It literally feeds off what is outside, and yet this all happens below ground, unseen, as the fallen leaves and branches of other trees, some long dead, provide warmth and nutrients. When the seed starts to grow, it changes radically and rapidly, reaching out towards light and deeper down into the dark earth.

Growth becomes visible when a seed becomes a *seedling* (2). As a seedling, nurture is still important; young leaves are delicate. If leaves reaching out to the light or roots seeking a firm foundation are stripped off through damage, the main stalk is unable to grow. The seedling looks very different to the seed and yet still does not always look very much like the fully grown tree.

In the wild, a seedling will grow into a *sapling* (3) if the trees around allow sufficient light to shine through their branches. Wherever saplings grow, there must be space for them to grow up beside the other trees. A bigger tree too close by and encroaching can cause a sapling to grow in strange ways. This sapling stage can be a time when much growth happens and when there can be damage from storms to still-young branches. As a sapling, branches appear and individuality begins to show. Sometimes these branches will be lost or damaged. Yet the shadow of these lost or damaged branches will be visible later in the fully matured tree. Some saplings put so much energy into growing more than one strong upward branch that other branches suffer later; the sapling ends up weakened and not fulfilling all its possibilities. Helpful training and even some trimming of over-extending branches can promote good growth. A sapling grown in a safe pot might need careful transplanting into more extensive and free ground to grow fully. When

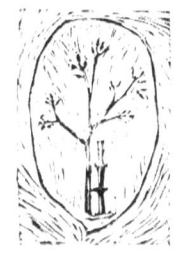  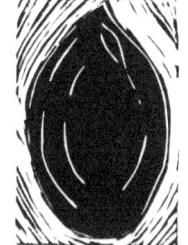

grown in controlled conditions a sapling can be supported closely by another piece of wood. This can seem helpful but can have unintended outcomes. There comes a point when the support for the sapling must be taken away; when the support becomes something that hinders the sapling becoming a young tree (4).

Trees don't grow in a single year. They are subject to the *seasons*. Growth is not only linear but comes in cycles. The seed, seedling and sapling experience the seasons; only the warmth of the earth and the rains of spring can enable the seed to sprout, and the seedling, no matter how small, will shed its leaves in the autumn. The sapling will blossom in spring and may fruit, even if the fruits are not fully formed, on branches not strong enough to hold them. Support can be needed to keep the sapling through the autumn and winter as these changing times and seasons can be disturbing; a time when there is not much light can seem like for ever and times of flourishing can feel too short-lived. Saplings can be disappointed in their fruits for that season, not realizing that times of fruitfulness are still to come.

For a *young tree* (4), some now for the first time without special support, the seasons suddenly become more apparent.

Bare branches of winter give way to new growth in spring blossom, in summer fruiting. Autumn leaf loss leads again to bare branches, but branches now changed since the previous winter, matured through the successive seasons. It is therefore the young tree when the seasons really begin to be significant. It learns to move with them, though still finds them changing and sometimes confusing. Now winter is a time of bare branches, focusing on the basics, of consolidating or of the dying back of some parts; a time when the light seems less bright and the young tree must rely on what it can draw from beneath. The young tree learns that spring is when new things begin, and growth from older branches produces the possibility of new branches in new directions. Then the foundations for fruits to come are seen in the blossom of spring. The summer is the time for flourishing, a time of abundant light when a tree feels so very alive. Autumn is the time for the tree to show its fruitfulness as it shows the results of its flourishing to offer up its fruit and prepare for the times when there is less light, a time to store up before it is winter again, with time for those new branches from the previous spring to consolidate themselves. A young tree will gradually mature, its strongest branches determining how the tree grows. It is still vulnerable, yet, by this vulnerability, more able to move with the storms of life while strong enough to endure them. Even if it loses some branches, it continues to grow both towards the light and in building good solid roots. The young tree is still versatile enough to be moved to new soil and continue to grow; to pick up its roots and re-establish somewhere new.

The *mature tree* (5) has solid core branches, established when the mature tree was a sapling and a young tree, which form the basic nature of the tree and the direction it grows. No slight storm can shake the core, although younger branches can move or even break away. The mature tree is less able to change. A great storm or some other external force can make big changes to the tree without destroying it, as the roots are more fixed and established. Yet growth is still possible, even from unexpected parts. Changing where a mature tree is planted is possible but can have detrimental effects; not done carefully, the tree can fail to survive. For the mature tree, the seasons are familiar. There is an expectation that there will be times when there is not much light and times for fruitfulness. Mature trees can focus their growth, allowing light to fall through their branches on to younger trees below, offering their leaves and even their lost branches as sources of nutrients to other growing trees.

Some trees as they get older require additional support to hold up great branches that might otherwise fall or break. Eventually all trees become older. Some mature trees will become great *totems* (6), still standing but no longer producing substantial new growth. Their main branches, formed so well over the years, can still stand despite a lack of growth. They can draw on the resources of their deep roots and present to the world a powerful image of the growth they have achieved. Even a hollowed-out tree can still show what a great tree it had been before and offer a sign of what a tree can be.

Ultimately, the tree becomes indistinguishable from the earth around it. Humbled to the point of rejoining the humus, it becomes *compost* (7) with all that it had been returned to the service of others, producing nourishment for other trees, young and old, and a place where seeds may lie untended.

Trees grow not just in one season but throughout the dark of winter, the burgeoning of spring, the flourishing of summer and the fruitfulness of autumn. The more mature tree endures such seasons with familiarity and much greater ease but can still be affected by too cold a winter or too hot a summer. Trees grow both progressively and cyclically. A tree in one spring is not the same tree the next; spring is familiar but the tree has changed since the last. The particular nature of these trees also determines how they grow. Oaks and beeches do not grow in the same way but vary in shape. They may look similar as seedlings, and even saplings, but, as they mature, their shape becomes more apparent; some grow tall and straight with one central trunk; others diversify into many branches, some of which produce fruit and others which may even wither and break off. As a totem, some of that shape remains, yet a totem is less distinctively of one shape or another and there is no distinction between compost as, all around, the ground in which trees are planted is made up of the roots of trees planted nearby and the richness left by trees gone before.

Notes

1 Fowler, James W., 1995, *Stages of Faith: The Psychology of Human Development and the Quest for Meaning*, San Francisco: Harper, p. 153.

2 Boyatzis, Chris, 2012, 'Spiritual development during childhood and adolescence', in Miller, Lisa, ed., *The Oxford Handbook of Psychology and Spirituality*, New York: Oxford University Press, pp. 151–64, p. 153; see also King, Pamela Ebstune and Boyatzis, Chris J., 2015, 'Religious and spiritual development in childhood and adolescence', in Lamb, M. et al., eds, *The Handbook of Child Psychology and Developmental Science*, Hoboken: Wiley, pp. 975–1021.

3 See for example: https://evolvingfaith.com/podcast/season-1/episode-3#:~:text=Worms%20devour%20things%20of%20death,the%20end%20of%20God's%20story, accessed 09.05.2025.

4 Fowler, James W., 2004, 'Faith Development at 30: Naming the Challenges of Faith in a New Millennium', *Religious Education*, Vol. 99, No. 4, Fall, pp. 405–21.

5 Fowler, James W., 1986, 'Faith and the Structuring of Meaning', reprinted in Dykstra, Craig and Parks, Sharon, *Faith Development and Fowler*, Birmingham: Religious Education Press, p. 37.

6 Fowler, 'Faith Development at 30', pp. 413–14.

7 See Evans, J., 2014, *God's Trees: Trees, Forests and Wood in the Bible*, Leominster: Day One.

8 See 1 Chron. 16.33; Isa. 55.12; Neh. 9.25; Ps. 96.12; Ps. 148.9.

9 Similitude Third, https://ccel.org/ccel/schaff/anf02/anf02.ii.iv.iii.html, accessed 09.05.2025.

10 Similitude Eighth, https://www.ccel.org/ccel/schaff/anf02.ii.iv.viii.html, accessed 09.05.2025.

11 Newell, John Philip, 2021, *Sacred Earth, Sacred Soul*, New York: HarperCollins, p. 118.

12 Ritchey, Sara, 2008, 'Spiritual Arborescence: Trees in the Medieval Christian Imagination', *Spiritus: A Journal of Christian Spirituality*, Vol. 8, No. 1, Spring, pp. 64–82, p. 64.

13 https://ccel.org/ccel/ugolino/flowers/flowers.iii.xlviii.html, Ch. XLVIII, accessed 09.05.2025.

14 https://ccel.org/ccel/maclaren/isa_jer/isa_jer.ii.iii.xii.html, accessed 09.05.2025.

15 *Dialogue of Catherine of Siena*, https://www.ccel.org/ccel/catherine/dialog, accessed 09.05.2025.

16 *The Dialogue: Truth and Love*, Chs 9 and 10, as cited by Wolski Conn, Joann, ed., 1986, *Women's Spirituality: Resources for Christian Development*, New York: Paulist Press, p. 180.

17 Teresa of Avila, 1979, *The Interior Castle*, ed. Kavanaugh, Kieran, London: SPCK, p. 40.

18 Traherne, Thomas, *Centuries*, IV.73, https://ccel.org/ccel/traherne/centuries/centuries.iv.html, accessed 09.05.2025.

19 https://hymnary.org/text/the_church_a_garden_is, accessed 09.05.2025.

20 https://hymnary.org/text/the_tree_of_life_my_soul_hath_seen, accessed 09.05.2025.

21 https://hudsonreview.com/1967/07/day-of-a-stranger/, accessed 09.05.2025.

22 Tolstoy, Leo, *War and Peace*, Bookbyte Digital, iBooks, Ch. VI.

23 Moustakas, Clark, 1990, *Heuristic: Design, Methodology, and Applications*, London: Sage, p. 12, citing Moffit, J., 'To Look at Any Thing', in Mecklenberger, J. and Simmons, G., eds, 1971, *Since Feeling it First*, Glenview: Scott, Foresman.

24 Buber, Martin, 1937, *I and Thou*, Edinburgh: T&T Clark, p. 8.

25 Buber, *I and Thou*, p. 75.

26 Westerhoff, John H., 2000, *Will Our Children Have Faith?*, rev. and expanded edn, Harrisberg: Morehouse Publishing, p. 88.

27 Westerhoff, John H. and Eusden, John D., 1982, *The Spiritual Life: Learning East and West*, New York: Seabury, p. 124.

28 Fowler, James W., 1996, *Faithful Change: The Personal and Public Challenges of Postmodern Life*, Nashville: Abingdon Press, p. 27.

29 Buchanan, M., 2010, *Spiritual Rhythm: Being with Jesus Every Season of Your Soul*, Grand Rapids: Zondervan, p. 250.

30 Hay, David and Nye, Rebecca, 2006, *The Spirit of the Child*, rev. edn, London: Jessica Kingsley, p. 20.

31 Csinos, David M., 2011, *Children's Ministry that Fits: Beyond One-Size-Fits-All Approaches to Nurturing Children's Spirituality*, London: Wipf and Stock, p. 152.

32 *Imagine: A Bigger Picture*, BBC, first aired 30 June 2009.

33 David Hockney in Bracker, Alison, 2012, *David Hockney: A Bigger Picture Educational Guide*, London: Royal Academy, p. 17.

34 See, for example, Holmes, S., 2021, '"Will my child have their own faith?" Exploring the impact of parental beliefs on childhood faith nurture', *Journal of Beliefs and Values*, pp. 430–47; Holmes, S., 2016, 'Observing Christian Faith During the Childhood Years', *International Journal of Children's Spirituality*, Vol. 21, Nos 3-4, pp. 177–90.

35 Miller-McLemore, Bonnie, 2006, 'Wither the Children? Childhood in Religious Education', *Journal of Religion* 86, p. 640.

36 Csinos, David M., 2017, 'An Exploration of Children and Culture in the United Church of Canada', unpublished thesis submitted to the Faculty of Emmanuel College and the Pastoral Department of the Toronto School of Theology, pp. 214–18.

37 Gayford, M., 2011, *A Bigger Message: Conversations with David Hockney*, London: Thames and Hudson, p. 29.

38 Ford-Grabowsky, Mary, 1987, 'Flaws in Faith Development Theory', *Religious Education*, Vol. 88, No. 1, Winter, pp. 91–2.

39 Streib, Heinz, Chen, Z. J. and Hood, Ralph W., 2020, 'Categorizing People by Their Preference for Religious Styles: Four Types Derived from Evaluation of Faith Development Interviews of Faith Development Interviews', *The International Journal for the Psychology of Religion*, Vol. 30, No. 2, p.115.

40 Ricoeur, Paul, 1960, *Philosophie de la Volonté: Finitude et Culpabilité*, Vol. 2, p. 327, cited by Belzen, Jacob A., ed., 2000, *Aspects in Contexts: Studies in the History of Psychology of Religion*, Amsterdam: Rodopi, p. 255.

41 Fowler, *Stages*, pp. 187–8, 289–90.

42 Fowler, James W., 1991, *Weaving the New Creation: Stages of Faith and the Public Church*, San Francisco: Harper, p. 94.

43 McLaren, Brian D., 2011, *Naked Spirituality: A Life with God in Twelve Simple Words*, London: Hodder and Stoughton, p. 234.

44 Zohar, Danah and Marshall, Ian, 2000, *SQ Spiritual Intelligence the Ultimate Intelligence*, London: Bloomsbury.

7

Exploring the Way Through the Trees: Application of the Model in the Parish

As with all the models we have explored, it is important to consider how this model might be used in a pastoral setting. I have shared this model with parishes, ordinands, academic conferences and colleagues. In each case, many people have found it something that captured their imagination. The metaphor is also not perfect. I wish it were but that would be impossible. It is neither an infallible recipe nor a scientific formula for perfect faith. It is not offered as a 'solution' to any perceived problem in the church and yet can, I hope, assist individuals to reflect on their own journey and ministers to consider how they are supporting the faith lives of others and how they might shape both ministry and mission within the local context to reflect on what the model can teach them.

It is important to note about the model that it is faith itself that is represented by the tree. The tree is not the person. The person is the one with primary care for the tree growing from the seed of faith planted by God. Other people, while caring for their own trees of faith, will also have some role to play in the care of people's trees of faith, especially in parent–child relationships, in ministerial responsibility, or in the care of those with reduced capacity such as dementia. The tree is singular for each person. A person's faith might suffer substantial damage at some point, though that does not mean it is destroyed or replaced. Like a tree, it regrows from that damage and might look very different from what it was before or what it might have become. Like any metaphor, it can be pushed too far and lose some of its meaning. In explicating it in the following paragraphs, my interpretation might not resonate with you as the reader. As with all creative endeavours, your interpretation has validity, even if it differs from that of the creator of the metaphor. If you find any dissonance between my explication and your reading of it, that might be fertile ground for digging further rather than you 'getting it wrong'. First, we will explore each of the stages of growth in the metaphor for certain key parallels with our faith experience and what that might tell us about ourselves, our ministry and mission, and our care for others. Thereafter, there are lessons to be learned from the model as a whole and some suggestions of how it might be introduced to people.

Untended, a Seed (1) can lie underground, unseen and unsprouting, for years. To begin growing, and in early growth, it requires nurture and development. It literally feeds off what is outside and yet this all happens below ground, unseen, as the fallen leaves and branches of other trees, some long dead, provide warmth and nutrients. When the seed starts to grow, it changes radically and rapidly, reaching out towards light and deeper down into the dark earth.

In our earliest faith life, how we construe the world can be like that seed, receiving and experiencing faith in terms of what others have experienced. As very young children, we each experience the faith of those around us, whether that is Christian, Sikh, Jewish, etc. or non-religious. This is not to say that there is no faith going on but rather that signs of it are less visible to the world. It certainly doesn't look how adults might expect faith to look. Recent research suggests that children's development is evident much earlier than some Faith Development models would suggest. Karen-Marie Yust has helpfully summarized the research of two separate studies by Bloom and Maria Harris that use new technology to observe the interactions of pre-school children. These studies show that children develop a sense of moral awareness and care at a much younger age than their verbal skills can communicate. Where previous researchers suggest that a sense of right and wrong was not present at this age, the use of videography to capture the length of visual engagement or the interaction by touch with different individuals showed that pre-schoolers appreciate fairness and justice and have a preference for those who help people over those who do harm.[1] So for those working in ministry or mission with pre-school children, I think the lessons from this model would be to approach their faith formation with openness and appreciative enquiry and ensure that they are surrounded by evidence of kindness and positive interactions and allow what is present, if not visible, to grow.

Growth becomes visible when a seed becomes a Seedling (2). As a seedling, nurture is still important; young leaves are delicate. If leaves reaching out to the light or roots seeking a firm foundation are stripped off through damage, the main stalk is unable to grow. The seedling looks very different from the seed and yet still does not always look very much like the fully grown tree.

If there are not sufficient examples around of religious faith and faithfulness, like a seed without fertile ground, faith does not grow, or worse still, ground that is infertile and damaged can result in stunted growth. In childhood, a negative experience of faith can mean that faith never grows or that a firm faith in there being no need for religious faith grows instead. Young children pay attention to those around them and if they experience an environment at home, church or school where Christian faith is normalized, their conception of the world will grow with a sense of openness to the place of religion in life. Of course, children can receive different messages from different contexts. The Growing Faith Foundation has emphasized the interrelation of three spheres of influence that play the most significant roles in the lives of children as the most important locations of faith formation: home, school and church.[2] Of course, not all children experience church or another place of worship. It is also possible that children will receive quite different messages about faith in each of those three environments and all three will feed the seedling of faith that a child is nurturing.

> *In the wild, a seedling will grow into a Sapling (3) if the trees around allow sufficient light to shine through their branches. Wherever saplings grow, there must be space for them to grow up beside the other trees. A bigger tree too close by and encroaching can cause a sapling to grow in strange ways. This sapling stage can be a time when much growth happens and when there can be damage from storms to still young branches. As a sapling, branches appear and individuality begins to show. Sometimes these branches will be lost or damaged. Yet the shadow of these lost or damaged branches will be visible in the fully matured tree. Some saplings put so much energy into growing more than one strong upward branch that other branches suffer later; the sapling ends up weakened and not fulfilling all its possibilities. Helpful training and even some trimming of over-extending branches can promote good growth. A sapling grown in a safe pot might need careful transplanting into more extensive and free ground to grow fully. When grown in controlled conditions, a sapling can be supported closely by another piece of wood. This can seem helpful but can often have unintended outcomes. The sapling will blossom in spring and may fruit, even if the fruits are not fully formed, on branches not strong enough to hold them. Support can be needed to keep the sapling through the autumn and winter as these changing times and seasons can be disturbing; a time when there is not much light can seem like for ever and times of flourishing can feel too short-lived. Saplings can be dis-*

appointed in their fruits for that season, not realizing that times of fruitfulness are still to come.

The sapling stage to me represents adolescence and the reader will not be surprised that this former youth worker considers it a particularly important stage. I hope this description helps raise our consciousness of just how big an impact we can have on the faith lives of young people even with the best of intentions. The concept of staking represents something of an overly prescriptive curriculum of faith nurture, which I have witnessed particularly in the UK in the last 20 years. On several occasions when I have shared this model, I have had horticulturalists, tree surgeons, gardeners or biologists in the room who have been particularly exercised at the idea of tree-staking. One such student pointed me to this caveat from a forester:

> Tree staking is done with the best of intentions but without regard to long-term tree health. Rather than helping a tree develop root and trunk growth that allow it to stand independently, improper tree staking replaces a supportive trunk and root system. This artificial support causes the tree to put its resources into growing taller but not growing wider. When the stakes are removed (if they ever are), the lack of trunk and root development makes these trees prime candidates for breakage or blow-down … When the wind howls and the rain falls, the young tree's roots react and push deeper into the soil. The winds make it stronger. In contrast, staked trees do not fully mature, despite their stability. What saplings need more than protection is the opportunity to grow. To stand on their own roots.[3]

The way we support young people in the faith needs to engage their faith not simply with a prop, a miniature version of our own faith, but with an engagement through the roots of their tree of faith with the richness of the Christian tradition, with the local community and by giving them space to grow their faith naturally. Teenage can be a maelstrom of emotional experiences and there's a real need for the accompaniment of mature Christians who can encourage and celebrate the times of fruitfulness; listen when times are tough; reassure that a dry spell is simply that, not the end of their faith. Teenagers can be full of energy and enthusiasm for new ideas and not always have the capacity to achieve all of them. Their faith can reflect this too. Accompaniment that helps with realizing some of those ideas and redirecting energies can be transformational to a young person's faith. A useful question for a church community might be: How much are we enabling the faith of teenagers to draw from the centuries of Christian heritage and how much are we getting their faith to rely solely on the support of church leaders rather than grow independently? Some adolescents will demonstrate more mature faith than that of the sapling if we give them the space and encouragement to grow that faith.

> *For a Young Tree (4), some now for the first time without special support, the seasons suddenly become more apparent. Bare branches of winter give way to new growth in spring blossom, in summer fruiting. Autumn leaf loss leads again to bare branches, but branches now changed since the previous winter, matured through the successive seasons. It is therefore the young tree when the seasons really begin to tell. It learns to move with them, though still finds them changing and sometimes confusing. Now winter is a time of bare branches, focusing on the basics, of consolidating or of the dying back of some parts; a time when the light seems less bright and the young tree must rely on what it can draw from beneath. The young tree learns that spring is when new things begin, and growth from older branches produces the possibility of new branches in new directions. Then the foundations for fruits to come are seen in the blossom. Summer is the time for flourishing, a time of abundant light when a tree feels so very alive. Autumn is the time for the tree to show its fruitfulness as it shows the results of its flourishing to offer up its fruit and prepare for the times when there is less light, a time to store up before it is winter again, with time for those new branches from the previous spring to consolidate themselves. A young tree will gradually mature, its strongest branches determining how the tree grows. It is still vulnerable, yet, by this vulnerability, more able to move with the storms of life while strong enough to endure them. Even if they lose some branches, they continue to grow both towards the light and in building good solid roots. The young tree is still versatile enough to be moved to new soil and continue to grow; to pick up its roots and re-establish somewhere new.*

This is the first stage that is not so clearly tied to an age group. It begins for some in adolescence though for most in early adulthood. That said, some adults will still be stuck with a sapling faith and in others the young tree of faith can continue for a considerable time. Early adulthood is a complex period and where faith fits in that world can be a real challenge. It's a time when many changes happen in someone's life and where faith fits within that will be a factor. This can be a stage of life where an individual either disconnects with formalized religion or indeed begins to engage with it due to other life changes (including independent living and first-time parenthood). In all honesty, this is not an age group the church has effectively engaged with in recent decades, as our regular membership shows. It maps in some ways with Fowler's Individuative-Reflective and therefore can be something experienced outside the church for many people. For me, there is something about this stage that points to the need for the church to present something dependable and familiar which can serve as something of continuity during changing times. Equally, if the church, through its members, can engage with the reality of the seasons of faith and help people navigate those changing experiences then we could have something to offer people. If the church has nothing to offer people when they don't feel able to celebrate life or nothing to offer in supporting someone in exploring how to lay the foundations for fruitfulness, then we will continue to fail to connect with those in this stage. There is a blurred line between this stage and the next because, essentially, this stage is a movement towards equilibrium and the next is the finding of that equilibrium. Just as it's difficult to point to a tree and call it mature or not, so with faith; it might be difficult to pinpoint when the change comes. Perhaps it's something we notice more once it has happened.

I think adults mature in their faith at varying speeds. Some may never get to this kind of level of maturity if they don't pay much attention to their faith life and simply live through the seasons without much reflection. After multiple cycles of spring, summer, autumn and winter as a young tree, suddenly we realize that we've weathered them all; that they've become familiar, and we have learned to weather the storms and not get overwhelmed by them. It's as tricky as defining when we settle into middle age. There are signs but often it might be other people who notice them more than we do. A young colleague commented recently that they were too young to buy a lawnmower and yet enthused about their recently acquired vacuum cleaner. Where is middle age? Where is the transition from young tree to mature tree? Perhaps, somewhere between vacuum cleaner and lawnmower.

The Mature Tree (5) has solid core branches, established when the mature tree was a sapling and a young tree, which form the basic nature of the tree and the direction it grows. No slight storm can shake the core, although younger branches can move or even break away. The mature tree is less able to change. A great storm or some other external force can make big changes to the tree without destroying it as the roots are more fixed and established. Yet growth is still possible, even from unexpected parts. Changing where a mature tree is planted is possible but can have detrimental effects; not done carefully, the tree can fail to survive. For the mature tree, the seasons are familiar. There is an expectation that there will be times when there is not much light and times for fruitfulness. Mature trees can focus their growth, allowing light to fall through their branches on to younger trees below, offering their leaves and even their lost branches as sources of nutrients to other growing trees.

As I said above, discerning the transition to this stage can be difficult and will not be automatic for everyone. This is the point where an equilibrium is reached. It maps roughly to Fowler's Conjunctive faith, which is the last of the substantiated stages (his universalizing stage being suggested on the strength of only one person in his research). In many models, this would be the pinnacle of the model; the intended self-actualization and fulfilment of all that has been. Yet, reading the mystical texts that we've explored should tell us that such a thing is not really achievable this side of heaven. Even a strong, mature tree can suffer damage from a significant storm or extreme heat or lack of rain. There is nonetheless something in this stage of a person's faith coming fully into itself. Trees at earlier stages may look similar although shape is more individual in intervening stages. This then is the stage of someone who has reflected on their faith and come to terms with some of their own foibles and doubts. This is someone who has been through one or more of those hiatus moments in the various seasons of faith. Mature faith is, as it sounds, something established and solid that comes with many benefits. The potential for people with this level of faith being able to offer wisdom to those at earlier stages is significant, just as mature trees shed many leaves and lose the odd branch that returns to the ground around it and feeds other trees.

Yet mature faith also has encumbrances. In our worshipping communities and in the wider community many ministers will have encountered people who are well rounded, mature in their faith and wise, while also having the potential to be intractable and sure enough about their own position that they are less willing to compromise. There is something else hiding in this stage too, the possibility of someone of mature faith having a real crisis of faith, especially those who, according to Erikson's psychological model, are looking back at their life and wondering if their life has amounted to achievement and meaning or if it has been meaningless and unfulfilled. Some people do radically change their lives as this existential crisis hits and, as the transplanting analogy indicates, this can be achieved, though with considerable cost. Grafting, however, is much more possible for an old stock. In supporting those of mature faith we should encourage them to add in new ideas rather than necessarily suggest they uproot entirely.

> *Some trees as they get older require additional support to hold up great branches that might otherwise fall or break. Eventually all trees become older. Some mature trees will become great Totems (6), still standing but no longer producing substantial new growth. Their main branches, formed so well over the years, can still stand despite a lack of growth. They can draw on the resources of their deep roots and present to the world a powerful image of the growth they have achieved. Even a hollowed-out tree can still show what a great tree it had been before and offer a sign of what a tree can be. The particular nature of these trees also determines how they grow. Oaks and beeches do not grow in the same way but vary in shape. They may look similar as seedlings, and even saplings, but, as they mature, their shape becomes more apparent; some grow tall and straight with one central trunk; others diversify into many branches some of which produce fruit and others which may even wither and break off. As a totem, some of that shape remains, yet a totem is less distinctively of one shape or another, and all around the ground in which trees are planted is made up of the roots of trees planted nearby and the richness left by trees gone before.*

This is the first of the two stages strongly influenced by Harris's work. As a totem, some of that shape which may have distinguished one tree from another remains, yet a totem is less distinctively of one shape or another. There is something incredibly powerful about the sight of a huge tree trunk that has long since been a fruitful tree. Sometimes branches remain as a sign of past fruitfulness. At other times simply a hollow remains standing, which, from some perspectives, appears strong.

Those with mature faith got to a point where their faith was visible, apparent and clear. This maturity continues as totem, even if faith is not as visibly active and fruitful as it has once been; even if some things that have seemed core to their being in the past are hollowed out and lost. Their faithfulness can be as imposing as those grand totems, full of life and still capable in spring of producing signs of growth even if they are not as productive in terms of bearing the fruits of 'work'. A totem is the kind of tree that Tolstoy described and that you go out to admire, to sit beneath and commune with. Likewise, the faith of those who have grown deeply in their spiritual journey is the kind that you don't expect to be frantically productive in activity but reliable and solid. We may have an abundance of these in our worshipping communities. People who have spent a lifetime of faithfulness. I certainly have one particular parishioner in mind when I talk about this stage. Someone who found joy in so many things and yet also lived a life of pain and limitation. I know friends in ministry who will talk about the person they visit with home communion who ministers to them more than they ever feel they minister back. And yet these people can be seen as 'unproductive' by those who consider faith and church to be something that should produce results such as new members, new projects and more money in the budget. Mark Yaconelli, writing about churches full of older members whom he called to pray for the young people they wanted to work with, shares many fabulous stories of the faithfulness these people offered.[4] If reading about this stage helps our worshipping communities value those who quietly and faithfully pray for the activity of others in the church then it will have done its task.

> *Ultimately, the tree becomes indistinguishable from the earth around it. Humbled to the point of rejoining the humus, it becomes Compost (7), with all that it had been returned to the service of others, producing nourishment for other trees young and old and a place where seeds may lie untended.*

Originally the model ended with Stage 6, and I would go on to speak about issues of terroir – the ground into which people's faith is being planted. Yet it was the power of the image itself that persuaded me that rather than speaking of terroir as an accompanying theme, it was instead a seventh stage. First, I had spoken about totem being a stage that encompassed both those of mature faith and those who had died but whose faith was still significant for others. However, as models from the Christian tradition (Porete, Eckhart and the author of the *The Cloud of Unknowing*) have shown, it is possible to speak of a faith stage after death. Second, although these seven stages are generally progressive (with regression in the model accounted for by the concurrent pattern of the changing seasons), in a sense this final stage gives these seven stages a cyclical quality whereby the final stage of compost offers a fresh place for the seed of the first. This does not mean I am suggesting anything like a sense of reincarnation. Rather, this cycle provides a context in which to understand some of the ways in which the trees of faith of individuals are connected as being a community, a 'great cloud of witnesses', in a forest of faith with individual trees and common ground. Terroir is about what surrounds the trees and much of this is made up of the inheritance of previous people of faith. Of course, faith also grows through the work of the Holy Spirit, just as water and sunshine work alongside the terroir. There is something important about what we leave behind, what we offer of our own faith to others and to the next generation.

> Trees don't grow in a single year. They are subject to the *Seasons*. Growth is not only linear but comes in cycles. The seed, seedling and sapling experience the seasons; only the warmth of the earth and the rains of spring can enable the seed to sprout, and the seedling, no matter how small, will shed its leaves in the autumn.
>
> Trees grow not just in one season but throughout the dark of winter, the burgeoning of spring, the flourishing of summer and the fruitfulness of autumn. The more mature tree endures such seasons with familiarity and much greater ease but can still be affected by too cold a winter or too hot a summer. Trees grow both progressively and cyclically. A tree in one spring is not the same tree the next; spring is familiar but the tree has changed since the last.

In addition to the specific considerations of the various stages of the model, and particularly when supporting those of young tree or mature tree faith, the model offers practitioners some insight into the possibility of seasonality in people's faith lives. For each of the seasons there are gifts and demands. In spring there is a sense of freshness and renewal while also a demand for energy and commitment to new things, with the possibility of frustration, the 'not yet'. In summer the Spirit feels close and warm, and there is the need for active engagement. Autumn is the season for enjoying the fruit of labours and there is a need to begin to let things go. In winter there is the gift of rest and opportunities to turn in and reflect, yet also the pain of loss, the bareness of branches, the cold chill of doubt and the chance of hiatus.

First, of all the seasons, it is worth ministers understanding the hiatus that winter can bring to people's lives of faith. It may be linked to life events such as bereavement, divorce, heartbreak, redundancy, mental and physical health troubles, addiction, supporting family members, being a victim of crime, or all manner of individual crises. It may also result from wider existential problems such as climate crisis anxiety, despondency at the enduring issue of world poverty, frustration with the church's response to survivors of abuse, the enduring power of the patriarchy, persistent racism, the impact of class divisions, or the weight of societal intolerance for the LGBTQIA+ community. Equally, some people will experience a winter of the spirit because they have not given themselves enough time to rest and have ultimately crashed mentally or spiritually. The psalms of lamentation (and equally Jonah's prayer from the belly of the whale [Jonah 2.5–7]) might be of use to those in this season, to give a sense of solidarity with the psalmist in their sorrow.[5] As we explored with other models, the hiatus is an important part of maturing in faith. It is challenging and yet offers the individual a new insight into their relationship with God, the world and themselves. With good support, a hiatus can lead to positive re-engagement in the spring. Sometimes, those in winter can struggle so much that it leads to such a crisis of faith that they feel they want or need to leave a worshipping community for a time. This can be challenging for those in ministry, though may also be important, for a season, for that individual. Being there with someone through the winter could mean that you will then also be with them through the spring. Springtime is that season for new beginnings and new ideas. This is a season that can be like a burst of youthfulness and it comes to people at all stages of faith. Supporting those in this season is about enabling them to focus on what God is growing in them and channelling their energies into something that will be productive for them and, hopefully, for the church and the kingdom. Like many plants in spring, there can be a lot of growth in lots of different areas, and helpful pruning and shaping by those with ministerial care promotes effective growth. The summer of faith is like the thriving 'mature tree' faith. It has a confidence in God's presence and the individual feels assured in their calling. Rejoicing with those in this season is important. Sharing in their delight at the enactment of what had been hoped for in spring will give them affirmation. It may also be worth being attentive to the possibility of vainglory and the importance of humility. The crash after vainglory is more painful than a gentle reminder to be humble from a wise counsellor. The autumn of faith combines the joy of seeing fulfilment of all that was hoped for and then done. It is a time for fruitfulness, which for Christians means a time of love, joy, peace, patience, kindness, goodness, gentleness, faithfulness and self-control, not simply a new project gaining new members. Growth and fruitfulness in our churches is much more about deepening and enriching than about numerical change. Autumn is also an important time of transition. After two seasons of rising energy and energetic engagement, now comes a season of wind-down in preparation for rest, of letting go while also storing up to see us through the winter when it comes again.

For those in ministry, supporting the faith lives of others, it's likely there will be people at all stages and in all seasons of faith. You may have saplings and mature trees in autumn to care for at the same time as you have a young tree in winter and a seedling in summer. Sometimes it might be more challenging to discern the seasons and at other times it will be obvious. As much as I suggest that there is the potential for nuance in the way you differentiate in supporting people, of course approaching people with love and compassion works in any season and attending to our own seasons might help us recognize when we need to be more deliberate about seeking our own centredness in order to do that most effectively. When we are in winter ourselves, we can still delight in the spring of others while being gentle to ourselves with a kind of spiritual hygge, and we must always remember that, just as we tend our own trees, others are caring for theirs. We can help and advise, but we cannot make faith happen in others. That is the work of the Holy Spirit.

I've had the delight of being able to share this model in a number of contexts and although conference presentations have been wonderful, there is nothing quite like exploring this with people in a formational context, whether that's in a parish or a theological college. I have found that using a number of images, both photographs and artworks (and even video of Groot from *Guardians of the Galaxy*, or a seed sprouting, or leaves falling from autumn trees), helps people settle into the world of the metaphor as I describe each stage. I suggest you read the metaphor as a whole to the group. Use the images provided in this book at the start and end of reading to demonstrate the whole model. You could also use either a screen or individual handouts to show other images of trees to inspire imagination. It would be wonderful to do this in a Forest Church setting or an arboretum. Although you would be in only one season, being surrounded by trees during the description would genuinely enhance the experience. I have found that some people find it easy to inhabit the metaphor, others get very excited about it and develop it further, and always some struggle either to associate faith with a tree or to comprehend any deeper meaning. A few find objections to some elements of the model and then struggle to engage with the rest. I have found that offering it humbly as a possibility rather than presenting it as the solution to all things usually means that people engage as much as they can. As the creator of the model, I then tend to take responses and questions. You could do the same and respond based on your reading of this book and your own knowledge. Alternatively, you could suggest people reflect on their response to the model either on their own or in twos or threes. If you are going to do this, it might help to offer people a two-sided handout of the model so they can discuss it. You could guide people to think about their own experience of faith so far and where they would locate themselves in terms of season and stage, with encouragement to think about what might be coming next for them in the next stage or season. These questions are one way of helping people explore it for themselves:

How is the tree of your faith growing?

- *Is it packed full of different branches, each with potential for fruit?*
- *Are its branches spread out wide with space inviting others to climb in and explore?*
- *Is it focused on growing upwards, reaching up towards the light?*
- *Or digging deep with roots into the soil from the trees of long before?*
- *Do you feel like you're in a particular season right now?*
- *Do you identify as a sapling, a totem, a young tree etc.?*

Similarly, you could ask them to think about what the forest of faith would look like in your particular community. Some groups might be well placed to respond creatively to this, either by drawing an image of 'my faith now' or their own version of a tree in various seasons or stages. For those keen but less confident to be creative, you could print a number of colouring pages featuring trees, or find a lot of pictures of different trees in different stages of growth and at different seasons and invite them to choose one to sit with and reflect further. If there are real trees nearby, exploring outdoors would be even better. Some participants will prefer to engage with words more than images, and having some of the passages identified in the biblical foundations section of this chapter for them to read might be helpful. Alternatively, you could challenge them to find as many different trees (cedar, fig, oak, terabinth, etc.) in scripture as they can, either by looking through, searching online or using a concordance, and read what scripture says about growth and what that might teach them for their own growth in faith. Ultimately, this model is intended not as a diagnostic tool but as a guide to encourage people to reflect on their faith and to grow from where they are.

Notes

1 Yust, Karen-Marie 'Let the Little Children Theologize: Moral development, critical thinking and preschool', in DeGaynor, E., ed., 2023, *Let the Children Lead: Exploring Children's Spirituality Today*, Alexandria: VTS Press.

2 https://www.churchofengland.org/about/education-and-schools/growing-faith-foundation, accessed 09.05.2025.

3 https://smorgasblurb.wordpress.com/2012/04/19/tree-staking-perils/http://www.smorgasblurb.com/2012/04/tree-staking-perils/, accessed 09.05.2025.

4 Yaconelli, Mark, 2006, *Contemplative Youth Ministry*, London: SPCK.

5 See, for example, Psalms 3—5, 7, 9—10, 13—14, 17, 22, 25—28, 31, 36, 39, 40—43, 52—57, 59, 61, 64, 70—71, 77, 86, 89, 120, 139, 141—142.

Bibliography

Adair-Toteff, Christopher, 2021, 'Friedrich Von Hügel's philosophy', *History of European Ideas*, Vol. 47, No. 7, pp. 1079–1093.
Astley, J., ed., 1991, *How Faith Grows: Faith Development and Christian Education*, London: National Society and Church House Publishing.
Astley, Jeff and Francis, Leslie J., eds, 1992, *Christian Perspectives on Faith Development: A Reader*, Grand Rapids: Eerdmans; Leominster: Gracewing.
Batson, C. Daniel, Schoenrade, Patricia and Ventis, W. Larry, 1993, *Religion and the Individual*, New York: Oxford University Press, pp. 74–75.
Bellous, Joyce E., Csinos, David M., Peltomaki, Denise A., Bellous, Karen L., 2009, *Spiritual Styles Assessment – Children*, Warsaw: Tall Pine Press.
Bellous, Joyce E. and Csinos, David M., 2009, 'Spiritual Styles: Creating an environment to nurture spiritual wholeness', *International Journal of Children's Spirituality*, Vol. 14, No. 3, August, pp. 213–24.
Blackaby, Richard, 2012, *The Seasons of God*, New York: Waterbrook Multnomah.
Boyatzis, Chris, 2012, 'Spiritual development during childhood and adolescence', in Miller, Lisa, ed., *The Oxford Handbook of Psychology and Spirituality*, New York: Oxford University Press, pp. 151–64.
Bracker, Alison, 2012, *David Hockney: A Bigger Picture Educational Guide*, London: Royal Academy.
Brush, S., 2014, 'Imaging Faith: Faith Development and Responses to Art', unpublished MA dissertation.
Buber, Martin, 1937, *I and Thou*, Edinburgh: T & T Clark.
Buchanan, M., 2010, *Spiritual Rhythm: Being with Jesus Every Season of Your Soul*, Grand Rapids: Zondervan.
Bunyan, John, *The Pilgrim's Progress*, ed. Keeble, N. H., Oxford: Oxford University Press, 1984.
Canlis, Julie 2010, *Calvin's Ladder: A spiritual theology of ascent and ascension*, Grand Rapids: Eerdmans.
Chater, Mark, 1994, 'In Stages or on Wings?' *New Blackfriars*, Vol. 75, No. 888, December, pp. 569–75.
Cloud of Unknowing, The, 1981, ed. Walsh, James, New York: Paulist Press.
Colby, A. and Kohlberg, L. eds, 1987, *The Measurement of Moral Judgment*, New York: Cambridge University Press.
Croft, Steven, ed., 2019, *Rooted and Grounded*, Norwich: Canterbury Press.
Csinos, David M., 2008, 'Including All Children: A qualitative exploration of spiritual personalities and children's experiences with God and church', an unpublished thesis submitted to the Faculty of McMaster Divinity College in

partial fulfilment of the requirements for the degree of Master of Theological Studies.

Csinos, David M. (2010), 'Four Ways of Knowing God: Exploring Children's Spiritual Styles', *Journal of Childhood and Religion*, Vol. 1, No. 8.

Csinos, David M., 2011, *Children's Ministry that Fits: Beyond One-Size-Fits-All Approaches to Nurturing Children's Spirituality*, London: Wipf and Stock.

Csinos, David M., 2017, 'An Exploration of Children and Culture in the United Church of Canada', unpublished thesis submitted to the Faculty of Emmanuel College and the Pastoral Department of the Toronto School of Theology in partial fulfilment of the requirements for the degree of Doctor of Philosophy in Theology awarded by the University of St Michael's College.

Csinos, David M., 2020, *Little Theologians: Children, Culture, and the Making of Theological Meaning*, Montreal: McGill-Queen's University Press.

Csinos, David M. and Beckwith, Ivy, 2013, *Children's Ministry in the Way of Jesus*, Madison: Intervarsity Press.

Cullen, Christopher M., 2006, *Bonaventure*, New York: Oxford University Press.

Cutting, Marsha and Walsh, Michelle, 2008, 'Religiosity Scales: What Are We Measuring in Whom?' *Archive for the Psychology of Religion* 30, pp. 137–53.

DeGaynor, E., ed., 2023, *Let the Children Lead: Exploring Children's Spirituality Today*, Alexandria: VTS Press.

Díaz, M., 2022, *Queer God de Amor*, New York: Fordham University Press.

Dykstra, Craig and Parks, Sharon, 1986, *Faith Development and Fowler*, Birmingham: Religious Education Press.

Eckhart, Meister, 1981, 'The Book of Benedictus: Of the Nobleman', in *Meister Eckhart: The Essential Sermons, Commentaries, Treatises and Defense*, trans. Colledge OSA, Edmund with an Introduction by McGinn, Bernard, London: SPCK.

Eckhart, Meister, 2009, *The Nobleman*, in *The Complete Mystical Works of Meister Eckhart*, trans. Walshe OC, Maurice with a Foreword by McGinn, Bernard, New York: Crossroad Publishing.

Edgell Becker, P., 1999, *Congregations in Conflict: Cultural models of local religious life*, Cambridge: Cambridge University Press.

Epstein, Robert, 2002, 'Interview of M. Scott Peck', *Psychology Today*, November–December, p. 72.

Erikson, E. H., 1950, *Childhood and Society*, 1st edn, New York: Norton.

Erikson, E. H., 1968, *Identity: Youth and Crisis*, New York: WW Norton.

Estep, J. and Kim, J., eds, 2010, *Christian Formation: Integrating Theology and Human Development*, Nashville: B. and H. Academic.

Eusden, John Dykstra and Westerhoff, John H., 1998, *Sensing Beauty: Aesthetics, the Human Spirit and the Church*, Cleveland: United Church Press.

Field, Sean L., 2017, 'Debating the Historical Marguerite Porete', in Terry, Wendy R. and Stauffer, Robert, eds, *A Companion to Marguerite Porete and the Mirror of Simple Souls*, Leiden: Brill.

Ford-Grabowsky, Mary, 1987, 'Flaws in Faith Development Theory', *Religious Education*, Vol. 88, No. 1 Winter, pp. 80–93.

Fowler, James W., 1984, *Becoming Adult, Becoming Christian: Adult Development and Christian Faith*, San Francisco: Harper.

Fowler, James W., 1986, 'Faith and the Structuring of Meaning', reprinted in

Dykstra, Craig and Parks, Sharon, *Faith Development and Fowler*, Birmingham: Religious Education Press, pp. 15–42.

Fowler, James W., 1987, *Faith Development and Pastoral Care: Theology and Pastoral Care*, Philadelphia: Fortress Press.

Fowler, James W., 1991, *Weaving the New Creation: Stages of Faith and the Public Church*, San Francisco: Harper.

Fowler, James W., 1995, *Stages of Faith: The Psychology of Human Development and the Quest for Meaning*, San Francisco: Harper, originally published 1981.

Fowler, James W., 1996, *Faithful Change: The Personal and Public Challenges of Postmodern Life*, Nashville: Abingdon Press.

Fowler, James W. 2001, 'Faith Development Theory and the Postmodern Challenges', *The International Journal for the Psychology of Religion*, Vol. 11, No. 3, pp. 159–72.

Fowler, James W., 2004, 'Faith Development at 30: Naming the Challenges of Faith in a New Millennium', *Religious Education*, Vol. 99, No. 4, Fall, pp. 405–21.

Fowler, James W. et al., eds, 1992, *Stages of Faith and Religious Development: Implications for Church, Education and Society*, London: SCM Press.

Fowler, James W. and Dell, M. L., 2006, 'Stages of Faith from Infancy through Adolescence: Reflections on Three Decades of Faith Development Theory' in Roehlkepartain, E. et al., eds, *The Handbook of Spiritual Development in Childhood and Adolescence*, Thousand Oaks: Sage, pp. 34–45.

Fowler, James W., Streib, H. and Keller, B., 2004, *Manual for Faith Development Research*, 3rd edn, Bielefeld: Universität Bielefeld/Research Centre for Biographical Studies in Contemporary Religion.

Furushima, Randall Y., 1985, 'Faith Development in a Cross-Cultural Perspective', *Religious Education*, Vol. 80, No. 3, Summer, pp. 414–20.

Gardner, Howard, 1999, *Intelligence Reframed: Multiple Intelligences*, New York: Basic Books.

Gayford, M., 2011, *A Bigger Message: Conversations with David Hockney*, London: Thames and Hudson.

Gilligan, Carol, 1982, *In a Different Voice: Psychological theory and women's development*, Cambridge: Harvard University Press.

Grundy, M., 1998, *Understanding Congregations: a new shape for the local church*, London; New York: Mowbray.

Hackett, Jeremiah M., ed., 2013, *A Companion to Meister Eckhart*, Leiden: Brill.

Hagberg, Janet O., 1984, *Real Power: Stages of Personal Power in Organisations*, Salem: Sheffield Publishing Company.

Hagberg, Janet O. and Guelich, Robert A., 2005, *The Critical Journey: Stages in the life of faith*, Salem: Sheffield Publishing Company, original edn 1989.

Hall, Richard, 1986, *For Everything a Season*, London: United Reformed Church.

Hamrick, T. R., 1988, 'Transitional Factors in the Faith Development of Middle Adults', PhD dissertation, University of Georgia.

Harris, Maria, 1989, *Dance of the Spirit: The Seven Steps of Women's Spirituality*, New York: Bantam Books.

Harris, Maria, 1996, *Proclaim Jubilee: A Spirituality for the 21st Century*, Louisville: Westminster John Knox Press.

Hawkins, Greg L. and Parkinson, Cally, 2007, *Reveal: Where Are You?*, Willow Creek: Willow Creek Association.
Hawkins, Greg L. and Parkinson, Cally, 2008, *Follow Me*, Grand Rapids: Zondervan.
Hawkins, Greg L. and Parkinson, Cally, 2009, *Focus*, Grand Rapids: Zondervan.
Hawkins, Greg L. and Parkinson, Cally, 2011, *Move: What 1000 Churches Reveal About Spiritual Growth*, Grand Rapids: Zondervan.
Hay, David and Nye, Rebecca, 2006, *The Spirit of the Child*, rev. edn, London: Jessica Kingsley.
Hernández, Gloria Maité, 2021, *Savoring God: Comparative Theopoetics*, Oxford: Oxford University Press.
Heywood, David, 2008, 'Faith development theory: A case for paradigm change', *Journal of Beliefs and Values*, Vol. 29, No. 3, December, pp. 263–72.
Hilton, Walter, 1957, *The Ladder of Perfection*, and trans. Sherley-Price, Leo, London: Penguin.
Holbrook, C., 1965, 'H. Richard Niebuhr', in Marty M. and Peerman, D., eds, *A Handbook of Christian Theologians*, New York: World Publishing Company.
Holland, Scott, 2014, 'The Return of Theopoetics', *CrossCurrents*, Vol. 64, No. 4, December, pp. 496–508.
Holmes, S., 2016, 'Observing Christian Faith During the Childhood Years', *International Journal of Children's Spirituality*, Vol. 21, Nos 3–4, pp. 177–90.
Holmes, S., 2021, 'Will my child have their own faith?' Exploring the impact of parental beliefs on childhood faith nurture', *Journal of Beliefs and Values*, pp. 430–47.
Holmes, U. T., 1980, *A History of Christian Spirituality: An analytical introduction*, New York: Seabury.
Hopewell, James, 1988, *Congregation: Stories and Structures*, London: SCM Press.
Hugh of St Victor, 1962, *Selected Spiritual Writings*, London: Faber and Faber.
Hull, John, 1985, *What Prevents Christian Adults from Learning*, London: SCM Press.
Hull, John, 1991, 'Human Development and Capitalist Society', in Fowler, J. Nipkow, K. and Schweitzer, F., eds, *Stages of Faith and Religious Development: Implications for church, education, and society*, New York: Crossroad, pp. 209–23.
Jamieson, Alan, 2002, *A Churchless Faith: Faith Journeys Beyond the Churches* London: SPCK.
Jamieson, Alan, 2007, *Chrysalis: The Hidden Transformation in the Journey of Faith*, Milton Keynes: Paternoster Press.
John Climacus, 1959, *The Ladder of Divine Ascent*, trans. Archimandrite Lazarus Moore, London: Faber and Faber.
John of the Cross, St, 1959, *The Dark Night of the Soul*, trans. and ed. Peers, E. Allison, Grand Rapids: Christian Classics Ethereal Library.
John of the Cross, St, 1962, *Ascent of Mount Carmel*, trans. and ed. Peers, E. Allison, Grand Rapids: Christian Classics Ethereal Library.
John of the Cross, St, 1987, *Selected Writings*, trans. and ed. Kavanagh, Kieran, The Classics of Western Spirituality, New York: Paulist Press.
Jones, Arthur, 2007, *The Road he Travelled*, London: Random House.

Jones, Benjamin, 2022, 'Reimagining Fowler's Stages of Faith: Shifting from a seven-stage to a four-step framework for faith development', *Journal of Beliefs and Values*, pp. 1–13.

Keefe-Perry, L. C., 2014, *Way to Water: A Theopoetics Primer*, Eugene: Wipf and Stock.

Kelcourse, Felicity B., 2005, *Human Development and Faith: Life-cycle stages of body, mind, and soul*, St Louis: Chalice Press.

Kim, Sungwon, 2021, 'Development and Validation of a Faith Scale for Young Children', *Religions*, Vol. 12, No. 197, pp. 1–14.

King, P. E. et al., 2021, 'The Measure of Diverse Adolescent Spirituality (MDAS) and Refined Findings from Mexican and Salvadoran Youth', in Ai, A. L., Wink, P., Paloutzian, R. F., Harris, K. A., eds, *Assessing Spirituality in a Diverse World*, Cham: Springer, pp. 383–410.

Kohlberg, L., 1969, 'Stage and Sequence: The Cognitive-Developmental Approach to Socialization', in Goslin, David A., ed., *Handbook of Socialization Theory and Research*, Chicago: Rand McNally, pp. 347–480.

Kohlberg, L. and Levine, C., 1984, *Moral Stages: A Current Formulation and a Response to Critics*, Abingdon: S. Karger.

Lamont, Ronni, 2020, *Faith in Children*, Oxford: Monarch.

Levinson, D., 1978, *The Seasons of a Man's Life*, New York: Knopf.

Loder, James and Fowler, James F., 1982, 'Conversations on Fowler's Stages of Faith and Loder's Transforming Moment', *Religious Education*, Vol. 77, No. 2, March–April, pp. 133–48.

Maidment, Pete, Mapledoram, Susie with Lake, Stephen, 2011, *Reconnecting with Confirmation*, London: Church House Publishing.

May, Rollo, 1972, *Power and Innocence: A Search for the Sources of Violence*, London: Souvenir Press.

McLaren, Brian D., 2000, *The Church on the Other Side: Doing Ministry in the Postmodern Matrix*, Grand Rapids: Zondervan, rev. edn.

McLaren, Brian D., 2011, *Naked Spirituality: A Life With God in Twelve Simple Words*, London: Hodder and Stoughton.

McLaren, Brian D., 2021, *Faith After Doubt: Why your beliefs stopped working and what to do about it*, London: Hodder and Stoughton.

Mclaren, Brian, 2022, *Do I Stay Christian? A Guide for the Doubters, the Disappointed and the Disillusioned*, London: Hodder and Stoughton.

Miller-McLemore, Bonnie, 2006, 'Wither the Children? Childhood in Religious Education', *Journal of Religion* 86, pp. 635–57.

Moseley, Romney M., Jarvis, David and Fowler, James W., 1992, 'Stages of Faith', in Astley, Jeff and Francis, Leslie J., eds, *Christian Perspectives on Faith Development: A reader*, Grand Rapids: Eerdmans; Leominster: Gracewing, pp. 29–57.

Moustakas, Clark, 1990, *Heuristic: Design, Methodology, and Applications*, London: Sage.

Newell, John Philip, 2021, *Sacred Earth, Sacred Soul*, New York: HarperCollins.

Ng, Greer Anne Wenh-In, 1996, 'Toward Wholesome Nurture: Challenges in the Religious Education of Asian North American Female Christians', *Religious Education*, Vol. 91, No. 2, Spring, pp. 238–54.

Nye, Rebecca, 1998, 'Psychological Perspectives on Children's Spirituality', unpublished thesis, Nottingham University.
Nye, Rebecca, 2009, *Children's Spirituality: What it is and why it matters*, London: Church House Publishing.
Origen, 1979, *An Exhortation to Martyrdom, Prayer and Selected Works*, trans. and Intro., Greer, Rowan A., New York: Paulist Press.
Oser, Fritz and Gmünder, Paul, 1991, *Religious Judgement: A developmental approach*, Birmingham: Religious Education Press.
Osmer, Richard R., 1990, 'Faith Development', in *Harper's Encyclopedia of Religious Education*, New York: Harper and Row, pp. 252–3.
Parker, Stephen, 2006, 'Measuring Faith Development', *Journal of Psychology and Theology*, Vol. 34, No. 4, pp. 337–48.
Parker, Stephen, 2010, 'Research in Fowler's Faith Development Theory: A Review Article', *Review of Religious Research*, Vol. 51, No. 3, pp. 233–52.
Parkinson, Cally, 2015, *Rise: Bold Strategies to Transform your Church*, Carol Stream: Navpress.
Parks, S., 1986, *The Critical Years: The Young Adult Search for a Faith to Live By*, San Francisco: Harper and Row.
Peck, M. Scott, 1988, *People of the Lie: The Hope for Healing Human Evil*, 2nd edn, London: Century Hutchinson.
Peck, M. Scott, 1990, *The Road Less Travelled*, London: Arrow Books, Original edn, New York: Simon and Shuster, 1978.
Peck, M. Scott, 1993, *Further Along the Road Less Travelled: The Unending Journey Toward Spiritual Growth*, New York: Simon and Schuster.
Piaget, Jean, 1950, *The Psychology of Intelligence*, London: Routledge and Kegan Paul.
Piper, E., 2002, 'Faith development: A critique of Fowler's model and a proposed alternative', *Journal of Liberal Religion*, Vol. 3, No. 1.
Porete, Marguerite, 1993, *The Mirror of Simple Souls*, trans. and Intro., Babinsky, Ellen L., New York: Paulist Press.
Power, C, 1991, 'Hard versus Soft Stages of Faith and Religious Development', in Fowler, J., Nipkow, K. and Schweitzer, F., eds, *Stages of Faith and Religious Development: Implications for Church, Education, and Society*, New York: Crossroad Publishing, pp. 116–29.
Ricoeur, Paul, 1978, 'The Hermeneutics of Symbols and Philosophical Reflection', in Regan, Charles E. and Stewart, David, eds, *The Philosophy of Paul Ricoeur*, Boston: Beacon Press, pp. 36–58.
Ritchey, Sara, 2008, 'Spiritual Arborescence: Trees in the Medieval Christian Imagination', *Spiritus: A Journal of Christian Spirituality*, Vol. 8, No. 1, Spring, pp. 64–82.
Roberts, Vaughan S. and Sims, David, 2017, *Leading by Story: Rethinking church leadership*, London: SCM Press.
Robinson, Joanne Maguire, 2017 'Marguerite's Mystical Annihilation', in Terry, Wendy R. and Stauffer, Robert, eds, *A Companion to Marguerite Porete and the Mirror of Simple Souls*, Leiden: Brill.
Rogers, Carl, 1959, 'A Tentative Scale for the Measurement of Process in Psychotherapy', in Rubinstein, E., and Parloff, M., *Research in Psychotherapy: Pro-*

ceedings of a Conference, Washington, D.C. April 9–12, 1958, Washington: American Psychological Association, pp. 96–107.

Rohr, Richard, 2009, *The Naked Now: Learning to See as the Mystics See*, New York: Crossroad.

Rohr, Richard, 2010, *The Art of Letting Go: Living the Wisdom of St. Francis*, Louisville: Sounds True Inc.

Rohr, Richard, 2012, *Falling Upward: A Spirituality for the Two Halves of Life*, London: SPCK.

Rohr, Richard, 2013, *Immortal Diamond: The Search for Our True Self*, London: SPCK.

Rohr, Richard, 2020, *The Wisdom Pattern: Order, disorder, reorder*, Cincinnati: Franciscan Media.

Scott, Mark S. M., 2012, *Journey Back to God: Origen on the Problem of Evil*, Oxford: Oxford University Press.

Slee, Nicola, 1999, 'The Patterns and Processes of Women's Faith Development: A Qualitative Study', unpublished thesis, University of Birmingham.

Slee, Nicola, 2000, 'Some Patterns and Processes of Women's Faith Development', *Journal of Beliefs and Values*, Vol. 21, No. 1, pp. 5–16.

Slee, Nicola, 2004, *Women's Faith Development: Patterns and Processes*, London: Routledge.

Slee, Nicola, Llewellyn, Dawn, Wasey, Kim and Taylor-Guthartz, Lindsey, 2024, *Female Faith Practices: Qualitative Research Perspectives*, London: Routledge.

Slee, Nicola, Porter, Fran and Phillips, Anne, eds, 2013, *The Faith Lives of Women and Girls: Qualitative Research Perspectives*, London: Routledge.

Slee, Nicola, Porter, Fran and Phillips, Anne, eds, 2018, *Researching Female Faith*, London: Routledge.

Spencer, A., 1982, *Seasons: A Woman's Search for Self through Life Stages*, New York: Paulist Press.

Stokes, Kenneth, 1989, *Faith is a Verb: Dynamics of adult faith development*, Mystic: Twenty-third Publications.

Stoyles, Gerard John, Stanford, Bonnie, Caputi, Peter, Keating, Alysha-Leigh and Hyde, Brendan, 2012, 'A measure of spiritual sensitivity for children' *International Journal of Children's Spirituality*, Vol. 17, No. 3, pp. 203–15.

Streib, Heinz, 1991, *Hermeneutics of Metaphor, Symbol and Narrative in Faith Development Theory*, European University Studies, Lausanne: Peter Lang AG.

Streib, Heinz, 2001, 'Faith Development Theory Revisited: The Religious Styles Perspective', *The International Journal for the Psychology of Religion*, Vol. 11, No. 3, pp. 150–2.

Streib, Heinz, 2003, 'Religion as a Question of Style: Revising the Structural Differentiation of Religion from the Perspective of the Analysis of the Contemporary Pluralistic-Religious Situation', *International Journal of Practical Theology*, Vol. 7, No. 1, pp. 1–22.

Streib, Heinz, 2005, 'Faith Development Research Revisited: Accounting for diversity in structure, content, and narrativity of faith', *The International Journal for the Psychology of Religion*, Vol. 5, No. 2, pp. 99–121.

Streib, Heinz, 2013, 'The Hierarchy of Religious Styles', contribution to the Discussion Forum on 'Religious, Faith, and Spiritual Development: Future Per-

spectives' at the Conference of the International Association for the Psychology of Religion in Lausanne, 27–31 August.
Streib, Heinz, 2019, 'How Religious Styles Develop: Typology and Longitudinal Perspectives', presented at the Conference of the Society for the Study of Human Development (SSHD), Portland, USA.
Streib, Heinz and Hood Jr, Ralph W., eds, 2024, *Faith in Development: Mixed-Method Studies on Worldviews and Religious Styles*, Bielefeld: Bielefeld University Press.
Streib, Heinz, Hood Jr, Ralph W. and Klein, Constantin, 2010, 'The Religious Schema Scale: Construction and Initial Validation of a Quantitative Measure for Religious Styles', *The International Journal for the Psychology of Religion*, Vol. 20, No. 3, pp. 151–72.
Streib, H. and Keller, B., 2018, *Manual for the Assessment of Religious Styles in Faith Development Interviews*, 4th edn, Bielefeld: Universität Bielefeld/Research Centre for Biographical Studies in Contemporary Religion.
Streib, Heinz, and Klein, Constantin, 2015, 'Do Religious Styles and Schemata Change over Time: Results with the Religious Schema Scale', presented at the Annual Meeting of the Society for the Scientific Study of Religion, Newport Beach.
Streib, Heinz, Chen, Z. J. and Hood, Ralph W., 2020, 'Categorizing People by Their Preference for Religious Styles: Four Types Derived from Evaluation of Faith Development Interviews of Faith Development Interviews', *The International Journal for the Psychology of Religion*, Vol. 30, No. 2, pp. 112–27.
Streib, H., Chen, Z. J. and Hood Jr, R. W., 2023, 'Faith Development as Change in Religious Types: Results from three-wave longitudinal data with faith development interviews', *Psychology of Religion and Spirituality*, Vol. 15, No. 2, pp. 298–307.
Streib, Heinz, Klein, Constantin and Keller, Barbara, 2021, 'The Mysticism Scale as Measure for Subjective Spirituality: New Results with Hood's M-Scale and the Development of a Short Form', in Ai, A. L., Wink, P. and Harris, K. A. eds, *Assessing Spirituality in a Diversified World*, New York: Springer.
Teresa of Avila, 1979, *The Interior Castle*, ed. Kavanaugh, Kieran, London: SPCK.
Teresa of Avila, 2014, *Autobiography of St. Teresa of Avila*, ed. and trans. Peers, E. Allison, Mineola, New York: Dover Publications.
Thompson, Ross, 2008, *Spirituality in Season: Growing through the Christian Year*, London: SCM Press.
Tournier, Paul, 1963, *The Seasons of Life*, trans. John S. Gilmour, Eugene: Wipf and Stock, reprint.
Tournier, Paul, 1971, *Learning to Grow Old*, trans. Hudson, Edwin, London: SCM Press.
Underhill, Evelyn, 1913, *The Mystic Way: A Psychological Study in Christian Origins*, London: J. M. Dent and Sons.
United Reformed Church, 1990, *URC Yearbook*, London: United Reformed Church.
Wahlgren, Gillian T., 2005, *Entering Teresa of Avila's Interior Castle* New Jersey: Paulist Press.
Ware, C., 2000, *Discover Your Spiritual Type: A guide to individual and congregational growth*, Bethesda: Alban Institute.

Watts, Fraser, Nye, Rebecca and Savage, Sara, 2002, *Psychology for Ministry*, London: Routledge.
Westerhoff, John H., 1985, *Living the Faith Community: The church that makes a difference*, rev. and expanded edn, Minneapolis: Winston Press.
Westerhoff, John H., 2000, *Will Our Children Have Faith?*, rev. and expanded edn, Harrisberg: Morehouse Publishing.
Westerhoff, John H., 2005, *Pilgrim People: Learning Through the Church Year*, New York: Seabury Press.
Westerhoff, John H. III and Edwards, O. C., eds, 1981, *A Faithful Church: Issues in the History of Catechesis*, Wilton: Morehouse-Barlow Company.
Westerhoff, John H. and Eusden, John D. 1982, *The Spiritual Life: Learning East and West*, New York: Seabury.
Westerhoff, J., and Willimon, W. H., 1980, *Liturgy and Learning through the Life Cycle*, New York: Seabury Press.
Williams, R., 1991, *Teresa of Avila*, Harrisberg: Morehouse.
Wink, Walter, 1991, 'Walking M. Scott Peck's Less-Travelled Road', *Theology Today*, Vol. 48, No. 3, pp. 279–89.
Wolski Conn, Joann, ed., 1986, *Women's Spirituality: Resources for Christian Development*, New York: Paulist Press.
Yaconelli, Mark, 2006, *Contemplative Youth Ministry*, London: SPCK.
Yeats, W. B., 1928, *The Tower*, London: Macmillan and Co.
Zohar, Danah and Marshall, Ian, 2000, *SQ Spiritual Intelligence the Ultimate Intelligence*, London: Bloomsbury.

Index of Bible References

Genesis
2.17	192, 193
8.22	131, 132
12	26
15.6	6, 22
24.27, 49	6, 22
28.10–19	29
32.22–30	19
42.20	6, 22

Exodus
4.1–9	6, 22
16—40	26
21.8	6, 22

Leviticus
5.15	6, 22

Numbers
5.6, 12, 27	6, 22

Deuteronomy
13.14	6, 22
17.4	6, 22
32.51	6, 22

Joshua
7.1	6, 22
22.16, 20–22, 31	6, 22
24.14	6, 22

Judges
9.15–16, 19	6, 22

Ruth
1.16	112
4.16	6, 22

1 Kings
3.6	6, 22
11.38	6, 22
18—19	113

2 Kings
10.1	6, 22
17.14	6, 22
20.19	6, 22

1 Chronicles
2.7	6, 22
5.25	6, 22
9.1	6, 22
10.13	6, 22

2 Chronicles
20.20	6, 22

Ezra
10.2, 10	6, 22

Esther
2.7	6, 22

Job
15.22	6, 22
29.19–20	193
39.12	6, 22

Psalms

1	193
3—5	220, 223
7	220, 223
9—10	220, 223
13—14	220, 223
15.21	6, 22
17, 22	220, 223
19.9	6, 22
25.5	6, 22
25—28	220, 223
31, 36, 39	220, 223
40—43	220, 223
52—57, 59	220, 223
61, 64	220, 223
70—71, 77	220, 223
78.22	6, 22
86, 89	220, 223
106.24	6, 22
120, 139	220, 223
141—142	220, 223
146.6	6, 22

Proverbs

11.28	193

Ecclesiastes

3	131, 132
12.10	6, 22

Wisdom

7.30	39
8.1	39

Isaiah

8.12	6, 22
28.16	6, 22
39.8	6, 22
61.3	193

Jeremiah

2.21	6, 22
8.13	193
12.2	193
17.8	193
33.6	6, 22

Lamentations

4.12	6, 22

Hosea

5.9	6, 22

Jonah

2.5-7	221
3.5	6, 22

Habakkuk

1.5	6, 22

Matthew

6.30	6, 7, 22
7.24-27	7
8.10, 26, 29	6, 7, 22
8.26	7
8.29	7
9.2	6, 22
12.33	193
13.31-32	6, 22
14.31	6, 7, 22
15.15	7
15.28	6, 7, 22
16.8	7
16.16	7
16.22	7
17.4	7
17.20	6, 22
18.3-4	8
21.21	6, 22
26.35	7
26.40	7
26.69-75	7

INDEX OF BIBLE REFERENCES

Mark
2.5	6, 22
4.30–32	6, 22
4.32	194
4.40	6, 22
5.34	6, 22
8.29	7
8.32–33	7
9.5	7
10.52	6, 22
11.22	6, 22
12.30–31	82
14.29	7
14.37	7
14.54–72	7

Luke
5.20	6, 22
7.9	6, 7, 22
7.50	6, 22
8.48	6, 22
9.20	7
9.25	6, 22
9.33	7
10.27	9
10.29–37	26
12.28	6, 7, 22
12.41	7
13.18–19	6, 22
13.19	194
15.11–32	26
17.5	6, 7, 22
17.6, 19	6, 22
18.8	7
22.33	7
22.55–61	7
24.12	7
24.13–25	26

John
1.45	112
3.3	8, 13
12.24	193
13.6	7
13.9	7
14.2	32
14.16	25
18.10–11	7
18.17–27	7
21.7–17	7

Acts of the Apostles
2.14	7
3.6	7
3.16	6, 22
3.17	6, 22
4.13	7
9.2	25
9.34	7
13.8	6, 22
14.9	6, 22
14.22	7
14.27	7
16.5	7

Romans
1.12	7–8
5.3b–4	13
6.4	132
7.6	132
9.32	6, 22
12	132
12.3	7
13.11	39

1 Corinthians
2.6	7, 8, 22
3.1–3	8
10.5	8
12.9	7
13.11–12	8
13.12	18

2 Corinthians
5.17   132
6.10   41
8.7   8

Philippians
3.15   7, 8, 22

Colossians
1.28   7, 8, 22
3.10   132
4.12   7, 8, 22

2 Timothy
3.7   7, 22

Hebrews
5.13–14   8

James
2.18   6, 22

1 Peter
2.24   192

Jude
12   193

Revelation
22.2   192, 193

Index of Names and Subjects

adolescence 10, 11, 12, 52, 77, 94, 102, 103, 107, 136, 148, 160, 207, 213, 214
adult 8–13, 16–18, 47, 51, 53, 59–64, 68, 70, 75, 77–8, 93, 101–3, 110, 148, 151, 153, 155–7, 159–60, 164, 167, 174, 189–91, 199, 211, 214–15
Anselm 6
apophatic 105, 106, 108, 164, 166
Astley, Jeff 6, 15, 22–3, 60, 83, 84
Augustine, 27–9, 109

Belenky, Mary 57, 105, 122, 136
Blackaby, Richard 4–5, 15, 126, 132–4, 141–2, 201
Bonaventura 3, 30
Brueggemann, Walter 77
Buber, Martin 128, 197
Buchanan, Mark 15, 129, 198, 201–2
Bunyan, John 3, 4, 33

Calvin, John 29
Catherine of Siena 3, 195
children 5, 8–12, 16–18, 28, 32, 36, 49–51, 53, 55, 59, 67–8, 70, 74–5, 93, 98, 101, 110, 117, 128, 131, 136, 139–40, 144, 153, 155–63, 189, 191, 199, 200, 210–12

Chrysostom, John 29
Climacus, John 3, 4, 30
Cloud of Unknowing, 3, 4, 26, 188, 218
compost 204, 207, 218
Csinos, David 4, 5, 15, 144, 157, 161–8, 188, 198–200

Dewey, John 98
Döbert, Robert 65, 69
doubt, 19, 39, 72, 102, 129–31, 136–40, 169, 189–90, 219
Doubt and Proud, 56, 81
Dykstra, C. 15

Erikson, Eric 11, 12, 18, 47–9, 62, 77, 105, 129, 145, 149, 216

Ford-Grabowsky, Mary 56, 58–9
Fowler, James W. 3–6, 11, 15–16, 19, 46–67, 69–75, 78, 89, 91–2, 95, 97–8, 100, 104–7, 109, 118, 129, 136, 138–40, 144–53, 156–7, 160, 162, 164, 167–9, 174, 179–81, 188, 191–2, 198–202, 207, 215–16
Francis of Assisi 109
Frye, Northrup 136, 169–71
Furushima, Randall Y. 58

Gardner, Howard 144–6
Gilligan, Carol 57, 61–3, 105

Gregory of Nazianzus 29
Growing Faith Foundation 212

Hagberg, J. and Guelich, R. 4, 77, 90, 109–14, 188–9
Hall, Dick 4, 5, 16, 126, 130–2, 201
Harris, Maria 4, 5, 16, 107, 111, 144, 174–80, 188, 191–2, 199, 201, 211, 217
Hawkins, G. L. 15, 90, 97
hiatus 13, 33, 35, 40, 69, 71, 77, 92, 95, 114, 117–18, 134–5, 159, 188–9, 202, 216, 219–20
Hildegard of Bingen 56
Hilton, Walter 3, 4, 31
Hockney, David 198, 200
Hopewell, James 4, 5, 15, 136, 144, 168–174
Hugh of St Victor, 3, 4, 26
Hull, John 13, 61, 156

infancy 10, 11, 15, 28, 32, 156

James, William 49
Jamieson, Alan 3, 4, 16, 46, 76–80, 146, 188–9, 192
John of the Cross 2–4, 31, 36, 77–8, 112, 116, 118, 139, 158, 189
Julian of Norwich 109, 116, 178

kataphatic 164–5
Kegan, Robert 105
Kelcourse, Felicity 15
Kim, Sungwon 17, 199
Kohlberg, L. 10, 11, 22, 47, 48, 65, 105, 118, 145, 147–9

Lamont, Ronni 6, 100
Levinson, D. 105, 126–8
Loder, James 60

Maidment and Mapledoram 103
mature tree 197, 204, 206–7, 215–16, 219–20
May, Rollo 110
McLaren, 4, 5, 15, 72, 110, 126, 135–43, 146, 188, 199, 202
Meister Eckhart 3, 4, 27–9, 177, 188, 218
Merton, Thomas 196
mid-life 1, 12, 15, 53, 129, 215
Miller-McLemore, Bonnie 6, 16, 18, 199
Moffit, J. 197 Moran, Gabriel 2, 174, 177

Niebuhr, H. Richard 47, 57, 63, 84
Nye 4, 5, 15–16, 18, 155–61, 164, 192, 198–9

Origen, Adamantius 3, 32–3
Oser, Fritz and Gmünder, Paul 3, 4, 16, 19, 46, 64–70, 131, 147, 148, 152, 188
Osmer, R. 56

Palmer, Parker 79
Parker, Stephen 15, 59, 79
Parkinson, Cally 16, 90, 97, 175
Parks, Sharon 3, 4, 15, 16, 60, 62–4, 77, 189
Peck, M. Scott 3, 4, 15, 46, 70–6, 109, 116, 136, 137, 188, 199
Pelagius 194
Piaget, Jean 9, 10, 47, 48–9, 62, 65, 105, 145, 149, 156
Piper, E. 59, 60–1
Polanyi, Karl 47
Porete, Marguerite 3, 4, 27, 188, 218

Ricoeur, Paul 47, 54, 83, 117, 136, 146, 192, 202
Rizzuto, A. M. 149, 157
Roberts, Vaughan S. and Sims, David 174
Rogers, Carl 12
Rohr, Richard 3, 4, 15, 80, 89, 90, 115–18, 136, 188, 199, 202

sapling 204–6, 212–15, 219, 222
seasons 5, 49, 126–37, 139, 190–1, 197, 199, 201–2, 204–7, 212, 214–16, 218–22
spring 126, 128–9, 131–4, 194, 197, 202, 205–7, 212, 214–15, 217, 219–21
summer 128–9, 131, 133–4, 138, 200–2, 205–7, 214–15, 219–21
autumn 128–9, 131, 133–4, 138, 193, 202, 205, 207, 212, 215, 219–21
winter 126, 129, 131, 133–4, 194, 200–2, 205–7, 212, 214–15, 219–21
seed 7, 27, 193–4, 201, 204–5, 210–12, 218–19, 221
seedling 190, 204, 205, 211–12, 219, 221
Shakespeare, William 126, 170
Slee, Nicola 3, 4, 14, 16, 48, 57–8, 60–1, 90–1, 95, 104–8, 136, 146, 155, 164, 179, 192, 199
Spencer, Anita 105, 126–8
St Paul 13, 18, 39, 66
Stern, D. 49–50
Stokes, Kenneth 1, 15
Streib, Heinz 4, 5, 16, 47–9, 57, 59, 62, 73, 144, 146–54, 159, 163–4, 169, 191, 201

Teresa of Avila 3, 4, 34, 36, 44, 77, 79, 87, 195
terroir 218–19
The Dream of the Rood 194
The Shepherd of Hermas 194
theosis 28, 31–2, 36, 54, 72, 118
Thomas Aquinas 39, 194
Thompson, Ross 5, 129
Tillich, Paul 47
Tolstoy, Leo 197, 217
totem, 204, 207, 217–18, 222
Tournier, Paul 126, 128, 141, 188
Traherne, Thomas 195

Underhill, Evelyn 42
Venantius Fortunatus 194
Von Hügel, Friedrich 42, 144, 146

Westerhoff, John 3–5, 15–18, 77, 89, 90, 95, 97–104, 111, 126, 129, 132–5, 138–42, 146, 162, 170, 176, 188, 191, 198–200, 208
Williams, Rowan 36
Willow Creek 3, 4, 19, 89–97, 100, 146, 149, 162, 169, 188
Wink, Walter 72
women 4, 16, 21, 57–8, 82, 89, 90, 104–8, 127–8, 146, 175–7, 179–80

Yaconelli, Mark 17, 218
Yeats, W. B. 131, 133
young children 17, 158
young people, youth 17–18, 69, 75, 91, 93, 103, 131, 147, 160–1, 189–91, 199, 201, 213, 218
young tree, 204–6, 213–15, 219, 221–2

www.ingramcontent.com/pod-product-compliance
Lightning Source LLC
Chambersburg PA
CBHW022048290426
44109CB00014B/1025